Bend Never Break

The Inside Story of UCLA Women's Soccer and Their Inspiring National Championship journey.

Madelyn Desiano

Bend Never Break

© 2025 Madelyn Desiano and TMJ

All rights reserved
No part of this book may be reproduced or transmitted in any form or by any electronic or mechanical means, including photocopying and recording, or by any other information storage or retrieval system, without written permission from the publisher.

First edition, first impression 2025
ISBN: 979-8-218-64889-3

Bend Never Break

The Final Countdown	1
Blank Slate	5
Hiring Process	8
Welcome to Westwood	14
Defense Wins Championships	20
The Turning Point	28
The Battle for LA	34
Building a Team Culture	39
The UCLA Soccer Baddies	46
Summer	52
Coach Wooden	55
Industriousness	58
Intentness	62
Cooperation	69
Alertness	76
Friendship	84
Team Spirit	93
Self-Control	99
Enthusiasm	112
Initiative	120
Confidence	126
Condition	132
Poise	162
Loyalty	168
Competitive Greatness	173
The Celebration	188
What's Next?	195

Bend Never Break

"Hard work beats talent when talent doesn't work hard."
Coach John Wooden

Bend Never Break

Part One

Chapter 1
The Final Countdown

November 12, 2021

It seemed like everything was happening in slow motion.

"**Ten.**"

I remember thinking, "There's no way this is happening."

"**Nine.**"

The announcer continued to count down as tears continued to fall down my face.

"**Eight.**"

I wrapped my arms around my fellow seniors, and we all cried.

"**Seven.**"

The fifth years and seniors dropped to the floor. Even though I still had another year of college soccer, my best friends were moving on. This was their last UCLA Soccer game, and it honestly couldn't have gone any worse.

"**Six.**"

I rubbed my eyes, pushing the embarrassment and frustration out of my face.

"**Five.**"

Even though I was so incredibly sad, I was equally as shocked. We, the second seed in the NCAA tournament, undefeated the entire year, would now lose to UCI in the first round of the tournament, at home.

"**Four.**"

Soccer is brutal; the best team does not always win. It's a 90-minute game that most times comes down to individual brilliance or a simple mistake.

"**Three.**"

They scored early on in the first half, and we were just waiting to tie it up. Shots hit the post left and right, formations were switched, subs were made, and bodies flew, reaching to block shots while voices were lost cheering on our teammates. Despite it all, we just couldn't find a way.

"**Two.**"

Months and months of dedication and sleepless nights, aimed at lifting that trophy. Yet tonight, our journey abruptly ended 90 minutes into the playoffs.

"**One.**"

To experience winning is to experience everything you've ever wanted. Losing stings.

Game over.

I looked up to the stands where my teammates who didn't roster were. They all stared solemnly out at the field, watching UCI dog-pile on our field. The whistle blew and girls on the field collapsed in tears. On the bench, we hugged each other tightly and walked to the circle that was slowly forming. The girls from the stands joined silently as we locked arms around each other. We came together as a team and not much was said. We thanked the seniors and we leaned on one another. My roommate, Maricarmen Reyes (Mari), had the flu and didn't play that game. She left our apartment and scootered to the field, and we all cried together. This was the end for my group of best friends. There were five of us. Throughout our four years, we all lived together, went on trips together, celebrated milestones together, and between the five of us, there were eight knee surgeries.

UCI was our opening game of the season back in August and we beat them 3-1. Despite both teams changing drastically since then, this time we came out a bit too confident and didn't prepare well enough. Our scout was sent out Wednesday night around 10 p.m. (I remember vividly because I was on the phone with my dad at 9 p.m. and he asked me what the game plan was, and I responded, "I wish I knew!"). Thursday's training was rough. We didn't have a specific game plan against UCI, and they sure had a game plan against us. This was a recurring problem. Yet despite the lack of preparation, we should still win. Player to player, we out-matched UCI in every aspect. We had better players and were technically and tactically sounder. Our program was made up of Olympians, national team players, and All-Americans. In any other situation we would've beaten them, but playoffs are a different animal.

I only played 17 minutes of that game, so I was wrestling with a lot of emotions. Being on the bench during an intense, must-win game is one of the hardest things an athlete can experience. You spend that time crossing your fingers that your coach will look down the bench and point for you to go in, while simultaneously crossing your fingers that your friends on the field can get the job done. It's not a sense of bitterness, but a sense of FOMO (fear of missing out). You want to be out on the field. You want to be running around contributing to the game. You want to be putting in tackles, making last-ditch efforts to score, and flying up the field. During my 17 minutes, I had a shot on goal and the goalkeeper came out of nowhere to make the save. Despite my efforts, I was subbed off quickly. I was frustrated and promised myself that this was the last time I'd be on the bench during an important game. I was going to do everything in my power to make sure that our coaches and my teammates would know to trust me in big moments.

After the game, I grabbed my bag and hurried off the pitch. I saw my parents who were just as shocked. My mom gave me a big hug and I remember that she didn't have much to say either.

We walked back to the locker room in silence. Some of the girls stayed back with their parents, but I wanted to be with my friends. My parents hugged me goodbye, and I went up to the locker room. The room was silent. I sat on the stool in front of my locker and watched the goal against us on repeat. Exposure therapy is what they call it. One of my best friends walked into the locker room. We looked at each other, and then she said, "Let's get out of here." After showering, some of us snuck into the UCLA men's basketball game and we watched them beat top-seeded Villanova in overtime; isn't that ironic?

Later that night I received a text from a sophomore asking if we had reserve training the next day. I laughed a little and reassured her, "No Megan, we have at least a week off." That's when it hit me – this was going to be my team now. I was now one of the oldest in the squad and I knew I could lead this team to where it should be, at the top. I couldn't sleep that night. I kept replaying the last 10 seconds of the game and I was just so anxious about my future, and the team's future. In the past two seasons, UCLA had won just one playoff game. It just wasn't good enough. That night I wrote in my journal -

Don't really know what's next. Squad splits up in December and it's going to be really hard. Planning on playing another year at UCLA. Feels weird knowing next year will be my last year playing college soccer considering this fall was the "first".

Really sad.
It's hard.
Soccer is weird man. End of the day didn't show up to win until the second half. And that isn't the player's fault….
Writing this at 1:50 a.m. mainly because I can't sleep. Also, because there is so much going on in my head. Don't know what the future holds….

I wish I could hold myself then and tell myself that everything was going to be okay, and that in a year from then, I would be a National Champion.

Chapter 2
Blank Slate

November is long and boring when you lose in the first round. Normally, we would be training, lifting, and preparing for our next opponent. This year, unfortunately, was not normal. I took the next few days off. When the weekend came, I went to support a friend playing for USC in the NCAA tournament.

During the game, I received a text from a former teammate that our head coach, Amanda Cromwell was leaving UCLA and our assistant coach was trying to take over. Simultaneously, an "anonymous" end-of-season evaluation was sent out to our team to complete. It asked us our opinions on staff members, UCLA Athletics, team culture, and player safety. At this point, I had been considering transferring for my fifth year. I didn't want to play for our head coach anymore and I really didn't want to play for our assistant coach.

To try and get ahead of everything, I created a new group chat with just the returning players on the team and got to work. I was worried that the girls on the team had missed the email with the survey, so I sent out a message encouraging everyone to fill out the questionnaire. This was an important opportunity for our voices to be heard. Then I asked the players to all meet at my apartment on Sunday morning.

Leading up to the meeting, I knew this was going to be my first obstacle as a future leader of the team. I wanted to remain as calm and as unbiased as possible, and I didn't want my own personal quarrels with the coaches to affect girls' opinions. My plan was to make everyone aware of the rumors and give people the opportunity to come up with a game plan. We hadn't heard anything from Amanda or the athletic department regarding these rumors, so it was up to us to gain some ground. There were conversations about transferring and speculation about who would be the new head coach. Would it be an outside hire? Someone currently on the staff? Would they be male or female?

Come Sunday morning there were around 16 players at my apartment along with six or seven on Zoom. It was the beginning of Thanksgiving break, so I knew not everyone was going to be able to meet in person. I rearranged all the furniture and we all squeezed into my apartment. I sat in front of all the girls, facing them, holding my laptop.

Growing up, I showed signs of leadership from early on. I was opinionated, bossy, and at times obnoxious. Playing club soccer, I was uber competitive on the field. After a few parents talked to my parents about how I talked to their daughters, my parents told me to chill out. They respected that I was competitive, but we were 10-years-old, and I needed to be a better friend than I was. So, I learned from a young age, it's both what you say and how you say it. I knew this was my first chance to prove my leadership qualities to my teammates. I took a deep breath, and then spoke:

"We can either watch everything unfold in front of us, or we can have a voice in what happens." We talked about how we wanted to be involved in this hiring process and what this could mean for the future of our program. The meeting was productive, and it was handled in a mature way. We had an open conversation, and the girls gave their takes on what we should do. The point of the meeting was to ease any nerves about the future and provide a space for everyone to voice their concerns. We came to the conclusion that we wanted to be as involved as possible. By the end of the meeting, these were the notes:

- *We as a team need to be involved in whatever is going on. It must be transparent. We've worked too hard on this culture to not be a part of it.*
- *We deserve the best coach possible that can win us a natty- it needs to be a nationwide search. It can't be a back-door job. Just like they would do for basketball/football. Fact of the matter is we've underachieved with the amount of talent we've had.*

At the end of the meeting, we decided to text our current head coach and address the rumors. This was so we could give her the space and time to message us whenever she felt she was ready, while also letting her know we wanted and cared about the future of the program. Naturally, I was voted to text her. Within two minutes, she sent a message to our team GroupMe asking for a mandatory team meeting the next day.

The night before our mandatory team meeting with the coaches, I was unusually anxious. I was excited and happy we were finally getting answers, but I was also extremely nervous about what these answers actually were.

I remember walking into the Acosta Film Room, seeing our entire coaching staff including our head Athletic Director Martin Jarmond, and associate Athletic Director Erin Adkins and thinking to myself, "shit is about to go down." We were all masked up, so it was hard to read my teammate's faces, but I am sure they were thinking the same thing.

Once we were all seated and the Zoom was set up for my teammates who were at home (this was the start of Thanksgiving break), Amanda immediately broke the news. She was offered and took the head coaching position at NWSL club Orlando Pride. She was emotional in explaining how hard this decision was but ultimately this was the next step in her coaching career. It was very quiet. There were mixed emotions. I was happy for Amanda and at the same time nervous for the future.

Erin Adkins stood up and reassured the group that she was going to do everything in her power to find the best candidate for the job and we would be involved in the hiring process, which would start that very day. She told the group she would be free for the next two days to discuss the hiring process and check in with whoever wanted to do it.

I played for four years for Amanda. I spent three of those years severely injured. Amanda, a defender herself, had also gone through ACL injuries, so she always had a soft spot for the injured girls. Amanda gave me a chance. Despite me having three knee surgeries and being out for two and a half years, she still believed in me. She trusted me in critical moments, and in important games, and I'll always be grateful for that. Now though, it was time to look to the future.

Chapter 3
Hiring Process

Winning a championship was the number one reason that I chose UCLA to begin with. I knew we were capable of winning, and I didn't want my final year at UCLA to be a "growing" year. But the truth is, we had been underperforming for a while now. When I would say this, though, people would say, "Maddi, you only lost one game in 2021 and won back-to-back PAC-12 Championships. How is this underperforming?"

Let's look at the facts. In the spring season of 2021, we took three of our PAC-12 games to overtime and lost in the second round of the NCAA tournament. In the fall of 2021, we took five of our 11 PAC-12 games into overtime, winning two of them and then losing in the first round of the tournament. In both the 2021 spring and fall seasons, we had a "comeback" personality. We continuously clawed our way back in overtime games. We would essentially play "fight or flight" defense. There was little structure or game plan for our defense. We didn't press, we didn't sit, and we didn't transition.

After the 2019 College Cup, where we lost 4-1 in the national semifinal, we started to decline. You can blame it on the 2019 class graduating or Covid or whatever excuse fits the book, but the truth is, for the amount of talent that comes through Westwood, we should have been a National Championship contender every year. We had the talent, depth, culture, and leadership to be Champions in 2022; we just needed a coach who believed in us just as much as we believed in ourselves.

Luckily, it seemed that the Athletic Directors were on the same page. Both Martin and Erin were very enthusiastic and wanted us to be involved as much as possible. They agreed to have an open-door policy. We all appreciated the transparency, and this showed us that they took our responses on the Google form seriously.

Erin Adkins was our senior Athletic Director in charge of football, men's basketball, and women's soccer. She cared deeply about our program and wanted to bring soccer back to where we belonged - the top. Throughout the year, Erin would become a confidant to me and someone I could go to for anything. With problems ranging from fan engagement to mental health screening, Erin was always on speed dial. She treated me like an adult and wanted the best for our program. She asked the right questions and challenged us to bring answers to the table, not just complaints. One of her first actions was to call the players who would form the core of the team next year and ask us our opinions.

My dad was a high school basketball coach, and my mom was a high school dance coach. Growing up, I saw my dad watch film until midnight, going over each game so he could prepare his team as best as possible. I watched him and my mom wake up at the crack of dawn for summer practices. I watched my mom make up choreography at 10 p.m. in our living room so she could teach it the next morning. They showed me what it took to be a dedicated coach, regardless of the level and sport you coached. They are my heroes and inspiration. Through them – I knew it was possible – I knew there was a coach out there who could lead our team to the top.

I was a bit emotional on my call with Erin. This was my career. This was my teammates' career. The conversation with Erin went great, though. We talked about the past, but we focused on the future. She asked me what I wanted in a head coach, the qualities I valued, and my insight into the past four years at UCLA. I told her I wanted a coach that cared. We needed a prepared and confident coach with experience. I wanted a coach with head-coaching experience who was hired outside of UCLA. I wasn't too specific when it came to gender, but I knew I wanted a diverse staff that wasn't made up of just one gender. Our previous staff was made up of four women, and I wanted something different. I value relationships, professionalism, and communication. I wanted a coach who was open to criticism, showed up in big moments, and took accountability when things went south. We didn't always have these qualities beforehand, and I knew in order for UCLA Women's Soccer to remain nationally competitive, we needed to face the truth. I also told Erin that the main reason I went to UCLA was to win a National Championship, and now I had one more shot. I told Erin that this hire shouldn't just be about the future of the program; it needed to be about right now.

I knew I was asking for a lot, but I trusted Erin and Martin and also had immense belief in our team. We didn't hear much over the next few days. We waited patiently, and eventually, after Thanksgiving, Erin texted me, Lauren, Reilyn, Kylie, Sunshine, Lilly, and Maricarmen that Martin wanted to meet with us. Lauren, Maricarmen, and I were all going to be fifth and sixth years, Sunshine and Kylie were going to be seniors, Reilyn was going to be a junior, and Lilly was going to be a sophomore. We all played big roles in the 2021 season and were trusted and respected amongst the team. These were my notes prior to the meeting:

My notes going into meeting with Martin Jarmond from 12/1/21:
- *Breeds a culture of competitiveness.*
- *How they talk about other teams, respect every opponent- how that's shown in film, scout training, game plans etc. Efficiency. We need to do small group film sessions (doesn't have to be just with head coach)*
- *Someone we can rely on when things get tough. Tied 0-0 down 1-0, and that's when WINNING, head coach experience comes in*
- *I played on great club teams with All-American forwards, all PAC-12 all ACC, and my coaches still COACHED us. They were critical of our best players.*
- *All 4 teams in the College Cup- blue collared teams, we need a coach that will coach us and push us to work hard. Wants to win as much as we want to*
- *Male coach - Women are too emotional and put feelings above facts*
- *Utilize every player- UNC style? Still keep the integrity of UCLA soccer- but we have depth. This can prevent fatigue and injuries.*

Once the day came around, we all marched up to the third floor of Morgan Center to the so-called penthouse. Both Martin and Erin were there, and we all sat in a half-circle around Martin's desk. This was my first real interaction with Martin, and this was the beginning of a great relationship. We all stated our names, positions, and ages, and then he asked what we wanted in a head coach.

Throughout the meeting, he took handwritten notes, asked us about the old staff, and was very straightforward. They treated us with respect and asked us about our previous years.

We told him we felt unprepared and our style of play for most games was "fight or flight." We explained to him how we underperformed the last two seasons. He sounded confused and told us we acted like we went 8-6 and not like we just won the PAC-12 back-to-back. Even though we showed grit and perseverance, we had limited game plans, poor scouts, and rarely felt prepared. He asked us questions about whether we would want a male or female head coach. For the last four years, we had an all-female staff. I felt that we needed a mixed staff and advocated for a male head coach with experience. Yet, I also expressed how I wanted a motivating and confident staff that cared about all the players and prepared us mentally and physically for every game, regardless of who our opponent was. My last statement to Martin was to say that I wanted a coach who would coach with no regrets. We, as players, are expected to play with no regrets. We are expected to play like it's our last game ever, and I wanted a coach who held the same standard for themselves.

After I said that, he gave Erin a knowing look. Almost as if what we just said had confirmed what they were thinking.

At the same time, unknown to us, on the other side of the country, coach Margueritte Aozasa was on a recruiting trip in Tennessee with Stanford. Like us, the Cardinal's season came to an abrupt end during the first round of the tournament to Nor Cal foe Santa Clara. Marg was hired as Stanford's assistant coach in 2015 and helped coach the Cardinal to two NCAA Championships in 2017 and 2019 and PAC-12 titles from 2015 to 2019. While out to dinner with her fellow Stanford coaches, Marg learned that both the UCLA Women's Soccer head coaching job and the USC Women's Soccer head coaching job were open. Paul Ratcliffe, Stanford's head coach, encouraged Marg to look into it. Marg reportedly always spoke of being a head coach one day. She had great success at Stanford, was on track to be associate head coach, and all of her family and friends were in Northern California. At this time, she was also about to get married in two weeks, on December 18th. After the recruiting trip, she decided to give it a shot with the USC job. After submitting the USC application, she thought, why not take her chances with the UCLA job too?

Not to her knowledge, Marg was already on the shortlist for the UCLA job. Erin Adkins was familiar with Marg and had heard great things. On Sunday, December 11th, seven days before her wedding, Marg was in a yoga class in San Jose when a notification popped up on her Apple watch. The message was from Erin Adkins, asking her if she would like to hop on a call and hear more about the head coaching position. Marg finished the yoga class. She walked out to her car and texted Erin back that she would love to chat. Erin wasted no time and asked if she could call immediately. In classic Marg fashion, she crushed her spur of the moment interview in the parking lot of the yoga studio.

Compared to the other available coaches, Marg knew our team the best. She scouted us, recruited a lot of us, and was familiar with the ins and outs of the program since so many of the Stanford players were friends with us. She told Erin that, on paper, we were a top-three team. Yet there should be no reason why we took so many games to overtime and were beating teams 4 to 3. She coached against UCLA in two College Cups and was familiar with some of the cultural shortcomings. Marg spoke authentically and honestly, and little did she know, but a lot of the things she was saying were verbatim what we spoke to Martin about. After 45 minutes, Erin told Marg that Martin was going to call her in 30 minutes. He did, and she crushed that interview too. At some point, Martin is said to have questioned her lack of experience with the USWNT. Marg was quick to name-drop the latest USWNT roster that was just announced, with over a third of the players coming from Stanford, a team that Marg had coached. She implied to Martin that, even though she had no direct USWNT coaching experience, she coached plenty of the current and future USWNT stars. He asked no further questions.

After she hung up with Martin, within minutes, Erin called her to schedule a trip down to Westwood. They wanted to fly Marg and her fiancé out later that week, so Marg had to break it to Erin that she was actually getting married on Saturday, so things were a bit time sensitive. Erin worked her magic, and 24 hours later, Marg and her fiancé landed at LAX on Monday night.

Marg was interviewed all day Tuesday. She met with Martin, Erin, and other staff members. She had breakfast at the Luskin Hotel at 7 a.m. and spent the rest of the day in and out of meetings. Most coaches show up with their coaching philosophy in hand, but Marg showed up empty-handed and in red pants. Martin and Erin still joke with her about that today. "Red pants to a UCLA interview." Regardless, Marg killed it and spoke with such professionalism and maturity. In one week, she flew to LA for an interview, got married, flew to Hawaii for her honeymoon, and was now about to be offered the head coaching job at UCLA. Erin called her the following Tuesday morning and offered the head coaching job at UCLA.

Chapter 4
Welcome to Westwood

I was 13 when I watched UCLA win their first NCAA women's soccer National Championship. I remember the exact play, the time on the clock, the names of the players, and the feeling of winning. I turned to my parents and said, "I want to go to UCLA and win a championship like that someday."

I worked hard towards my goal, and when I was 15 years old, I committed to UCLA. I was a highly-recruited defender, and from the second I stepped foot on campus in January of 2018, I was in the starting lineup. I had started every one of our spring games as an early enrollee at right back. My future looked bright. It looked set to be a four-year starter. It looked like there would be no hiccups. My journey looked unstoppable. It looked like I was on track to be a captain and graduate early to go play professionally. Yet, that's the funny thing about goals and dreams: you really can't plan everything out. Things will come up and change the trajectory of your future in a split second. Months after arriving on campus, I tore my left ACL in our last spring game. I had been to back-to-back USYNT camps in Switzerland and Spain and was playing 90 minutes in our spring games. I started and played against the professional teams, OL Reign and Utah Royals, and held my own out there. I was so excited for the fall, and then, in a split second, everything stopped. I had never been injured before, and now I was going to be out for a very long time.

It took about 10 months to come back from my first ACL. It wasn't a smooth journey, but the week before spring break, I was cleared for contact. I was so excited to be back with my friends and was looking forward to my team's trip to Italy in June. During my first contact practice back, and almost exactly a year from when I tore it the first time, I re-tore my ACL. I was defending and went to cut inside, and my knee gave out. I knew immediately that I hurt it, and everyone around me was crying. It truly was one of the worst seasons of my life. I never got the feeling of being back, and that haunted me throughout my second recovery.

My second recovery was horrible. For every gain I made, there were multiple setbacks. My surgeon used my right patella tendon and put it in my left knee, so I was rehabbing two knees. I spent six months in pain, not really being able to run or jump. Towards the end of the year, I found out I had tears in both my labrums and considered getting labrum surgery. We decided to put the ACL recovery to the side and rehab my hips. There were nonstop setbacks for over a year. I went home in March 2020 for the pandemic and finally felt pain-free. That was short-lived, and after a few weeks of running, I started to get dreadful pain in the inside of my knee. I called my PT and surgeon, and they ordered an MRI. To none of our surprise, we found a meniscus tear. My surgeon was able to squeeze me into Ronald Reagan Hospital, at the peak of the pandemic, for a scope. Without the medical team of Amanda Pruden, Jeremy Vail, Dr. Miller, and Dr. Jones, I wouldn't have come back. They believed in me more than I believed in myself and pushed me to keep going.

After I got the scope, things looked like they were turning around. We found out we weren't going to be playing in the fall of 2020 and that our season would start in February 2021. This would give me even more time to come back and feel confident. I was able to train non-contact the entire fall and felt fit coming into January 2021. I missed our first few games due to Covid, and then finally, almost three years later, I got the call from the surgeon that I was cleared to play against University of San Diego. The game was two days before my 21st birthday, and I will never forget receiving that FaceTime with my trainer and surgeon, giving me the thumbs up to play. I cried. My roommates cried. My parents cried when I told them. It was finally happening, and I was so excited. I hadn't played in a soccer game since April of 2018, and it was almost March of 2021.

Since there were no fans, my parents watched from outside the gates of Wallis Annenberg (Wally). They cheered when I was subbed on in the second half. I will never forget when our assistant coach, Sam, told me I was starting the second half. I broke down in tears and couldn't stop crying. My teammates around me hugged me and were crying too. Sam told me to "pull it together" and gave me a hug.

I ran out onto the pitch with a big smile on my face as my teammates cheered from the sideline. That was a peak moment in my life, and I will never forget feeling so loved and supported by my teammates and friends. I continued to play limited minutes for the rest of the spring. My parents finally saw me play in person, and my confidence grew every game that I played. In the fall of 2021, I earned a starting spot, led the team, and ranked fourth in the PAC-12 for assists. I played freely and creatively. I was finally getting my groove back when our season suddenly ended. My family and friends came to all my games, and I was so thankful to be back doing what I love. It was a long journey, and there was still so much more to accomplish, but I had put in three years of hard work to be back on the pitch. My time at UCLA, being injured, wasn't easy. Most of the time, I felt on the outside. My close friends were there for me, but I didn't always feel valued by the team. Now, I had one more year at UCLA to achieve everything we hadn't managed to achieve over the last three seasons. Being a senior, I wanted to change that for the younger girls. I wanted to make sure they were being checked in on, felt included, and knew that their role on the sideline was appreciated.

I had all these hopes for my final year, but I was nervous. New Year's Eve was approaching. I was in New York City with juniors Brianne Riley, Kylie Kerr, Jackie Gilday, and Hannah Mitchell, a trip we had been planning for a while. Walking around the city, we received a message saying that we needed to attend a Zoom meeting to meet our new coach.

We found a quiet Mexican restaurant, and Kylie, Bri, and I set up our phones on Zoom and waited patiently for the meeting to start. Faces started to pop up, and both of our Athletic Directors were on the call. Within a few minutes, our new coach appeared on the screen. That was the moment we all officially knew – our head coach would be Margueritte Aozasa, the Stanford Women's Soccer assistant. I will never forget that Zoom call. Martin introduced her, and then she introduced herself and said how excited she was for this opportunity. You could hear the gratitude in her voice. She said that she was planning on meeting with all of us individually. I smiled. She was already prioritizing relationships! It was a little quiet after she talked. I remember going off mute and saying on behalf of the team how excited we were and looking forward to this New Era. This was now the start of a New Era, and it was exactly what our team and program needed. After the meeting, we toasted to a new beginning and finished our margaritas.

Marg sent a message to our GroupMe with a sign-up sheet for meetings with every single player. The following week, we flew from JFK straight to LAX and immediately started week one of classes. Because of Covid, classes were online for the first few weeks of the winter quarter, and we needed to have negative Covid tests to lift, enter the Acosta Training Center, play pick-up, and meet with Marg.

Bend Never Break

When I got back to LA, I got my negative Covid tests and scheduled my meeting with Marg. Unlike the previous meetings with Erin and Martin, I didn't have anything prepared. I was excited to meet her and hear her plans for our team. Marg also reached out to all of our support staff and managers to meet as well. She lined up meetings with our strength and conditioning coach, Paige, and our athletic trainer, Nikki. She also reached out to our managers, Kian, and Anish, to schedule meetings and get their perspectives on the program. Even though it seems so obvious to meet with the people who put in hours and hours of work for our program, it went a long way and made everyone feel valued and appreciated.

In the past, individual meetings with the previous coaches were rigid. Sometimes, they were scary or intimidating, or they felt like an interview. I remember always trying to find the right words to say or dance around how I really felt. The older I got, the less scary these meetings were, but as a younger player, I definitely felt nervous going into individual meetings. I had no expectations for that first meeting with Marg. At that point, I had talked to my friends at Stanford, and they all raved about her. They said she was such a smart coach who looked after their best interests. They said how lucky we were.

Even so, knowing this was her first time being a head coach, I was a little wary. There's a difference between an assistant coach and a head coach. For the past eight years, she made suggestions and pointers to Paul Ratcliffe. Now she was calling the shots and listening to the suggestions and pointers from her assistant coaches.

My meeting with Marg went great; it was informal, not scary at all, and she was very easy to talk to. I remember my main takeaways being that she valued fitness, the weight room, culture, and defense. She was going to make us love and appreciate the weight room and wanted us to respect Paige, our strength coach, and her plan for us. Prior to Marg coming, in my four and a half years at UCLA, we ran the beep test maybe three times. We didn't prioritize the weight room and rarely ran in the off-season or pre-season, and it showed. In previous years, we couldn't use our bench because of our lack of fitness, and we played a slow style of soccer that reflected the lack of speed and endurance on our team. I told Marg that this team had the drive and passion to buy in; we just needed a coach to lead us. She wanted our "defense to reflect our culture." She explained that defending as a team, recovering for each other, and putting our bodies on the line shows our commitment and love to one another, which will be embedded in our culture. All I could do was smile. I knew that things were already better than before, and I was excited about our future, but I was also aware that there was a certain level of trust needed.

When the new year began, I also started a master's program in Transformative Coaching and Leadership. This was a year-long program, and we would learn about different types of coaching philosophies, leadership styles, and how to build a successful team culture. My first class for my master's program was called "Coaching Philosophies," and it was taught by legendary UCLA gymnastics coach Valorie Kondos Field and our supervisor, Arif Amlani. Every week, we read a book by a different coach and had discussion questions due. These coaches ranged from John Wooden, Pete Carroll, Miss Val, Bobby Knight, Vince Lombardi, and so many more. We would spend half the class discussing their coaching philosophies and the other half listening to a guest speaker.

Learning about these legendary and transformative coaches while being coached by a first-time head coach was eye-opening. While these coaches had decades to develop their coaching philosophies, I realized that Marg didn't have that luxury; she was expected to return a championship to UCLA in one season. It took John Wooden 18 years until he won his first National Championship, and then he went on to win 10 in the span of 12 years. He created his Pyramid of Success in 15 years. Learning about different coaching philosophies made me respect and view things differently. It's not easy being a coach, yet I learned what certain coaches did that made them successful. Through years of trial and error, coaches created their own coaching philosophy that had a lasting impact on their players, coaching staff, and millions of young athletes, coaches, business managers, and leaders around the world. The John Woodens or Pete Carrolls of the world valued similar things. Their principles ranged from the importance of preparation and focusing on the details to the significance of coaching with love and valuing relationships. Marg was already showing signs of being one of the greats too, someone to be studied one day.

Before our first training, we had a team meeting via Zoom with Marg. She set her expectations for the winter quarter:

1. Be respectful, be professional, be competitive, be brave, be accountable.
2. Respectful to staff, teammates, program, environment.
3. Professional: Arrive on time, wear proper attire, train with a purpose, efficiency, proactive communication.
4. Competitive: Win everything, compete with each other, come with your best self.
5. Brave: Embrace chance, invite challenges, value adversity, suffer together.
6. Accountable: Own your development, own your actions, standards, help each other.

Rules:
- Communication: Respond to text messages.
- Pre/post practice surveys: Complete to train.
- No food/drink in the training room.
- Proper attire for weights and training.
- Mandatory attendance.

Some may think this sounds pretty routine for a coach, but our team finally had clear and explicit expectations. We knew what she wanted, and she knew what she wanted. I appreciated the honesty, and even though she was a first-time head coach, she was confident. A nervous yet excited energy filled the locker room. Even though the expectations were clear, we still were jumping into the water headfirst. None of us had experienced an off season dedicated to fitness. We didn't know her coaching style or philosophy, and we still didn't have assistant coaches. We would soon find out.

Chapter 5
Defense Wins Championships

Since UCLA was on the quarter system, for the first couple of weeks of the winter quarter, we trained four days a week for one hour and were in the weight room or running for the remainder of the time. These were 10-hour weeks that allowed us to hone the details, and eventually our regiment would increase to 20-hour weeks. We could focus on a topic for a week and spend every training working on it. From the beginning, it was clear that Marg knew what she wanted from us and that it wasn't going to be easy.

Marg started off her trainings with a technical exercise involving passing patterns, dribbling, and ball mastery work. As basic as it sounds, our team needed it. Balls were bouncing, we weren't checking our shoulders, and the quality was poor overall. Marg would stop the drill soon after it started and said, "Every single one of you told me how much you wanted to be the best team in the country. In order for that to happen, we have to be the very best at every single thing we do."

She let us know that if we wanted to lift up a trophy in a year, we needed to train like the best. Every drill needed to be executed to the highest ability. We needed to hold each other accountable, ping passes into each other, and focus on the smallest of details. Goodbye to the days of cruising through training. From Day One, Marg set the precedent that we were to train like National Champions. It was up to us to hold each other to that standard.

Defense was up first. We wanted to be the best defensive team in the country. Being a great defensive team requires more than just having a solid backline. Defense requires everyone. It takes everyone tracking runners, communicating, and playing smartly. The two seasons before, our defensive record was not something to brag about. We were slow in transition, gave up soft goals, and relied on our goalkeeper too much. We knew that if we stood any chance of getting to a College Cup, our defense needed to be outstanding. Every single position on the team contributed to defense, and it was imperative that we took it seriously. So, how do you improve on team defense?

We needed to go back to the basics. We did 1v1s, 2v2s, 3v2s. We did drills that focused on shifting and sliding. We worked on ball-winning and clearances. We worked on transitional drills. Everyone was involved; not just the back line. We played small-sided games where getting scored on resulted in a punishment. We hammered down the importance of communicating. This lasted for about a month; for 30 days, defense was the only priority. At this time, we never worked on shooting, crossing, finishing, or how we were going to press. During one of our first intrasquad scrimmages, the score was 4-3, and Reilyn scored a hat trick. Marg joked on the sideline, "Reilyn is a great player, but there is no reason why she should be scoring a hat trick in 25 minutes." Yes, we scored seven goals, but we also collectively gave up seven goals. Marg wanted us to realize that this was not good enough.

On top of giving up unnecessary goals, we also wouldn't tackle. Marg threatened that if we didn't start tackling, we would wear shin guards in training (something we weren't used to). She wanted us to be reminded, at every point, that everything we did was with the intention of being the best defensive team in the country.

While we were becoming defensive maestros, we worked on another part of the game no one liked: fitness. After practice one day, Marg asked us, "Guys, what's going to happen if we aren't fit?" Lilly responded confidently, "We're going to lose!" The team laughed a bit and then stopped when Marg didn't laugh back. She looked at us seriously and responded, "Well, we aren't going to lose, but we're going to be forced to play a sub-based strategy. Every 15 minutes, I'll be making subs." None of us wanted that, so we were going to have to buy in and get on the line. We had much to be nervous about; we knew brutal fitness tests were coming.

Hell Week arrived in the fourth week of January. It consisted of training four times a week, and lifting twice. The notorious beep test was set for Tuesday, the 300s test on Thursday, and a six-minute assault bike test on Friday. The anxiety was at an all-time high. Mind you, I had been at UCLA for five years, and this was our fourth beep test ever. Even though there was no "pass," or "fail," number, people were still nervous.

Training that week was particularly tough. Defense is not easy on the body. Our legs were tired from 1v1 battles, transition games, and the constant shifting and sliding. The weekend before Hell Week, you could feel the stress in the air amongst the team. Nobody went out, everyone went to bed early, and we were chugging water like there would be no tomorrow.

First up was the beep test. The beep test is a 20-meter run, down and back, with a 10 second rest in between each run, with one "miss" allowed. A miss is counted if one does not make the cut on time at the halfway line or does not make it back in time. The beginning stages of the beep test are fairly slow but ramp up pretty fast. Every time the clock ramps up, a new level is reached, and the goal is to run as many levels as possible. By the 20th round, you are running less than six seconds down and six seconds back.

The beep test is something that truly never got easier. Yes, the fitter you were, the more levels you'd be able to run. But everyone got tired. Your legs felt heavy after every cut, and the 10 second rest felt like nothing. Even though there was no standard yet, everyone wanted to make a good first impression on Marg.

Come testing day, it was not pretty. There were a few people who hit 40, but there were definitely more who were in the 20-30 range. A 40 on the beep test was considered "passing" come the fall. Most teams expect between 35-40, so we had some work to do. After the beep test, Marg said, "Some of you killed it, and some of you got killed." I remember us laughing nervously. The idea was that the more we ran the beep test, the less stressed we would be. Preparation equals confidence, right? The more we ran during the winter quarter, the fitter we would be in the fall. We wanted our base fitness to be as high as possible. This would allow us to taper down in the summer, save our legs, and still be fit come August. I was particularly proud of myself after the test, I got the highest score and was the "last man standing."

We didn't know it at the time, but this early preparation would allow us to play three overtime games in the tournament using just 14 players. We couldn't have known it then, but the work we were doing in January was going to help us come December.

Next up was the 300s. None of us had ever run these before, so we spent the days prior Googling things like "What's a good 300 time?" or texting our Stanford friends for tips and tricks. All we knew was we were going to run 50 yards six times, and the goal was to average our time to 55 seconds. My nerves and anxiety were a bit higher than during the beep test. I didn't know how to pace myself. "Do I go full throttle the whole time? Do I take the first two cuts slower?" I had no idea how I was going to run this. As we stepped up onto the line, my heart was pounding. Drake was blasting on our speaker. I took a deep breath and repeated the time to myself. "10 minutes. I can do anything for 10 minutes."

Bend Never Break

The 300s kicked our asses. After the first rep, my butt cramped up the second I stopped running. The first rep was equally as bad as the sixth one, and my average was 56 seconds, which was definitely on the faster end. A lot of girls finished in 62 seconds. After the test, we were standing in the huddle, and I almost blacked out as Marg explained the passing drill we were about to do. I looked to my left. Michaela Rosenbaum looked up at me, and we both gave each other the "I'm dying" eyes. I looked to my right and whispered to Jackie, "I think I'm going to pass out." She replied, "Same." We survived the next 15 minutes doing the passing pattern; our jello legs moved in slow motion as we bounced the ball back and forth to each other. After training, we laid down on the grass in exhaustion. Just like the beep test, the goal was for us to become more and more familiar with the 300s. We would continue to run similar workouts to help prepare us for the next test.

Last was the six-minute assault bike test. Most of us were familiar with this test. Since freshman year, the six-minute assault bike test was a staple in the weight room. All we had to do was push as hard as we could on the bike for six minutes. This wasn't a normal stationary bike; it was a resistance bike, which made it a lot harder. The more calories you burned, the better. This test allowed someone who maybe didn't crush the running to do well. Unfortunately for me, it was not my strong suit. The bike focused more on strength and stamina, and I was not very strong. We split up into two groups. Every girl had a partner, and the entire time, we were yelling at each other to keep going. I stared straight ahead, didn't look at the calories, and used the music to help me keep going. The entire time I was thinking about how much I wanted to quit, but I told myself to just keep going.

Hell Week was officially over. I was so proud of all my teammates for pushing through and having a good attitude throughout the week. We leaned on each other, and it allowed everyone the space to set goals for the future. These were some of the moments where our team felt closest. You could feel the motivation, determination, and love in the room. The music was blaring, we were cheering everyone on, and we knew that we were putting ourselves in the best possible position to win a championship less than 10 months later. At that moment, it was hard to imagine, especially with how our 2021 season ended. None of us had ever won a National Championship before, and the majority of the team had only won one playoff game before. Our coach's commitment to fitness and the weight room was giving us the confidence that we may just be able to achieve the impossible.

During the beginning of the winter quarter, UCLA hired two assistant coaches. Gof Boyoko from UCSB was hired as the first assistant coach. Gof grew up and played in France and brought a European style of soccer with him. He brought such great energy with him and truly brought the best out of the players. He was encouraging and instilled confidence in all of us from day one. His fun-loving and infectious personality made you want to work hard for the team. His knowledge of the game and tactics helped us grow as players, as well as people outside the pitch. While Marg was very steady and remained calm, Gof had an exuberant personality that hyped us up. Marg and Gof worked very well together and balanced each other well.

UCLA also hired assistant coach Molly Poletto. Molly was a goalkeeper coach who coached at Missouri. Molly primarily worked with the goalkeepers and backline, but she also had experience in psychology that helped us with the mental aspect of the game. Between her and our team's psychologist, mental health and team culture were prioritized. The three of them meshed together perfectly.

Marg did a great job recognizing what holes she needed to fill. Marg also hired our fourth coach, Chelsea Tudela. Chelsea was a UCLA Women's Soccer alumni who played for Amanda and was on the team when they won back in 2013. She played with Sam Mewis, Katelyn Rowland, Caprice Dydasco, and Abby Dahlkemper. Chelsea and her husband ran a youth soccer club in The Valley, and she was now going to be on our staff. Chelsea ran technical sessions and filled in when the coaches were recruiting. She also helped out with our social media and created content during our spring trainings. She was a useful tool for us and someone who we could relate to playing under our old coaching staff.

Our team was growing, and now we had a large squad. This was a blessing and a curse. We had close to 30 girls on the team in the spring and were inheriting a large freshman class. Only 11 could start, and only 22 were on the roster for PAC-12 games. Marg came from a program that kept a much smaller roster. Here at UCLA, we always had a large roster. In some cases, like injuries, having a big roster saved us. We had one of the deepest squads in the country. The other side of that is that it's hard to keep an average of 36 people happy. In fact, you can't. All players want playing time. Everyone wants to start. Everyone wants to travel. But that's not how it works. There were training sessions when girls had to sub in or got limited reps because of our roster size. During one training, Marg sat us down after the training had finished. She told us that having a big roster had its pluses and minuses but that it was ultimately difficult to keep this many players happy. She told us that she had a goal for us. She wanted us to be able to look back after our time here and say we got everything we wanted out of our four years. She wanted to help us grow as players, people, and leaders, and to keep everyone happy, she was going to have conversations with us individually about our futures.

Her biggest concern was understanding our roles. If your role was to be the best teammate you could be, and you knew that and were happy with that, you could be on the team. Yet, there was no room for bitterness or negativity. There was no room for shit-talking the coaches or your teammates. There was no room for drama, ego, or unreal expectations. She wanted to be transparent with all of us and agreed that you could fight to change your role, but ultimately, she would have to have some tough conversations. I looked around at my friends and saw tears brimming in some of their eyes. While I agreed with everything she was saying, I remember walking away from that meeting and thinking, "Woah, she has just gotten here and basically threatened to cut people."

This was a reality check for a lot of players. Gone were the days of just being content being "on the team." We were reminded that being at a school like UCLA was an immense privilege. Some players were recruited with the intention of playing for four years, winning titles, and going on to play professionally. Other players were not in the same boat. They came to UCLA for the academic experience and then to play soccer. While both priorities are equally as respected and as important, when trying to build a National Championship winning team, you need a roster that is fully dedicated to that quest. I also knew that, in order for us to win, we needed everyone on the team to buy in. You had to work for your spot, and if it didn't work out, you had to fully accept your role as being a great teammate who wasn't going to travel or get minutes.

I appreciated Marg's honesty and transparency, but I was also confused about the timing. We hadn't played any spring games, and she had only been in Westwood for a few weeks.

Despite Marg's intimidating moments, she also worked hard to create an open-door policy. She encouraged us to pop in for informal meetings and "catch-ups", and the coaches told us they were always there to support us on and off the pitch. We were told this in the past, but I never took advantage of it. I was never going to pop into our old coaches' office to say "Hi." It wasn't because of what I thought they would say, our relationship with the old coaches was just more rigid. With Marg and the new coaches, everything just felt more welcoming and encouraged. I'll never forget one day in the winter quarter; Sunshine and I were in Morgan Center at the computer lab doing homework. Morgan Center was the Athletics building where all the coaches and Athletic Directors' offices were. After about an hour or so, I said to Sunshine, "Hey, let's go see what Marg is up to."

We walked into the office, and they were all hanging out there watching the U20 qualifying games, so we pulled up chairs and hung out for about an hour. We talked about soccer and school, gossiped, and laughed. It was small things like this that we weren't used to. We walked out of their office and looked at each other and said, "Wow, we did that."

At the beginning of the winter quarter, we got wind that the two inaugural NWSL teams, Angel City and San Diego Wave, were going to be on our spring schedule. Panic swept through the Snapchat group chat as we sent memes back and forth about playing Alex Morgan and Christen Press. We had only been training for a few weeks before our first spring game against the San Diego Wave rolled around.

This was San Diego's first season; we were their first opponent, and it was also our first game under Marg. We had spent the last month working on defense and fitness, so that was our main priority. We had no real attack and knew we just needed to defend with our hearts, and then maybe we could give San Diego a tough game. We drove down to San Diego and were so excited but nervous to start our spring season.

Our families and friends were allowed to watch so I was excited to see my parents, especially because my birthday was just around the corner. We piled like sardines into their locker room, listening to music on full blast. We joked about how the game would go as we made our way out to the field. I remember before kickoff I said to the team, "This is the start of our quest of winning a National Championship. Have fun and kick ass." There were a few smirks and maybe some eye rolls, but I didn't care. I knew the will to win a

Bend Never Break

National Championship didn't start in August, it started whenever we wanted it to.

We held SD Wave to 0-0 for the first 40 minutes and then, unfortunately, gave up two goals in the last five minutes from Kelsey Turnbow. Despite not having the ball for almost the whole half, we played great team defense, had aggression, and were constantly communicating with one another. Throughout the first half, Marg made subs and the game had its ebbs and flows. Kelsey Turnbow scored her third of the match in the second half, and we ended up losing 3-0. As disappointed as we were, our coaches were still encouraging and proud. We let one player score three goals, kept the game scoreless for the majority of the first half, and created some quality chances. We had a lot to build on, but our fitness showed as we were able to keep up and compete with a professional team.

Chapter 6
The Turning Point

I was in class on the first of March 2022 when I received a text from Marg asking me to call her. Within 10 minutes, I got another call from Jen Alvarado. This was unusual. My class took a break, so I went outside to take the call. She told me the news: Stanford star Katie Meyer had passed away.

I was in shock; tears rolled down my face. I hung up, and Jen texted, saying she was going to pick me up from class. I remember sitting in the stairwell, just shaking. Of course, the class I was in at the time was *Mental Health in Sports,* so I pulled my professor aside and told her what had happened. She started crying too and we both just sat in silence. I remember going back into class and everyone asking if I was alright. I just nodded and kept looking at my phone, waiting for Jen to text me. She finally did, telling me to come down. I packed up my stuff quickly and bolted right out of there. Once I got into the car, Jen and I sat in silence.

I called Marg back, and we were silent for most of the call. Marg had coached Katie for four years. I then called my mom, who was out celebrating my dad's high school's basketball playoff win, and my dad said he was going to come pick me up. By that night, the entire team had found out. I remember us all texting each other in the group chat, saying how much we all mean to each other. I kept thinking about the Stanford girls.

I had known Katie since I was 12 years old. We did ODP together, and we played on the youth national team together. We were both from Southern California, so we played on rival clubs. Katie was a ball of light. She was a tenacious and confident keeper, but she was also a loyal and compassionate friend. She was everyone's biggest hype-woman and lifted those around her. When I tore my ACL for the second time, she and her family sent me an edible arrangement. After we beat Stanford in the fall of 2021, I went up to her family and gave each of them a hug. With tears in her eyes after a hard 0-1 loss, she told me how happy she was for me that I was finally back out there. Her mom and dad told me the same thing. I thanked them and told Katie she played great and that they would kick USC's ass in their next game.

Katie played the biggest role in Stanford's 2019 National Championship. People were upset after a controversial PK incident in the semifinal against us, but I remember telling my friends at the time that she "gives Stanford an edge." We, along with 99% of the teams out there, didn't have an edge. But Stanford did. Their edge was Katie Meyer. I think most people watching the National Final knew Stanford was going to win before the penalty kicks even started. Why? Because of Katie's energy. She was cheering the crowd on, hyping her penalty kickers up, all with a big smile on her face. I knew she was going to be the hero, and she was. No one was more deserving than she and her team of winning the National Final in 2019. After her saves, she turned to the camera, pointed at the Stanford logo, and said, "Let's go, Stanford!" She was performing, and we were all just lucky enough to watch her live out her life on her stage. That one moment doesn't define who Katie was, but it sure taught me a lesson on how to own your stage when the spotlight is on you.

Practice the next day was canceled, and the team took a team walk to Starbucks instead. I struggled to process it all. I had just seen her at our San Diego Wave game. I called some of my old national team friends, and we cried together. We also laughed at our memories with her and with each other. Some of them were planning on flying out for the candle lighting service. Towards the end of the week, I was sitting in my grandma's backyard and just felt the need to call Marg. She answered, and I told her that she needed to leave and go back up to Stanford. I told her that we were going to be okay. That we could lean on each other and that she needed to go back home to be with her people. She needed to be up in Palo Alto with those girls, Katie's family, and the whole Stanford community. She paused before responding and then said that she would think about it.

The next day, she texted me, saying that she would take my advice and head up to Palo Alto with her husband.

We resumed practice the next week. Our coaches scheduled a team meeting with Melinda, our sports psychologist, and encouraged all of us individually to talk to her. Katie's passing was all over social media. Most news outlets posted about Katie. Millions of people interacted with these posts, showing their condolences for Katie's family and the Stanford community. The soccer community was shaken to the core. Teams from across the country reposted or posted something for Katie. There was also a general push for mental health awareness in college sports. I remember thinking that not knowing who to go to, who to call, or where the best resource could be found, could no longer be an excuse. The Athletic Directors, coaches, and team leaders have to provide resources to their teams. UCLA made a PDF that had different numbers and URLs for athletes to access mental health resources, and it got sent out to every student-athlete.

During our meeting with Melinda, we sat around in a circle. We started off the meeting with an icebreaker, something lighthearted. Then we started talking about Katie. Most were silent. A lot of the girls on our team were friends with girls at Stanford or knew Katie personally. I remember saying, "Katie was such a fierce competitor. She lived for big moments." I also said I was going to miss her sending me TikToks. She had also just started a podcast called "Be the Mentality." Her first episode was out; she did it with her dad.

Throughout the meeting, a few girls shared personal and sensitive stories about their experiences at UCLA over the last few years and the impact it had on their mental health. There wasn't a dry eye in the room. There were many stories. I remember Marg and I locking eyes. A lot of the girls had trauma from their past experiences with UCLA soccer. If you weren't a starter or a major contributor to our team, you didn't feel valued. Injured girls were always on the outside. I will never forget the incident that happened during my first game back after my long recovery from injury, when our coach gave the "Come with Me" award (MVP equivalent) to our 90-minute starting center-back. Tears brimmed my eyes as I looked down at my feet when she announced it to our team. I wasn't mad that I didn't get the award. I was mad that she watched me claw back from three years of heartbreak and couldn't even acknowledge it. Lucy Parker accepted the award, and her voice broke as she turned around and presented the award back to me. She told me how proud everyone was and how inspiring it was to watch me back out there. That was the leader that I wanted to be.

I knew a lot of my teammates felt worse than I did, and perhaps they felt it would be better to just step away from it all. Being a high-level, elite athlete isn't easy. Being in a competitive, do-or-die culture every single day isn't easy. Being belittled, forgotten about, and tossed to the side isn't easy. I knew my teammates were using this New Era as a literal chance to have a fresh start. I don't think Marg will ever forget her first individual meetings back in January. Tears rolled down player's faces as they spoke about their experience so far at UCLA. I think in those moments, she realized that the problems she thought she would face: drama, ego, not wanting to buy in to her vision, weren't really going to be the real problems.

After that meeting, I began pushing for mandatory mental health screenings for all student-athletes, as well as mandatory therapy for freshmen. Every summer, student-athletes should have a baseline mental health screening, and freshmen should be mandated to meet with a psychologist at least three times a quarter. I reasoned that this could help break the stigma and allow student-athletes to feel comfortable when seeking out help. For the next two months, I consistently brought this up to our coaches, Athletic Directors, mental health professionals, and other student-athletes. I'm proud to say that UCLA implemented some of these changes in 2022 and hired more psychologists.

Amidst the beep tests, heavy days in the weight room, and tiring trainings, our team was evolving in more ways than just on the field. A lot of girls were trying to move on from negative experiences with our team culture in the past. Even though it was such an exposing and vulnerable moment, there was such a tightness that began to develop in the team. I have one younger brother, and all my cousins are boys. I didn't grow up with sisters or even close girl cousins, but I did have 35 girls that I considered sisters. To lose a sister because of a mental health crisis (Katie suffered what therapists term an acute stress reaction) is devastating. We worked hard over the next few weeks to create a culture that respected mental health, and in return, we grew closer.

Since Katie's passing, Katie's parents have created Katie Save Foundation. They just passed a law in September 2024 called Katie Meyer's Law. If a student on campus in one of California's public schools is involved in any administrative conflict or disciplinary action, they are allowed to choose an "outside the university" designated advisor for extra guidance and support. This person is also trained in the processes and procedures. Katie Meyer's Law provided a common-sense solution, with the intent being that the student does not feel alone or remain isolated when navigating difficult scenarios. Thanks to the legacy of Katie Meyer, this initiative would now support, protect, and save students in the future.

By the end of the winter quarter, we entered 20-hour weeks. We trained every day for an hour and a half, ran twice a week, lifted three times a week, had Champ Camps on Fridays, and sometimes had games on the weekend. We had meetings on team culture or team bonding at least once a week. Champ Camp took place every Friday. Every UCLA sport out-of-season would compete for the best times and to make the leader board in the weight room. These short HIIT workouts usually last 6 minutes and incorporated anything from the assault bike, rowing machine, ropes, jump rope, or burpees. Despite us dreading Champ Camps, they built character, stamina, and culture.

During the first few weeks, there was a lot of whining. People were tired and sore, and there was tangible anxiety and nerves from all the running. After a few weeks, though, we shifted into a more intense lifting schedule. After one of our lifts, I brought everyone in and said, "We deserve this. We deserve a coach that values fitness and the weight room. If we want to win, we have to be fit and strong, and this is only going to prepare us for the fall." I made it clear that we deserved a coach who wanted us to be prepared. Preparation creates confidence. The fitter we were, the stronger we were, the smarter we were, the more prepared and confident we were going to be in the fall.

Our last game of the winter quarter was against Pepperdine in Malibu. This was a heavy game. The head coach of Pepperdine, Tim Ward, was a close family friend of the Meyers. One of Katie's best friend's little sisters was also on the team that day, the same day as the candle lighting service.

Leading up to the game, we wanted to wear something that represented mental health. For our fall season, we planned on wearing warm-up shirts with the number 19 on the back, as well as Katie's saying, "Be the Mentality," on the sleeve of the shirt. For this game, we decided to wear green ribbons in our hair to represent mental health.

Before the game, both teams came together in a circle, and the Pepperdine coach prayed over us. We all locked arms with each other and looked down at the ground. Something came over me during the prayer; tears streamed down my face. I was standing in between two Pepperdine players, and they started crying too. Here we were, playing in Malibu on their stunning field, while Katie would never play a soccer game again. As I walked back to our bench, Marg came up to me, and we hugged before the game started. I wiped away the tears and tried to focus, I still wanted to finish the winter quarter with a win. The game was a blur; I don't remember much. All I remember was that at halftime, Marg was pissed off that we didn't know what formation they were playing. Regardless, we won 2-0. It felt good to end the winter quarter, the most transformative quarter of my career, and probably my life, on a W.

My family came up for the game, so I showered, and then we went and met some of my youth national team friends for lunch who flew in for the candle lighting service. I hadn't seen them since high school, and it was so hard seeing them in this capacity. We met at a Mexican restaurant in Malibu and sat around the table, reminiscing on our USYNT trips. We had so much fun. That night, 20 of us met at Katie's high school for a vigil held in her honor. We all wore our black UCLA puffers and sat together as a team. As we walked into Katie's high school, we crossed paths with the entire Stanford Women's soccer team. I started crying immediately as I went up and hugged my long-time friends. We walked onto the football field and sat next to each other, looking up at the jumbo screen that was set up. Before the service began, they played a slideshow, flashing through memories of Katie. Pictures from her youth soccer days, club days, national team days, Stanford days, and pictures of Katie just being Katie. We sat in teary silence. Her best friends and parents went up to the podium and took turns speaking. It was both beautiful and heartbreaking.

Chapter 7
The Battle for LA

After our Pepperdine game, we didn't have any more soccer obligations until after spring break. The quarter system is 10 short weeks long, ending with finals week. Most classes have finals throughout week 10 and finals week, so we had no mandatory workouts for two weeks. We still met up to get touches in and play small-sided, but the coaches weren't involved at all. What is unique about athletic programs in the quarter system is that we got to train and prepare for the fall season from January to June. Most semester programs ended in May, and then reported for summer training in July. We grinded for five months straight and then reported on August 1st, thus giving us six weeks at home. So, after a tough 10 weeks of soccer, we now had two weeks to taper down. We had a beep test scheduled the week we came back from spring break, so we still needed to maintain fitness, but it was nice to have a little bit of a break. There were still optional workouts throughout these weeks, and we still had a few games during the spring quarter to prepare for, but everyone was very excited going into spring break.

Leading up to spring break, we were all figuring out our plans. Cabo? Road trip? Going home? Jackie and I had planned a trip to Rio with some of the graduating seniors, so my spring break plans were taken care of. By February, everyone had figured out their plans. I think a lot of teams would consider themselves close or maybe even best friends, and we definitely did. We did everything together. Everyone was invited to Starbucks after practice or Rubio's at Ackerman. All 30 of us would show up to parties together. We hosted parties and were notorious for being "That Team."

That Team who would lead Pauley Pavilion in chants for volleyball games. That Team who would organize athlete formals. That Team who would heckle the opponent at men's soccer games. That Team who would go on spring break trips together. Even after spending every single day with each other for the last 10 weeks, we all spent spring break together. Jackie and I went to Rio with some friends, eight girls went down to Cabo, while 12 others took a road trip up to San Francisco. I think there was one girl who decided to go home and see her family, but everyone else chose to spend it with each other. We spent the break sending updates on our team Snapchat and hyping up one another on Instagram. We had a huge team with four different age groups; there were going to be differences, cliques, and stronger friendships. Yet, in order for us to trust each other on the field and be willing to work for each other, there needed to be a level of compassion and friendship off the field. This was built in the spring.

After playing soccer on the beach, hiking up to Christ the Redeemer, and partying in Copacabana, it was time to head home. Jackie and I said goodbye to our friends who were headed up to Sao Paulo and got on our flight back to LAX. On our 14-hour flight home, I reflected on the past couple of months. Our team and I had gone through so much adversity throughout the winter quarter, and we all handled it with such grace and love.

On my flight back from Rio, I wrote in my journal that it was time for me to own my stage. "Owning your stage" is something legendary UCLA gymnastics coach and one of my professors, Miss Val, created. She described it as owning your life and owning the choices that you make. The dancer in me really resonated with it. To me, there are moments in your life when you might be in the audience cheering your friends on, moments when you're patiently waiting backstage, or moments when you're in the back of the performance. Those moments are to help you grow as a person, teammate, and performer. However, there will be moments in your life when you are center stage with the spotlight beaming down on you. In those moments, it's time to own your stage. For me, it was time to own my stage. After coming back from two ACL recoveries, finally getting to play again in 2021, and now getting one more shot at winning a National Championship, it was my time to be center stage. I knew the spring quarter was going to be pivotal for our team. We made so much ground in the winter quarter; now it was time for us to shift our mentality and work on our culture.

We were back into 20-hour weeks right away when we came back from spring break. We survived our second beep test of the year with scores much better than the first. You could see the improvement and confidence in our running, and it showed during that beep test. More people ran in the 30s than the 20s, and our leaders continued to lead. We continued to have surprise shuttles, Champ Camps, and trainings solely focusing on defense. We spent the next week and a half preparing to play our cross-town rival, USC.

This game was interesting for several reasons. First, we never play USC in the spring. Our coaches were shocked when they found that out; *why not play one of the best teams in the country?* We never knew why and never questioned it. Secondly, we hadn't lost to USC in years. Obviously, we have a rivalry with them, and our games were always competitive, but we weren't going to let our winning streak end, even if it was just a spring game. Lastly, two of our previous UCLA coaches were now at USC.

Jane Alukonis was now the head coach, and Saskia Webber was the goalkeeping coach. We were excited for Jane and Saskia; it just added another layer of competition between our programs. Since we didn't want to ruin our home pitch, we were going to play at Drake Stadium. While we normally played at Wallis Annenberg, Drake could host 10,000+ people. We advertised the game on social media, and to our surprise, there were thousands of people who flocked in through Drake's gates. I remember being on Aux and looking at my friends, thinking, *there's no way this many people are here to watch us play a spring game*. Students, athletes, little girls and boys, families, and members of the community all made their way up Drake's stairs to watch two high-level women's soccer teams battle it out. We were going to play three sets of 30 minutes, and we wanted to dominate every single minute.

We had played in front of huge crowds before, and the UCLA/USC rivalry is the biggest college sports rivalry in history. We were separated by 12 miles, and UCLA held the second most NCAA championships, while USC held the third most NCAA championships. Our "Battle for LA" games during our fall season are filled with rich history, and our programs constantly go back and forth.

The top five NCAA Women's soccer attendance records, excluding NCAA tournament games, are held by UCLA vs USC games. In 2017, 2014, 2018, 2010, and 2016, more than 8,500 people, with the most being 11,925 in 2017, packed Dignity Health Stadium and Drake Stadium to break records. The third most attended soccer game in NCAA history, including NCAA tournament games, was in 2017 at Drake Stadium. I was a senior in high school at the time and was in the stands as I watched UCLA rally to beat USC 3-2 in overtime. In my freshman year in 2018, I was on the bench when I, along with 9,000 people, watched Olivia Athens score in double overtime to beat USC at Dignity Health Stadium in Carson, California. It was insane. Up until 2022, there were no professional women's soccer teams in California. We were the best women's soccer teams in California, and Los Angeles showed out for us year after year. To be able to play in front of thousands of people was a privilege and an unreal experience. Professional women's soccer teams in England or France don't even get this kind of support, and here we were doing it on the collegiate level, and we were doing it at a spring game. It was unreal.

The game started off a little rough. Like usual, USC came flying out the gate. Penelope Hocking and Croix Bethune were relentless in their attack. We withstood their first wave of danger, held on, and defended well, and then finally, Sofia Cook hit a banger at the end of the first 30 minutes. Little freshman Sofia Cook, who had just stepped on campus a few months ago, scored a huge goal for us against a great USC team.

The crowd went wild. The bench went wild. What a moment for Sof. We all cheered and high-fived each other as we started the second 30 minutes. I had been battling the Flu for the past couple of days, so I knew my minutes would be limited.

Nonetheless, it was so fun to be back out there playing in front of such a huge crowd. We continued to dominate the next 30 minutes. Micky scored twice, and Sunshine hit a banger to give us a 4-0 lead. We scored three goals within 20 minutes, and the momentum was flowing. We were putting on a show in front of thousands of people, scoring team goals, and defending in an organized and disciplined way. Next thing you know, USC pulls back two goals, and we ended the half up 4-2.

We knew we needed to pull it together for the last 30, there was no way we were going to let USC come back and beat us. We defended hard and finished the game with a 4-2 W. While Jane didn't play all her players (weird), Marg rotated every single person on our team, and it was amazing to see players like Micky and Sunshine score. Sunshine didn't score a single goal in the fall, and here she was now, running circles around USC's midfield. We felt fit, fast, and creative out there. Our weeks of running and time in the gym were paying off, and you could see it on the field.

Easter Sunday rolled around, and we had practice scheduled on Saturday. Before training, our coaches set up an Easter Egg Hunt around Wallis Annenberg. They split us up into teams, and whoever found the most easter eggs got a prize! The only rule was that everyone had to walk so the injured girls could participate. My team was My, Jackie, Kelly, and Lexi. Of course, the easter egg hunt ended in a tie, so we had a "walk off egg off" between my team and Reilyn's team. Each team nominated one member to walk 10 yards down and then 10 yards back, balancing an egg on a spoon. Whoever made it back fastest without dropping the egg would win.

Naturally, we chose Jackie. The calmest, most level-headed member of our group. Funny enough, the other group chose Rei, the opposite of Jackie. They started on the line together and got ready to walk. I stayed in the back of the group, since I was too nervous to watch. Rei was beating Jackie on the cut, and then Jackie started to speed up. Rei could feel the pressure and tried speeding up and ended up tripping and falling. Jackie calmly walked across the finish line, and we won. We celebrated obnoxiously and posed for a social media picture. Lastly, we followed up by doing an egg toss. We each had a partner, started close together and then we backed up to increase the distance. We laughed and yelled at each other in frustration as eggs dropped left and right. Activities like this brought us closer. In the past, all our team bonding was done outside the soccer field.

Chapter 8
Building a Team Culture

Creating a championship culture starts from the top down, from the Athletic Directors to coaches, support staff, and finally, our student-athletes. Luckily, at UCLA, we were surrounded by incredible people who worked tirelessly to give us student-athletes everything we needed and more. Our Athletic Directors listened to us student-athletes, showed up to our games, and made it a point to involve us in hirings, marketing initiatives, and special projects. They supported us in more ways than one, even bringing in guest speakers and always finding creative ways to inspire us.

When Marg took over the position in January, she immediately started working on our culture. Marg was a level-headed and composed coach, but still lived for competition and winning. She desperately wanted us to win a National Championship, but more importantly, she wanted to make sure that every single one of her players still loved the game after four years. She knew it wasn't going to be easy, but she emphasized that if we could cultivate a strong team culture, the soccer stuff would take care of itself.

On top of the physical work Marg was demanding of us on the training field, she was also adding the culture layer. We met once a week for team building activities. These would either involve a psychologist or just the team. During one of the meetings, we agreed that we needed a "Core Four." Four words that described our culture as a team and who we wanted to be.

There were moments during these meetings when I felt as if we weren't looking at the bigger picture. We were just throwing around words like "confidence" or "hard work." One day, I stood up in front of the group and said, "Let's create a legacy. We have the opportunity here to create a New Era with Marg."

We started in small groups, deciding what words and phrases described our team and our future. Then, we would have bigger discussions with the team. We spent hours and hours trying to come up with what defined us. I remember one meeting we went back and forth over whether or not we should add "accountability" into our core four. At this point, we had Family, Consistency, and Resilience, and we were deciding between Trust and Accountability. One side believed that to hold others accountable, we needed trust. While others believed that trust was innate, and accountability was its own entity. We went back and forth for a few meetings and then ended with the following list:

Family

Family came most naturally to the groups. We all moved away from our families and spent every day with each other. Even though a lot of our team was from California, we still weren't home. We lived with each other, took classes together, and were there for each other during all the ups and downs. The college soccer season is intense. Freshmen walk onto campus on August 1st and immediately have to adapt. Unlike other sports, there is no acclimation period. You are a student-athlete from the first day. We had to be big sisters to the freshmen and lean on each other through tough times.

In September, one of our teammate's mothers passed away. The room was heavy when the coaches broke the news to us. We sat in silence and hugged each other. On the day of the funeral, that next Sunday, we had a game against San Diego State at home. Our team bussed down to Orange County to support our teammate and her family. We bussed back to Westwood that day for our game. Usually, my pre-game speeches were filled with F-bombs and hype, but on that day, I told our team, "There are things bigger than soccer."

We won that night, and our team displayed family values in times of celebration too. After being injured for pretty much her entire career, senior Kali Trevithick clawed her way back to play for her final year at UCLA. She got cleared at halftime during our game against Fullerton, subbed on, and scored two goals. The bench exploded in joy, and there wasn't a dry eye in the stadium. We led the crowd in a "Kali! Kali! Kali!" chant that echoed through our campus. After the ref blew the whistle, we ran onto the field, jumped around, and hugged her. We took a team picture, all pointing to her in front of the most beautiful fall sunset.

Consistency

Consistency highlighted everything we had been doing up to that point. We had dedicated the winter quarter to playing team defense. We spent weeks and weeks doing the same drills and hammering down the same points so it would become ingrained in our heads. We ran the fitness tests every few weeks to build confidence in our running. We remained consistent in our goals of becoming the fittest, hardest-working team we could be. We knew that in order for us to lift that trophy in December, we had to focus on one game at a time. Consistency is something we could control. Before going away for the summer, I sent out a message to the team in our GroupMe. I told them, "We worked so hard this spring to let it all go to waste. Let's put everything out on the table and get your mind, body, and spirit ready for the fall."

That fall, we were the fittest UCLA team I had seen in my five years of being there. Everyone put in the work that summer. We were consistent in the weight room. One of Coach Wooden's principles is to Make Each Day Your Masterpiece. This principle emphasizes the importance of doing your best every day by focusing on the basics. By doing the little things consistently, like checking your shoulder, not cheating during running, playing to the correct foot, and bumping your runner, we were giving our 100% effort every day. Making Each Day Your Masterpiece values discipline and hard work, which are characteristics that we all held close to our hearts. By doing the little things and trying our best every day, we were growing closer to that trophy.

Resilience

Being resilient *and* having a good attitude at the same time was not easy. There were seniors who didn't roster and barely played. There were freshmen already in the transfer portal. There were injuries throughout the season. There were tough losses. Yet, every single day, people showed up to work for the person next to them. Sometimes, with a smile on their face, and other times, it was shown through work ethic and communication. Our senior class was especially resilient. A lot of us faced adversity throughout our whole career at UCLA, on and off the field. The adversity held us back in some ways, but it also made us the best leaders we would become.

After getting limited playing time during her comeback season in 2021, Sunshine Fontes led our team in points. Maricarmen Reyes, our captain, did not play much during the NCAA tournament but, when called upon, performed her best. There were seniors who didn't play much but still led by example and worked hard every day. There are so many personal stories that showed how resilient our team was, and it ultimately created a feeling throughout our team. We knew that when things went south, we were going to find a way to pull out the win. I had joked early on that our season was "already written." Our personal and team resilience was the backbone of our team and allowed us to trust that everything was *supposed* to happen.

Trust

The last piece of our Core Four was trust. In order for us to hold each other accountable and win throughout the fall, we had to have undeniable trust. Trust in each other, the game plans, our coaches, and trust within ourselves. Our team displayed trust on all fronts. In order for my team to trust me, I had to lead by example. I had to show up in fitness, I had to be vocal, and I had to trust the coaches. This was hard for me. When the coaches first came in, I didn't trust them. I didn't think Marg was totally qualified because she had never been a head coach before. It took me a while to become 100% bought into her vision. I respected her and the other coaches, and I was excited for the future, but I knew that trust was a two-way street. While Marg had been there for a few weeks, I had been there for four years. I knew what my teammates had gone through with our previous coaches, and I knew things weren't automatically going to be sunshine and rainbows.

 As the winter and spring quarters went by, my trust in them grew. The more we prepared for the fall, the more I realized how much they cared for our team. After Katie's passing, I felt a shift in energy with the coaches and within myself. When we opened up about mental health and the girls talked about their past experiences on the team, the coaches were finally able to see what people went through.

 Our trust in the coaches and in each other would become vital in the fall. As we switched formations the night before we played Duke or during overtime against Virginia, we had to trust our coaches' game plan. We had to trust each other after losses, throughout the summer break, during a Covid scare, and when we were seconds away from losing. Trust was embedded in our culture early on and remained one of the key components in our team's championship run.

 As the spring quarter went on, we met with Melinda, our UCLA Athletics sports psychologist, for team building activities. I had met with

Melinda individually for the past couple of years and was very familiar with her. Up until I got to UCLA, I had never been to therapy before, so I didn't really understand the benefits until I met her. I knew that if Melinda could help me on a personal level, she would be able to help our team.

In the past, our team never had organized independent meetings on mental health or team culture. Our previous coaches led everything, which made it hard for people to really speak out about their feelings or connect with one another on a personal level. I was grateful that our new coaches were viewing therapy in a healthy light, thus showing all of us that therapy is normal and a positive experience.

Our first meeting with Melinda was all about leadership and conflict. We met in the meeting room at Morgan Center and started off with a few icebreakers. They began trivial and became more personal with every question: *Chocolate or gummy, favorite candy? If you had to pick a sport other than soccer to play, what would you choose and why? What is one bad fashion choice you made?* In the second round, the icebreakers became more meaningful: *Which two characteristics do you most admire in a teammate? What's one thing that annoys you? In one word, what comes to mind when you think of conflict?*

Everyone went around in a circle and shared trivial answers like Skittles, gymnastics, and wearing Justice. Then we all went around and shared a bit more vulnerable answers, such as being an inclusive and hardworking teammate or being annoyed at people who are always yelling and complaining.

Melinda then facilitated the next exercise, which focused on what our tendencies are when dealing with conflict. She explained that we all have tendencies when we're feeling vulnerable - When conflict arises, when we feel under attack, or when we witness conflict. She broke down the tendencies with five different animals: The Lion comes in hot – the lion might attack or come on the offensive when feeling vulnerable. The Rabbit bolts when under attack. The porcupine gets prickly so that others step back. Owls intellectualize but struggle to engage on an emotional level; they stay focused on the content of the argument. Turtles hide under their shells when they feel attacked.

We all took a few minutes to read over the tendencies and decide which one we all were. I sat there reading back between Lion and Porcupine.

Eventually, I walked over to the porcupine group, which was a small portion of the total team, and we all laughed at each other. I looked across the room and saw my teammates in their respective corners, and everything made sense. All of my closest friends were exactly where I expected them to be. My porcupine group went around in a circle and shared tendencies regarding conflict. We all agreed that sometimes we are so quick to get upset or confrontational that people tend to back away. I knew that I needed to do a better job at giving people the benefit of the doubt and looking at the bigger picture when dealing with conflict. Not everything needed to be solved or talked about right away. As we all came back together, each group shared their tendencies. We pulled out themes and reflected on how this relates to team dynamics regarding conflict and management. A lot of my teammates talked about how tone matters; it's not what you say, it's how you say it. We talked about how pulling someone aside to have a conversation in training is more effective than yelling at them on the field. We talked about how compliments and positive reinforcement can go a long way. A lot of the time, we know when we made a mistake on the field. We know that we shouldn't have passed it out of bounds or taken a bad touch into the defender. Getting on each other for obvious mistakes wasn't solving problems, and it definitely wasn't lifting the team up. Holding high standards in training is a different situation. Demanding more from your teammate is part of the game, whether that be sharper passes in a passing pattern, running through your tackles, or better communication. We all understood that things could get intense, and there would be moments when things get ugly. That is part of playing at UCLA and competing for a National Championship.

Our second meeting with Melinda was a bit more personal. It focused on learning about emotions through our families. We started off with icebreakers again: *What was your favorite breakfast cereal growing up? If you could give a piece of advice to your younger self, what would it be? What is your favorite family tradition? What is one feeling you like to experience? What is one feeling you find difficult to tolerate?*

As we all went around the circle and shared, some answers were funny and light-hearted, while others were more emotional. After this, Melinda gave us an introduction about feelings. In it, she said that:

- *We learn about emotions through our families—our parent's model how*

- *they manage emotions, and different family dynamics impact how we experience emotion, our relationship with our own feelings, and also how we manage conflict within a system.*
- *Some of us may have developed roles in our family—typical roles are mediator or hero, or sometimes we are what's called the "identified patient." These roles develop to help us cope and to help the family system cope with something difficult. They are functional in the system that you grew up in but not always so helpful as you get older (aka, we often repeat our family dynamics in other systems/relationships).*
- *Many families struggle to manage intense and difficult emotions, which leads us to learn to suppress our feelings. College athletics is also an environment where we learn to push away feelings.*
- *Some families talk in healthy ways about feelings, express feelings openly, talk things through, hear others' perspectives, honor different feelings, and work to resolve conflicts.*

We all then split up into three groups to talk about our families. We spoke of the three different types: families who ignore feelings, families who erupt with feelings, and families who validate feelings. We went around and took turns speaking about our feelings. Melinda said that she wanted us each to think about which feelings were more difficult for us to tolerate. She encouraged us to invite curiosity and build awareness around emotions. She emphasized that when we speak more specifically, we tend to get our needs met. She also emphasized that it is important to understand our feelings so we could be effective in managing conflict. Feelings give us a lot of information, and when we aren't in touch with them, not only are we more vulnerable to depression and anxiety, but we can't use them as a guide. This exercise allowed us to get to know each other on a deeper level. We learned about each other's families, whether it was about past trauma or Christmas traditions. Some grew up in similar households where emotions were never shown, while some grew up in households filled with emotion. We were able to draw similarities from our experiences and build connections with each other. In some ways, I think this explained to all of us why each player was the way that they were.

Chapter 9
The UCLA Soccer Baddies

Throughout the spring quarter, our team continued to grow closer off the field. We put in more effort to bonding through socializing, and we wanted to put all the things we were learning into practice. This didn't just apply to soccer. We partied like we trained as well. Following on from our sessions with Melinda, where we all identified as one of four animals in conflict resolution, we decided to throw a jungle-themed party for Maricarmen's 22nd birthday.

Three years prior, we were freshmen and hosted a jungle-themed party for Mari's 19th birthday. We hosted the party at an older girl's apartment, and it ended up being a flop. Turns out, a lot of people don't want to come to celebrate a freshman turning 19. To redeem ourselves and celebrate Mari's last birthday at UCLA, we decided to give our jungle party one final attempt. We made a hilarious flyer, sent it to every student-athlete we knew, and told them to dress in their best jungle-themed attire. This ranged from animal print to greens and costumes. A good friend, Liv, lived in an apartment with great front yard space, so she and her roommates offered to host us. We borrowed the men's soccer massive speaker and began getting everything ready for Saturday night. We first had to take care of business against Long Beach State.

The day before our big party, we bussed down to Orange County to play Long Beach State for our final spring game of the year. We played them in the fall at home and walked away with a narrow 1-0 win. Long Beach advertised the game, and as we walked out to their pitch to start warmups, so did hundreds of fans. I walked past the same spot where I first tore my ACL almost four years prior. I clutched onto my ACL brace and walked right over the endline where my circle first started. I thought to myself, *Here I am now, about to close that circle.*

Our game against Long Beach State went great. We looked incredibly fit, explosive, and confident. Everyone played substantial minutes, and we ended with a 3-1 win. We beat Long Beach in front of a pretty big crowd, and at the end of the game, we took a team picture and celebrated a successful spring season.

Bend Never Break

I was personally happy because this was my first completed spring season with UCLA Soccer. I had played every spring game and remained healthy the entire time. I was planning on transitioning out of my knee brace for the next couple of weeks, so I could fully be ready by the fall. Not only were we excited about winning our game, but we were excited for a fun-filled Saturday. As we took the bus back to Westwood, the vibes were high as teammates discussed their outfits, sent out the flyer, made playlists, and schemed for the weekend. The next morning, we woke up excited to celebrate Mari! We pregamed at Lauren and Jackie's apartment, made TikToks, and took pictures. Mari wore a super cute cheetah dress, and I wore a leopard sheer skirt with a black top. Our teammates had zebra sets on, cheetah skirts, and tiger-print pants. Everyone looked beautiful and festive.

Our second attempt at the jungle party was a huge success. Everyone looked amazing in their animal print and jungle greenery. Cheetahs, zebras, trees, and birds flocked up and down Roebling Ave. Jungle juice was poured, music blasted, and the cops were eventually called. It was significantly better than Maricarmen's 19th birthday, and it was a party I will never forget. The pictures and videos will live on forever, and I can't wait to show my kids one day what their mom and her friends did in their senior year of college. The next morning, we helped clean up Liv's front yard, returned the speaker to Men's soccer, and went over all the happenings of the night before with the team at Starbucks.

From the very beginning of the spring quarter, we knew we wanted to host an athlete formal too. In the past, UCLA baseball would put one on, but after Covid, there hadn't been one. We believed that if we planned it, we could rally the troops and get the word out to every student-athlete. I'll never forget sitting at Starbucks with Kylie and Sunshine and calling the venue to book the date of the party. Everyone Venmoed Kylie the $16 deposit, and we got to planning.

Before we knew it, our athlete formal was creeping up. Jackie put together a clever flyer for us to send out to everyone. It was a play on words with John Wooden's Pyramid of Success. We switched out some of the blocks with "W's Only", "Competitive Drinking", "New Era", "Buy in", "Dress to Impress," "Go for #120," "Friendship," "Team Spirit," and "Enthusiasm." Jackie photoshopped John Wooden next to a Bruin with a spotlight shining down on both of them. We decided it would be even more fun if we all went to the party together, so we rented a party bus for the night.

We were so excited in the lead up to the party. It's what got us through a week filled with running, lifting, and Champ Camps. We spent the entire week talking about our outfits, shoes, how we were going to do our hair, and speculating who was going to show up. Girls would send their outfits in the Snapchat group chat. Whether you had a date or not, it was the first event, outside of athletics, since Covid where all the student-athletes were invited to something fun. The date finally rolled around, and our coaches told us to "stay out of the streets" over the weekend. We all laughed.

On the agenda, we planned to take sunset pictures in our dresses at Royce Hall. This was a core memory. Everyone looked amazing. There was an array of colors, and it was the first time in a while we all got glammed up together. Everyone met at the top of Janss Steps for a beautiful spring sunset. We took pictures for close to an hour, and then all went over to Jackie and Lauren's apartment before going out. We took pictures, played games, and danced and sang. We all boarded the party bus and arrived fashionably late to our own party. When we were first planning our party, we figured there would be at least 100-150 people and told the location to plan on 100 people coming. There turned out to be closer to 400 people, half the student-athlete population at UCLA, and we quickly needed to "hire" a bouncer- per the manager's request. We called up one of our team managers and told him he needed to man the door.

Throughout the night, random people who I had never met thanked a few of us for planning such a fun night. When looking back at my college experiences, it's nights like those where I look back and smile. Not only did we have the best night, but it was also great to spend the night with other athletes. It was also moments like this where I was so grateful for my teammates and friends. Everyone was included in every decision. Everyone was invited and could invite whoever they wanted.

Not only were we social butterflies, but we also were Intramural (IM) Football Champions. That spring, a group of girls, along with managers, Kian, and Leo, put together an intramural Football team. Every week, "Kitchen United" would destroy sorority sisters and fraternity brothers. Sunshine was QB1, and Reilyn, Jayden, and Lexi would score touchdowns left and right, and we would blow teams out of the water.

Bend Never Break

There would be weeks where the opponent would forfeit before the game even started. As the weeks went by, Kitchen United became a hot commodity. We would show up in numbers to support our girls, and eventually made it to the final. Our Athletic trainer's husband, Coach AB, was a strength coach for UCLA Football, so he would come and draw up plays for our girls to run. During the final game, our friends who were on the football team showed up and helped run plays. We heckled the other team and were obnoxious on the sideline, cheering for every touchdown, interception, and flag pulled. We won the final comfortably and rushed the field when the clock struck 0. Our girls put on their IM Football championship shirts, and we made a tunnel for them to run through. This was the start of our championship journey and foreshadowed how our fall season would end up.

We ended the spring quarter with a bang. Our coaches planned the "Bruin Olympics." They split us up into teams, and we all dressed up. My team dressed up as John Wooden and the UCLA basketball team. I dressed up as Coach Wooden, and my teammates dressed up as the basketball players. One of the girls made a whiteboard and attached a string to it to wear it around her neck. The Bruin Olympics had several events, all ranging from juggling, PKs, trivia, and a shoe tying competition. Each team nominated members to compete in each event, and whoever won got the most points. Our coaches played up the "Olympic" aspect by having an opening and closing ceremony as well as having gold, silver, and bronze equivalent prizes.

While we were having a blast hosting our parties, we were still putting in the work on the field. While most of the country finished up their spring season weeks before, we were still running shuttles on Wallis Annenberg. Our strength coach, Paige, was given full control and pushed us to the max every week. At the beginning of the year, there were three groups for fitness, with each group running five seconds slower than the next. By the end of spring, there were two groups, and the times were greatly improved. Fitness anxiety subsided and our names were plastered all over the Champ Camp wall for the best times.

Soon, the spring quarter was coming to an end. The grand finale of what was truly the most fun six months was graduation. The week of graduation was filled with so much joy. Practice was over, so we didn't have any obligations during the day. Some of us had finals that week, so we were getting everything done early so we could enjoy every moment together.

Bend Never Break

My original freshmen class took graduation pictures together one morning. We woke up at 6 a.m., got ready, and met the photographer at Janss Steps. We all wore white dresses with "fun heels." Even though the weather was overcast and gray, the pictures turned out beautiful. Later that day, we all went to the beach, the same spot we went to during the last week of our freshman year and had dinner. The end of the spring quarter was bittersweet. I was sad saying goodbye to my old friends. We reminisced on our adventures in the dorms, our dingy sophomore year apartment, drama with boys, and everything in between. We laughed while looking back on all the embarrassing moments college brought. Those girls will always be my best friends and a huge reason why my time at UCLA was so incredibly memorable. At the same time, I was looking forward to the encore that was coming. It really was a New Era, and we had spent the last five months grinding in the dark.

UCLA has a unique graduation celebration with only its student-athletes. It's held in Pauley Pavilion, and anyone can attend. To walk at graduation, each senior had to attend three workshops that UCLA Athletics organized. They all covered a different topic in life after college athletics. They ranged from exercise, diet, taxes, mental health, and resume building. This was the first graduation held inside since 2019, and it was a magical day.

The seniors walking were me, Lauren, Mari, Hannah, Cassidy Tshimbalanga, Kylie, Shana Flynn, and Idalia Serrano. Earlier that day, everyone's families met for lunch in Santa Monica. Our moms planned a special brunch; they decorated our table with little signs and flowers, and the mimosas were flowing. Our families hadn't seen each other since the fall, so they were living it up as well. After brunch, we went back to our apartments to freshen up before graduation. It was madness. My parents were changing at our apartment, my grandmothers were over, Mari's boyfriend was getting ready as well, and we were rushing to meet everyone for drinks before graduation. I wore a gold sequin mini dress and black heels. My roommate, Maricarmen wore a tight, white dress and looked stunning. We packed up my mom's Mazda and drove to the Luskin Hotel, UCLA's on-campus hotel. At Luskin, our teammates and coaches met us. We took pictures, had drinks, and got ready to walk across the stage. I will never forget feeling so loved and happy in that moment. We were surrounded by our family and best friends, and it was the perfect day.

Bend Never Break

We headed to Pauley Pavilion, where we met up with all the other student-athletes. We took pictures together and with all the other student-athletes. Our Athletic Directors greeted us before it was time to head up to the arena. While we were walking into the arena, our friends were outside Pauley Pavilion, cheering us on. They were banging on Pauley's wall as we jumped up and down. We walked into Pauley and immediately heard our friends and family screaming for us. I broke down in tears as my mom waved a poster of me in the air. Hannah and Kylie told me to pull it together as we walked to our chairs. Graduation started, and as Women's Soccer got ready to go on stage, our teammates cheered loudly for all of us. My mom and dad took me out to dinner that night, and then we went back to our apartment to get ready to go out. This was our last big hurrah of spring quarter, and of course, we were going to spend it out partying. After dinner, Jackie and I met up with the rest of our team at a local bar. I wore my graduation sash around my neck with a white lei my mom bought me. We got to the bar and met up with the rest of our team. Older sisters were buying drinks, we were dancing and singing, and the vibes were at an all-time high.

After graduation, we all said goodbye and left to go home. Some girls were coming back to Westwood for summer school and summer workouts, while others were going to be gone until August. Since UCLA was on the quarter system, we only had six weeks of summer. Luckily, we trained from January to June together, so we put in a lot of work during the spring. By the time we left in June, our team was fit. The goal of summer was not to train so hard that we would burn out come August but to maintain fitness from the spring. I added the incoming freshman and two transfers to our GroupMe, and I sent out a message to our team saying,

"Failing to prepare is preparing to fail" -Coach Wooden. One month out!! Hope everyone is having a fantastic summer and doing everything we can to get our mind, body, and soul ready for season. We've worked so hard the last 5 months to let anything go to waste. Let's put everything out on the table and have no regrets!!"

Chapter 10
Summer

Over the first six months of 2022, our team grew expeditiously. To think that in December, we didn't have a coach and had no idea what the future held. To think that they hired a rookie head coach who, unbeknown to her, inherited an emotionally broken team that couldn't play defense. To think that I had six more months being a Bruin. The last six months were transformative, physically exhausting, and filled with resilience. A lot of girls faced their fitness fears, made huge strides in the weight room, and showed vulnerability in our culture meetings. We leaned on each other during the hard moments; whether that involved pulling someone off the ground during the beep test or giving a hug when talking about low moments in our personal lives.

For me personally, I put myself out there and intended to never look back. There were moments in training when I snapped at people to drive a higher standard. There were moments when I yelled during our 300s to run harder. There were moments where I told people to stop screwing around in the weight room. There were moments where I had to check myself: was I being the best teammate I could be? Was I leading in a way that could be relatable to my teammates? I always wondered, if I never called that team meeting back in November, what would have happened? If I never texted Amanda, asking her what the hell was going on, what would have happened? I was so adamant that we be involved in the hiring process and that our voices should be heard; what would have happened if I wasn't? The *what if* factor always played in my head, and at that moment, I never thought anything of it. I showed more bravery than I ever had, and I wouldn't have been able to do that if I didn't have an army of supportive and compassionate women behind me, allowing me to be myself.

This was going to be my last year playing at UCLA. I had two more years of eligibility left, but I knew deep down this would be my last season. At this point, I felt that I had given everything to this program and the school, and I knew my time would be done come December. There was little to no part of me that thought I'd go play professionally. Up until this point, I had only played one season of college soccer, and our team had been kicked out in the first round of the tournament. I didn't have a lengthy list of accolades to my name. At the same time, I felt as if I had nothing to lose. In a way, not knowing my future allowed me to pour everything into my team. That summer, I decided I would do everything in my power to leave UCLA with no regrets.

I knew if I was a demanding, inspiring leader in every aspect, I could lead this team to win a National Championship. This wasn't an easy decision. I had to not care what people thought about me. If I was going to yell and snap at people at training, I would have to leave training knowing they'd go home and gossip about me. If I spoke up in film or in meetings, I knew I'd get eye rolls and heavy sighs (from players and from coaches). If I wanted to hold our team to the highest standard, I knew I'd get push-back. But, quite simply, I really didn't care. Talk about me, roll your eyes, hate me, or love me; none of that would matter when we were champions.

Luckily for me, I had built strong relationships with the majority of the team, and there was already respect and trust established. I could also relate to everyone on the team. Throughout my entire career at UCLA, I had been in every role you could think of. I was in the injured role, the comeback role, the sub role, the starter role, the lost-my-spot role, and now I got to be in a leadership role. Every role comes with its own stressors and demands.

Being injured, you are expected to come back and play at the highest level. Every day, you wake up, go to rehab, squeeze in an extra lift, run after practice, come back in the afternoon for more rehab or treatment, make sure you eat enough calories to build muscle, and still be a loyal and energetic teammate. Being injured is taking two steps forward and then one step back. For every milestone you hit, there is pain and discomfort around the corner. You never feel as if you are truly making an impact on your team's success. You just do whatever you can to be back on the pitch as soon as possible.

Once you're cleared from a major injury, it takes a few months to feel like yourself again. This role is difficult because you're always in between. In between still feeling as if you're behind, but also so excited and happy to finally be back playing. In between feeling satisfied and giving yourself grace, but also looking ahead and wanting more from yourself.

Being a sub brings its own challenges. Having to understand your role and perform to the best of your ability while still being an encouraging and positive teammate isn't easy. In training, you're a part of the scout team, but you are also trying to retain any information about what the starters are doing so you feel prepared going into the game. You still feel a part of the team because you get to play and make an impact, but deep down you always want more. Losing your starting spot is a different feeling. You become the underdog, fighting to prove something to your coaches, teammates, and yourself. You are in a different position than being a normal sub because you have something to earn back.

During the first part of 2021, I started every game at left back. I led our team with nine assists and was playing well. This was my first full season back from injury, and I was just so happy to be back playing with my best friends. Being a starter comes with its own set of responsibilities. You prepare differently. Watch film differently. Maybe you have a different pre-game routine. Your body knows when you are about to start a game. There is a heightened level of nerves and anxiety. There is also a sense of pressure to get the job done, because if you don't, you could get subbed out. Every starter is expected to be a leader out on the pitch. We all had our own ways of leading; we were expected to communicate, be prepared with the game plan or scout, and execute during the game. Going into our 2022 season, I had no idea what role, or roles, I would be playing that year. Of course, I wanted to be a starter and lead our team to a National Championship, but I also knew I could only control so much.

Our summer was short and sweet. We only had six weeks at home to unplug and get ready for our season. I was at my best friend's wedding, went to Mexico to watch Maricarmen play for Mexico vs. the USWNT, worked at UCLA camps, and got myself ready for our season. I ran at my local fields, the beach trail, and at the gym. I trained with a local group of college girls that included some of my teammates and lifted as much as I could. I didn't want to burn out or overwork my body because I knew pre-season would be tough, but I also wanted to have no regrets. In order for me to earn a starting spot, I knew that I had to check all the boxes. I had to work. Everything I did that summer was to give our team the best possible chance to make it to the College Cup.

Chapter 11
Coach Wooden

As I lay in my bed the night before our first day of pre-season, I couldn't help but think that I wasn't ready for this to all be over. I wasn't ready to move on, honestly. I had spent so much of my career at UCLA unable to walk, run, or kick a soccer ball, and here I now had four months until it was all over. I thought about John Wooden and how he would lead his team.

John Wooden, also known as the Wizard of Westwood, was a legendary basketball coach at UCLA. He led the Bruins to 10 National Championships in a 12-year span, seven of those in a row. At the time of writing, no other program has won more than four. During his time at UCLA, his teams won 88 games in a row, which was a NCAA men's basketball record for most consecutive games won. Coach Wooden was loved by his former players, including Kareen Abdul-Jabbar and Bill Walton; his inspiration continues to motivate many coaches and athletes.

Throughout my master's program, John Wooden quickly became one of my favorite coaches. Not only is he a UCLA basketball legend, but he also created the Pyramid of Success. My father played college basketball at San Jose State, so basketball has always been a part of my life. Ever since I was a little girl, the quote, "Hard work beats talent when talent doesn't work hard" had been ingrained in my brain. Whenever I could choose to write about a coach, I would always choose John Wooden. The coaches and girls on the team called me "Coach Wooden," and I carried the nickname with pride, humility, and humor.

Throughout his career, Coach Wooden stayed true to his values and beliefs. He didn't let others change his standards. "The highest, purest, and most difficult standard of all, the one that ultimately produces one's finest performance and the great treasure called peace of mind; that which measures the quality of your effort to reach Competitive Greatness." He applied this standard throughout his career and succeeded. Coach Wooden's Pyramid of Success is taught in businesses, sports teams, and schools. The key principles within the Pyramid of Success left a championship legacy at UCLA and beyond.

John Wooden spent decades curating and identifying the most important traits that helped define a successful person and team. These life principles in the Pyramid of Success had no reference to basketball and athletics; they are a roadmap to becoming the best version of yourself. The building blocks included in the first tier are Industriousness, Friendship, Loyalty, Cooperation, and Enthusiasm. The second tier includes Self-Control, Alertness, Initiative, and Intentness. The third tier involves Skill, Team Spirit, and Condition. The fourth tier involves Confidence, Poise, and lastly Competitive Greatness.

My favorite one is Team Spirit: "A genuine consideration for others. An eagerness to sacrifice personal interests of glory for the welfare of all." It's easy to have team spirit when things are going your way. However, it's hard to have it when things are looking down. Coach Wooden describes Team Spirit as one of the most tangible intangibles. It's something you feel. Industriousness and Enthusiasm make up the foundation because, without their presence, nothing can be accomplished. These are the "qualities of the heart," such as Friendship, Loyalty, and Cooperation. These qualities allow for a powerful bond between teammates.

The second tier of the pyramid is the disciplines of Self-Control, Alertness, Initiative, and Intentness. Combined with the foundation, these disciplines add to a powerful, positive, and relentless leadership force. The center of the pyramid and third tier is made up of personal assets such as Condition, Skill, and Team Spirit. The last three blocks, Poise, Confidence, and Competitive Greatness, rely on the 12 other blocks for support. Coach Wooden describes Poise as remaining steady no matter the situation. Being able to hold Poise under pressure is what makes a great leader. Lastly, there is Competitive Greatness. He defines this as "A real love for the hard battle, knowing it offers the opportunity to be at your best when your best is required." It's not measured by success or defeat but rather by the feeling or knowing that you did everything you could to be the best.

Whether we realized it or not, I knew we had the ability to possess each building block and could reach Competitive Greatness by the end of the year. It was going to take time, but this group was special. We had immense talent, squad depth, and coaches that had nothing to lose. We spent the entire spring curating our culture.

We had everything that it took to build the Pyramid of Success, and to reach Competitive Greatness, it was going to take every single person to believe that we could do it. We were going to spend the fall chasing Competitive Greatness, checking off one block at a time.

Bend Never Break

Part Two

Chapter 12
Industriousness

There is no substitute for work. Worthwhile results come from hard work and careful planning. "Nothing will work unless you do." One of John Wooden's cornerstones of the Pyramid of Success is Industriousness. Throughout pre-season we displayed industriousness on and off the pitch.

We arrived on campus on August 1st. After a busy day filled with expectation-setting, back-to-back meetings, and my final media day, it was time to get to business. Our first training was the next day, followed by an afternoon training. We had mandatory breakfast as a team in the morning and mandatory team lunch in between trainings. The night before practice I was so anxious, I barely slept. I was excited. Stressed. I was a lot of things. I wanted to perform my best, and I wanted our season to be a dream. I had put so much time, effort, and passion into this program, and I had four months left to show the industrious spirit.

The first few days went well. It was hard. The sessions were competitive, fast-paced, and demanding. We worked a lot on our shape, counter-press, and our identity. We were a really dynamic group. We had long-legged, gazelle-like forwards who could run for days. We had an incredibly smart midfield who were all different types of players. Mari brought creativity and flair, Sunshine brought vision, Ally Lemos brought calmness, and Jackie brought wisdom. They all were physical, strong ball-winners.

Our defense was experienced, fast, and organized. Our center backs and goalkeeper were leaders, and our outside backs could join in the attack. Our bench was stacked. We had seniors and freshmen who could come on and change the game. After a week of training together, you could tell our team had something special going for us. We trained in 90-degree heat with our tank tops and long socks on. Marg decided that since we weren't a physical team in the spring, wearing shin guards would help us be more physical. Pre-season is grueling because it's so short. You don't have much time before your first exhibition game, and there is so much to go over, so you're just constantly learning new information.

At the end of the summer, our coaches gave us the option to run the beep test prior to stepping on campus. Paige scheduled the beep test for the last week of July for whoever could make it. Half of our team was either already in Westwood or So Cal, so there was a large group of us that were going to run. The "standard" in the fall was a 40. If you hit 40, then you wouldn't have to run it in August when the rest of the team got to Westwood. I hadn't moved in yet, so I drove up the night before and stayed at one of the girls' apartments. The next morning at 6 a.m., we woke up and got ready to run the beep test.

That day, there were probably a dozen of us that ran. Most of the group hit 40. People who had never gotten 40 hit it. I was proud of the group. Not only did people push through mentally and physically that day, but I knew people had spent that summer staying fit and putting in the work to be prepared for our season. Most, if not all, of the seniors pushed over 40. The senior group continued to drive the standard during the spring, and now we were going to drive an even higher standard during the fall. Paige told the coaches who passed, and we were all cleared from running the beep test during August. Those who didn't pass were going to have to run again with the rest of the team. After the beep test, we all sat there for a little bit and then we set up the field to play small-sided. We played for a little bit, on tired legs, and it was fun to just be back playing soccer with your friends.

Since there was a second group that needed to run, we ran the beep test one last time a few days into August. It was set up on our intramural field, and the group running all took their spots. Everyone else was standing behind them and cheering people on. Maricarmen and I stood next to Sunshine, telling her over and over that she's got this. She can do it. She can run one more. Shine had her best beep test score ever, and as she collapsed on the turf, we all rallied around her in encouragement and love. Most of the group pushed through and got between 35-40. It was our best beep test showing all year. Everyone put in the work during the summer and came to pre-season prepared and ready to go. Our base fitness was so high because of the work we did in the spring, and now everyone in the country was going to watch us run circles around them. And that's exactly what we did.

Bend Never Break

    The first 10 days of August were filled with double days. Music blasted as we warmed up. The mornings were filled with possession drills, 1v1s, and small-sided games. We touched up on our defensive principles and played 11v11s. Since everyone crushed the beep test, we didn't have to run as much at the end of training. If you didn't hit your top speed or distance, Paige had you do individual running at the end. In between sessions, we were in the weight room. It was imperative that we keep up with our strength training before games started, so we were down in the weight room putting in work.

    After three hours of working out, we went up to the locker room to shower and hang out before going to mandatory team lunch. Everything revolved around our team and soccer. If we weren't training or eating together, we had meetings, mandatory ice baths and recovery, or watching film. After lunch and maybe a quick nap, we headed back out to Drake Stadium for our afternoon session.

    These were usually "bigger picture" trainings where we focused more on tactics and started incorporating set pieces. After training, we headed back up to the dining hall for mandatory team dinner before finally going to bed. My legs would sink into my bed; they were so tired. Even though we spent so much time together and soccer seemed to take over our lives, no one really complained. Yes, we were tired. Yes, we wanted some separation. Yes, we wanted to eat our own food. However, we knew this was what it was going to take to be the very best. Our first couple of games were against Santa Clara, Duke, and UNC. We needed to be ready to go by the end of the month, and the work we were putting in now was hopefully going to pay off.

    Our first and only exhibition game was against Fresno State. We played them on August 13th, 10 days after we started our pre-season. Exhibition matches are a great opportunity for teams to see their progress against another team. I was excited to finally get to play against an opponent and see how our team looked. We were hosting Fresno, and it was my last, first college game. Prior to the game, Maricarmen, Lauren, and I sat together on Wally, looking out onto the field. Tears brimmed my eyes as I knew my time at UCLA was coming to an end. I didn't want to be emotional, but I couldn't control how I felt. I turned to my left and looked at Lauren; she smiled and told me, "Maddi everything is going to be okay," I turned to my right, and

Maricarmen was crying as well. You could tell how much this program and team meant to us. Gof saw us sitting together and came up and gave us all hugs. He told us there was no need for tears and then told us to lead this team.

My family and family friends made their way into Wallis Annenberg to watch warmups. I waved to my mom and grandmas as they walked in. My mom had made a cut-out of my head and was waving it in the air. Jayden and I kept the vibes light as we danced through pre-game. Our teammates smiled back and laughed as we brought the energy. We ran out and came together as a team. This was my first pre-game speech, and to this day, I will never forget it. I told the team, "We have always been talented. We have always been badass defenders with superstar attackers. We have always had a strong culture with strong leaders. We have always had a deep bench. We have just never had the opportunity to show it, and now we finally do. Go out there and have fun."

Our team always had what it took to be the best, but now we had coaches who were motivating, passionate, and cared about players 1 to 35. We finally got to show everyone what we had been working on for the past seven months.

The game started, and immediately, transfer Ally Cook scored. Shortly after, Mari scored, and we were up 2-0. Twenty minutes in, Fresno broke free and scored on a fast transition. The score was 2-1 heading into halftime. Marg told us one of her famous quotes, "You can either sprint back on defense, or you can sprint back to me on the bench." We all looked at each other with wide eyes. Very rarely did Marg ever reprimand anyone, so when she did, we knew she meant business.

From then on, everyone worked hard to get back on defense, and that would be the last time we would be scored on from a lack of defensive effort. As for Marg, she kept her word. As our season went on, she had a commanding presence and never hesitated to sub someone out.

We finished the exhibition game with a 5-1 win. It wasn't our best performance, but we adapted as the game went on and finished our chances. Comparatively to the year prior, we struggled to punish teams and let teams hang in games. Scoring five goals was already a promising sign. Our next match was the following week against Iowa.

Chapter 13
Intentness

"Set a realistic goal. Concentrate on its achievement by resisting all temptations and being determined and persistent."
John Wooden

Everything we had done in the spring was with the intention of being the very best team in the country. When Marg first came in, she told us that if we wanted to win a National Championship, we had to train like National Champions. We emphasized the importance of team defense, team culture, and fitness. We went back to the basics, and everyone was involved in learning defensive principles. We had team meetings and team activities focused on culture, communication, and the future. In the fall, we applied everything we learned in the spring and focused on building a team culture, emphasizing both on and off the pitch intentions.

In pre-season, we came up with a few goals. We wanted to be undefeated at home, win the PAC-12, and win a National Championship. We knew we had a long way to go, but anything was possible. To reach these goals, we all knew we had to win big games. The NCAA soccer season is short. You have to be able to move on quickly from bad performances and mistakes. Every game is a battle, and being at UCLA meant that other teams usually had their best performances against us.

The coaches decided it would be beneficial if we scouted ourselves. They broke us up into groups, and we had to put together a scouting report of ourselves. We needed to cover attacking and defending tendencies, weaknesses, strengths, key players, and whatever else we wanted to include. I had never done something like this before, and I thought it was important for us to think like coaches. To think tactically. To think holistically. To think outside the box, but to also just think about ourselves. From the very first day, our coaches challenged us to think like coaches. They wanted us to understand why we played certain shapes or why we switched formations during halftime when things weren't working. They trusted us and believed that we would be able to see the game from a coaching perspective. They encouraged us to ask questions, challenge them, and lead with our soccer brains. My group came together, and we tried to think about what it is that we do best.

In a way, this exercise gave us confidence. We didn't just have one or two key players like most teams; we had a whole arsenal of weapons. We could play different shapes, adapt on the fly, and were unpredictable in our attack. If we struggled to come up with a scout report of ourselves, our opponents would too.

Our coaches decided we should come up with a mission statement or something that encompassed our team's goals. We broke up into groups and all worked on a sentence or two that captured everything we worked towards. My group's sentence was chosen:

By instilling a selfless, inclusive, and competitive culture based on the foundation of relentless hard work and personal growth, it's our mission to create a championship legacy that inspires and lifts up those around us.

Yes, we wanted to win. But we also wanted to do it in a way that would inspire the thousands of little girls watching us to want to grow up and win one day. We wanted to inspire our Bruin Bubble to win championships and set the standard across the whole athletic department. It was Marg's goal for every person to walk through her program and to leave knowing that they became the best version of themselves, and I think our mission statement showed that. We read it aloud, like a cult, once a week before a game or a meeting.

Iowa Game

"The best competition I have is against myself to become better." - John Wooden

Our opening night game was against Iowa. A familiar foe. We had faced Iowa a year and a half prior in the 2021 spring tournament, where Reilyn scored two goals from behind in five minutes to lead us to a 2-1 victory. They were a gritty, Big 10 team, and we knew that they were coming to Westwood to prove a point. We didn't have much film on them because it was their first match as well, but we knew they were tough defensively and played a 4-4-2 with a diamond in the midfield. It was our first game under the "New Era" and our first chance to cement ourselves in UCLA's history.

Iowa started off the game hot. They took advantage of their extra player in the midfield and baited our outside backs to step. I struggled through the first half, unable to get in a rhythm. I was subbed out within 20 minutes, along with a few others. We went into the halftime break 0-0. This was our first test. One of our team goals was to win every game at home. Overtime wasn't a thing anymore in the NCAA, so we had 45 more minutes to get the job done. Marg sent out a different lineup in the second half as she tried to get a spark going. All of a sudden, Quincy exploded up the left side flank and ran past her defender with speed and power. Our offense ran with her and got numbers in the box. As she cut the ball back, Maricarmen was there to tap it in. She ran to Ally Cook and embraced her. We went up 1-0 and defended hard the rest of the half. I got subbed back on towards the end and tried to redeem myself as the game went on, but I continued to struggle to do the simple things right. We continued to defend and finish with a gritty win. Maricamen scored our first goal of the season, a game-winner from a Quincy McMahon cross, foreshadowing how our season would end up.

It was Marg's first career win as a head coach. The athletic department gave her a ball that said, "First career win," and we celebrated around her. Molly and Marg Griddy-ed through the circle, and we all cheered them on. Marg said, "This could be a long season," and it turned out to be a longer season than any of us could imagine. In the moment, I was happy for Marg, but I also was so mad at myself for not performing well. I wasn't upset about getting subbed out or not starting the second half; I was upset that I didn't do the little things right. I barely slept the night after and just kept replaying my mistakes over and over.

Molly came up to me at the end of training and noticed I had been down all day. I was shocked because I thought I had done a good job of concealing my emotions. I told her that I felt like I let everyone down. I was embarrassed about my performance and wanted to learn from it and move on. Earlier that morning, we watched film from the game, and one of my turnovers was highlighted. Molly comforted me and laughed a little, but then she told me, "Mad Dog. It's a long season. There are many more games in your future." I appreciated Molly recognizing that I needed her at that moment, and instead of being a hardass coach, she was empathetic and supportive.

Our coaches were more than just that. They served as mom and dad, therapist, friend, confidant, and coach. Many of us had sat on their couch and cried to them about problems ranging from family adversity, partner fights, school stress, soccer anxiety, and so much more. They truly heard it all, and our team was so open and vulnerable to them because of the amount of trust-work we had done in the spring. During my first individual meeting in the fall, tears welled up as I told them how sad I was that this was my last season. They passed the almost empty tissue box and looked back at me sincerely. I was told how excited they were for me and how grateful they were for the past seven months. They encouraged me to try and enjoy every moment I got on the field. That wouldn't be the last time they saw me cry.

Team Dinners

Marg didn't bring much over from her time at Stanford, but one thing she did bring was post-game meals with our families. Molly coordinated with the local Orange County moms and put together a committee that would help plan meals after every home game. Families paired up together and decided where they were going to cater from. Families who lived out-of-state sent money to help pitch in for "their" weekend. I'm sure it was stressful for our moms to plan, but it truly was special for our team.

After every home game, every player and their family and friends were invited to our post-game meals. We had them right outside Acosta Training Center, and UCLA Athletics helped provide tables and coolers. We would eat standing up and, on the steps, outside with music blasting and, sometimes dance parties would take place. Thankfully, we won every single home game, so there weren't any bad vibes after a game. Even after games where I didn't think that I played well, it was nice to come together after and socialize with all our friends and family. Our coaches would be there too, and they would make their rounds, talking to parents and members of the community who supported our team. Our parents catered anything from Italian food, Greek food, a taco truck, Chipotle, and so many other places in Westwood.

My favorite post-game meals were after our NCAA tournament games. Since it was so dark and cold out, they were held inside, and everyone gathered around the few Acosta tables with our families and friends. We would all go upstairs to our locker room, celebrate, shower, change, and go back downstairs with our people. There was a different feel in the air as we all knew we could potentially be having our last meal after a win together. The post-game meals represented family. They represented inclusivity and allowed our families to meet each other. Not everyone lived in Southern California, so when families flew in, these meals allowed everyone to come together outside saying "Hi" to each other in the stands.

In addition to having post-game meals, our families would meet before the game at the Luskin Hotel. Right across from our stadium, the Luskin served a great burger and fun drinks. Our parents would pregame our pregame warmup. They all took Fireball shots together before heading into the stadium. This tradition would carry onto away trips as well. Our parents would tailgate our games and toast with Fireball. I knew my parents were going to miss hanging out with their friends, so they too were enjoying every moment of UCLA Soccer that they got.

Lauren Brzykcy

When I was eight years old, I joined the So Cal Blues. I made the U9 A team and started my first year of club soccer in 2009. At that age, we didn't really play specific positions. Our coach rotated us in every position so that we all got to try different spots. This included playing goalkeeper. While most of us dreaded getting the ball smacked at our faces, Lauren Brzykcy loved it. Even though we were both from San Clemente, I didn't know Lauren before, but she would become one of my best friends.

Lauren and I played club soccer together from when we were eight years old to when we were 17, and then five years at UCLA together. I watched Lauren blossom into the badass keeper that she is today. When we were 15 years old, we won the ECNL U15 National Championship together. Our Blues team, filled with NWSL stars such as Penelope Hocking and Kennedy Wesley, beat powerhouse teams including Sophia Smith and Jaelin Howell of Real Colorado and Alexa Spaanstra of Michigan Hawks. Lauren committed to UCLA that year, and shortly after, I committed there as well.

Lauren arrived at UCLA in 2017 as the third string keeper. She shortly earned the second spot and red-shirted that year. Lauren spent her freshman year adapting to the style of play, and intensity, that came with college soccer and improved her distribution.

In the next two seasons, 2018 and 2019, Lauren was the back up. Australian Women's National Team keeper Teagan Micah was a fifth year starter. Lauren played a few games when Teagan was hurt or sick, but she never really got a shot. In 2018, Lauren was selected to the PAC-12 All-Freshman team. During Lauren's sophomore year in 2018, Teagan was hurt going into the Stanford/Cal weekend, so Lauren got the call-up to start against Stanford in Palo Alto.

Most inexperienced, young goalkeepers would've crumbled under the pressure. Lauren didn't. She rose. Lauren made a season-high seven saves while facing 24 shots. We lost to Stanford 1-0, and without Lauren, it would've been way worse. In 2019, Lauren played in six games and started four, earning two solo shutouts against Colorado and Washington.

Once Teagan graduated, it was finally Lauren's time to shine. And how brightly she did. Lauren's first season as a starter was in 2020/2021. During the 2021 spring season, Lauren was named the PAC-12 Goalkeeper of the Year, selected to First-Team All-Conference, First-Team Scholar All-American, and Scholar All-Region, and helped lead us to our first PAC-12 title since 2014. She led the PAC-12 in wins with 13 and ranked second in shutouts (seven in total).

She continued to shine through 2021. Lauren did not allow a goal in her first nine games played and had an 849-minute shutout streak from May 5th to September 30th. She was nominated to the MAC Hermann Trophy Watch list and was named PAC-12 Goalkeeper of the Week three times. She only allowed 11 goals in 1805 minutes of play and led the PAC-12 and ranked in the Top 10 nationally with a 0.55 goals against average. In 2021, Lauren moved into sixth on UCLA's career lists for saves (161), shutouts (20) and wins (37). She helped lead us to our second PAC-12 title in just as many years.

Lauren's most decisive, confident, and commanding self was between the goalposts. She was an unbelievable shot stopper; reaching to the top corners, excellent in 1v1 scenarios, strong in the air, and reacted to everything. As a defender, I never felt worried about Lauren. In any 1v1 situation, I knew the forwards had no chance of scoring. I had full faith in Lauren to make the save, and in her three years starting at UCLA, there was never a goal against us which I felt Lauren should've saved. She never made any dumb mistakes and never faltered under pressure.

In 2022, Lauren was our hero. She won us big games every single weekend, and when we couldn't put the ball in the back of the net, she showed up for us defensively. Throughout 2022, she started all 25 games and tied the school record for single-season victories with 22. She allowed just 13 goals in 2,108 minutes of play and ranked 10th nationally. She led the PAC-12 with nine solo shutouts and also had five shared shutouts, while recording 73 saves on the year, including a career-high-tying nine saves in the 2-1 win at second ranked Duke on September 1st. She was twice named to the Top Drawer Soccer Team of the Week, selected to the MAC Hermann Trophy Watch List, and moved into UCLA's Top 5 for goals against average (0.65), career saves (234), career shutouts (29) and wins (59).

Lauren could've transferred. She could've left UCLA and started at any other school in the country. Instead, she put her head down and waited for her shot. She waited three years to earn the starting spot. When Lauren did earn her shot, she didn't waste any time messing around. She immediately made a name for herself and helped lead our program to two PAC-12 titles and a National Championship. It's no coincidence that the three years Lauren started were the three years we got rings.

Chapter 14
Cooperation

John Wooden defines cooperation as something one should do "with all levels of your co-workers. Listen if you want to be heard. Be interested in finding the best way, not in having your own way." Coach smiled, then repeated slowly and carefully: "Make sure the people in your department know that they're working with you, not for you."

There were seven graduating seniors on the team, eight including Sunshine, and all of us individually experienced the highs and lows of college soccer. All of us knew the feeling of being a starter, playing 90 minutes, feeling valued, and playing with confidence in big games. At the same time, all of us knew the feeling of being benched, cut from a lineup, not feeling valued, and clawing back from injuries or personal adversity. This made us all resilient, adaptable, and, most importantly – relatable. None of us were four-year starters. None of us had pro contracts set in stone. None of us were handed anything. And I think this was an essential reason that contributed to us winning.

Every single player on the team - girls who were starters, girls who were on the bench, girls who were injured, girls who were redshirting - had someone to go to. Everyone had a mentor. Everyone had a big sister who had been in their shoes before. Everyone had an inspiration. At the time, this wasn't something we talked about. This wasn't some crazy realization or forced team culture tactic; it was natural. It allowed us to lead with our voices, by example, from the bench, locker room, or from the pitch. We were all leaders in our own way.

While Mari, and I were in our fifth year, and Lauren was in her sixth, we also had a very strong senior class who held up the standard. Sunshine and Jackie led in their own, quiet ways from the midfield. Defenders Kylie Kerr and Brianne Riley were true seniors who had the option to transfer for their last two seasons in the spring. Kali Trevithick had the Comeback of the Year, and Janae Defazio spent her four years at UCLA working hard every day in training. The younger girls had seen us at our lowest points, as well as our highest points, and everywhere in between. We carried our team in fitness and in the weight room. We didn't complain or whine during double days. We worked hard for every minute that we earned. I think just being us and having our own experiences allowed us to lead in more ways than we realized at the time.

Leading up to us electing the captains, I felt confident that I would be voted. I felt as if I had proved everything that I needed to my team and coaches in order for me to be picked. Our team voted for two captains and four council members. Being captain wasn't going to make or break my season, but I felt as if I deserved it. When the day finally came around and the results were tallied, we sat in our film room, and Marg explained how the process was going to work. There were going to be two captains named, as well as five members of the leadership council. She said that everyone on the council would have different roles, and it didn't matter to her who would "go up to the refs before the game," and then she glanced at me. My heart sank a bit because I am a very self-aware person, and I knew it wasn't going to be me. She named sophomore Lilly Reale and Mari as captains and the council was going to be made up of Quincy, Lauren, My Haugland Sorsdahl, Bri, and myself.

I tried not to let my face react. I could see my friends looking at me. I walked out of the meeting, and I texted Sunshine, *"Bruh…"* and she replied, "I'm shocked." Kylie texted me later that day, "How are you doing?" I look back and laugh now, but in the moment, it hurt. I questioned a lot that day. Did people not like me? Did they not vote for me? Is this the coaches' decision? What's going on?

I told Kylie that maybe I was just an emotional ticking time bomb, and the coaches knew that. Or maybe I was a shitty leader. Both Lilly and Mari have an alter ego on the field. Nothing shakes them. They exude confidence. I did not have those qualities. I had this inner dialogue all day long. I got back to my apartment and Mari seemed just as shocked as me. I texted one of our council members, My, that night. She always knew what to say, and I knew she would be honest with me. She had the perspective that I would lead no matter what, and naming Mari captain would encourage her to rise to the occasion. I agreed but was still wary. It was still a hard pill to swallow. There was a small part of me that felt like saying, *"F you. F all of you! I pour so much into this team and program every single day."* I let myself be upset for a bit and question what happened, but I knew I had to pull it together and keep moving forward. I knew no matter what, I would be a leader.

I would continue to be myself, and I had such supportive and inspiring friends who would have my back every step of the way.

Kylie and Bri were two of my closest friends, and they both helped define our culture and buy in attitude we demanded of everyone. Both played many minutes in 2021, but with the coaching change, everything regarding minutes and starting positions was up in the air. Nothing was guaranteed. Both of them could have transferred and have guaranteed playing time for two years elsewhere, but decided to stay at UCLA for one more season. They crushed every single fitness test in the spring. They worked extremely hard in training, motivated people left and right, and were involved in our team culture meetings.

Throughout the fall season, both of them competed for starting spots and minutes. Bri subbed at outside back while Kylie played limited minutes. I know it was hard for both of them, but I admired the attitude and work ethic they brought to training every single day. They pushed our teammates during reserve training and set an example. Even if you weren't a starter or played limited minutes, you could still make a difference and prove to those around you what type of player you were. They led the scout team every week and made sure those girls were focused. They easily could have been bitter and selfish about their situation, and in moments alone, they may have been, but they never showed it. They were the epitome of loyalty and showed what it meant to be a true teammate. They celebrated when the team won, picked others up when they were down, and constantly made sure everyone felt included, valued, and seen. We wouldn't have won our National Championship if players like Kylie and Bri said, "F you and F the team." We needed everyone to buy in, including those who didn't see the field as much as they probably deserved.

At the end of the day, we seniors wanted to win. We wanted to bring a National Championship to Westwood. We had experienced the 2019 College Cup and saw what it took to make a run in the tournament. We played with Olympic Gold Medalists and World Cup rostered players. We sat in the stands and watched from the bench. We played 90 minutes and scored game-winners in dramatic fashion. We had yearlong recoveries while coming back from surgery after surgery. We left school for six months during the pandemic and woke up for 8 a.m. mandatory team Zoom meetings. We patiently waited for our earned opportunities. We had something worth fighting for, and more importantly, we had something worth winning for.

Every emotional decision that we all made, individually and collectively, was aimed at helping us win. The emotional decisions involved were not made lightly. It's not easy being a 22-year-old senior and showing up to lead the scout team filled with 18- and 19-year-olds, or being a passionate leader despite not being voted captain, handling conflict, or buying-in to our coaches' game plans.

A lot of the time, we put our own agendas aside to help our teammates out. To listen to them. To inspire them. To cheer them on. I think the beauty of it is that we brought that winning mentality out of a lot of players. A lot of our teammates were going to be four-year starters. They were going to have professional teams reaching out while they were still in school. They were going to have long, healthy, decorated careers at UCLA, even though winning a National Championship might not have been at the forefront of their minds when they walked through the Acosta doors at 18 years old. The will to win takes an unselfish, resilient mentality that we brought out of all our teammates. As our season went on and we started to win more and more games, you could see it in their eyes. You could see that they started to believe we could do it. It was in our control, and it was going to take all 35 players to make it happen.

Santa Clara Game

We were scheduled to play Santa Clara on Saturday, Duke on Thursday, and UNC the next Sunday – all on the road. Going into the Santa Clara game, we had only played two games prior. We scraped by against Iowa 1-0 and wanted to make a statement against Santa Clara. Santa Clara had been to the last two College Cups, while Duke was ranked second in the country and UNC was ranked first. We knew this week would present its challenges, yet we also knew we could take care of business one game at a time. Before we could even step on our first flight of the week, we were presented with an old friend: Covid.

The morning of our flight to San Jose, Mackenzee Vance, and my roommate, Maricarmen tested positive for Covid. Panic spread through our team. Even in 2020 and 2021, we didn't have any Covid positives during the season, yet now, in 2022, we had multiple leading up to the biggest week of the year. Our team quickly took rapid tests, and everyone waited on pins and needles for the results. Everyone was on edge. Unfortunately, we lost one more, Brianne. I will never forget being on Facetime with Bri while I was at Target when she told me. We both held back tears and were just hoping everyone would be okay for our North Carolina trip.

UCLA and Santa Clara have a unique rivalry. There were a lot of So Cal girls on their team, and we had a lot of Nor Cal girls on our team. They were fast, aggressive, could score goals, and were well-coached. Thankfully for us, the game was during the day. Their night games were usually sold out, and their fans were definitely rowdy. That year, there was another level of competition between us, as Santa Clara was Marg's alma mater. Marg prepared us well for that game. She told us how they defend differently than most teams we played. Most teams we played forced us wide, so our midfield wasn't on the ball. Santa Clara was going to force us inside. They were going to funnel us and then trap us into turning the ball over. This was something we weren't used to, but through preparation in our scout and training, we were ready.

Due to our Covid scare and missing three players that would play good minutes for us, we needed other players to step up. Jackie Gilday, who had been injured for the last two and a half years, was finally healthy to play again. With the first start of her career, Jackie took the field alongside Ally Lemos and Sunshine in the midfield. With Brianne out, Quincy and I were going to have to play 90 minutes against Santa Clara's speedy forwards. This was the first 90 of my career. The game went exactly how we predicted. They were fast, athletic, and dynamic. We started off slow, and through composed passing, we set Sunshine up for a banger outside the box. We went up 1-0 in the first 15 minutes.

Marg would always laugh at us because nothing was ever good enough for us. We barely celebrated Sunshine's goal because we wanted to use that time to fix the issues at hand. We were always trying to come up with solutions and communicate with our coaches for their insight. At halftime she told us that we needed to be more in the moment. Take a breath. Celebrate each other. "Don't be satisfied but be proud." This would be the start of "Bend, Never Break." Marg joked that we needed to be like bamboo. Even though bamboo is a type of grass, it is three times stronger than timber. It has a tensile strength of 28,000 pounds per square inch, allowing it to withstand more tension and stretching pressure before breaking.

We knew that we were going to have to defend throughout the second half, and it wasn't going to be easy. Marg and Gof explained at halftime that we needed to keep the ball in front of us and explained that it's okay not to have the ball. We didn't need to panic or get desperate. We would have our chances and our possession with the ball, but we just needed to be patient. At first, this wasn't easy to process. There were moments of frustration and moments where we felt like we should press and go, but that's not what the game called for. For the next 45 minutes, we bent, but we never broke. We played stellar defense and took our chances in attack. We were disciplined and patient and fought through the heat with limited subs. We would go on to win 1-0 and start the week off strong. Several players stepped up and played 90 minutes, and it was the perfect way to give us confidence going to North Carolina.

Lexi Wright

We had Reilyn Turner. We had Sunshine Fontes. But we also had Lexi Wright. When I came in early winter of 2018, I gave 15-year-old Lexi a recruiting tour. I showed her and her dad around Acosta, Wally, and the dorms. I answered their questions, told them funny stories about girls on the team, and did everything I could to get Lexi to commit to UCLA. She came from the same powerhouse So Cal Blues club team that included Reilyn and Trinity Rodman. She was from San Diego and was a tiny little thing with a big future. She committed a few months later in May of 2018.

Lex is one of the best wingers I have ever played with. She has no weak foot, can run for days, and has the heart of a champion. She dribbled hard at defenders, making them look silly. She was unpredictable to defend because of how shifty and quick she was. Beyond her raw talent, she was also an empathetic person. She was always there to give you a hug or to make a TikTok with you. We danced together before every pregame and called each other twins. Our curly hair and long legs ran alongside the left and right sides of the field in unison. She was a great friend, and even though she was only a sophomore, she played at a level beyond her years.

Bend Never Break

During our 2022 season, Lex battled through a back injury that took her out from a lot of trainings. She constantly was getting MRIs and X-rays – trying to figure out what was wrong. She spent much time in Acosta doing physical therapy and getting treatment. She did everything she could to be ready to go for game days. She had a game face like no other and fought through adversity that 2022 season, a lot of the time, alone. She never let it show.

Lex missed half of her freshman season in 2021, coming back from an ACL tear that happened the year prior in high school. Even with the few minutes she played in her freshman year, we all saw what she was capable of. She would sub onto games and immediately provide a spark. No one could keep up with her. In the spring, Lex continued to grow into her "comeback." She got super fit and strong and played without fear in our spring games. We knew 2022 was going to be a big year for Lex.

Throughout our season, Lex was involved with, or even scored, big goals for us. During our UNC/Duke weekend, she was involved in all four goals. That weekend, you could tell that she and Rei had played years of club soccer together. Every PAC-12 game, she played her heart out, and in our first playoff game, she scored two huge goals for us that propelled us through the rest of the tournament. Lex was a secret weapon for us. Teams tried to shut out Reilyn, Shine, or Ally Cook. They forced us to play out wide and keep the ball away from our creative and steady midfield. Lex and Quincy took care of the left side, combining up the field together, setting each other up, and defending any speed that struck their side. They played great together, and it was impossible for teams to shut them down. In her own quiet but unstoppable way, Lexi made a name for herself that season.

Chapter 15
Alertness

"Be observing constantly. Stay open-minded. Be eager to learn and improve."
John Wooden

Leading up to our North Carolina trip, we had been playing a 4-3-3 formation. Four defenders in the back, three in the midfield, and three up top. It had worked for the past three games, and we were getting the job done. We had just played a tough Santa Clara side and held them to a shutout while walking out with three points. We played Santa Clara on a Saturday and then left on Tuesday morning for North Carolina. At this point in time, we were ranked third, Duke was second, and UNC was first. For all of us, these were the highest ranked teams we had ever played. Prior to the Santa Clara game, our staff made predictions on how we would do against the three big teams. Marg said we would go 1-1-1, Gof said 2-1-0 (1 loss), Molly said 1-0-2 (two ties), Chelsea said 2-0-1, and Anish, our director of operations, predicted we would go a perfect 3-0-0.

For the trip, there was a travel roster. Both Mari and Mac still had Covid, and thankfully, on Monday, Bri tested negative and was safe to fly with us. I felt for Mari. She was a fifth-year captain and was going to miss out on two huge games. We were going to miss her presence on the field. I also felt bad for Mac. She was finally healthy, and her family was from South Carolina. I knew that they wanted to be there more than anything. Once we got to North Carolina Tuesday night, we had a team meeting to go over the practice plan for Wednesday.

Duke was notorious for playing a 3-5-2 formation. They played with rapid wingbacks, three strong center backs, three in the midfield, and two finishers up top. Marg decided to match them. We were going to play a 3-5-2 as well. Marg thought that our best chance of beating them was to go player-for-player. We were going to play slightly more defensive; instead of having wingbacks that played like forwards, we were going to play with wingbacks like fullbacks. We were going to force Duke to play their own game.

The next day, we trained at Duke's field. Practice was rough. Marg mixed players around, trying to find the perfect combinations. I remember being initially left out of the starting group, and after a few rounds Marg switched me to the starting team. Then, we went over how we were going to defend. We decided that we didn't have time to learn how to press. We were going to sit in a mid-block and shift side to side. We were going to "Bend Never Break." We were going to keep them in front of us, screen passes, and shift hard. We were okay with them having the ball, possessing it around us, but the second we picked the ball up, we were going to punish them. And that's exactly what we did that weekend.

On the day of the game, we had a meeting with the leadership council. We went over the game-day routine, and Marg went over roles and responsibilities. She provided us with a lot of clarity and told us that she trusted us. She trusted us to play this new formation, and if it was going south, she could switch it on the fly. At that moment, I knew we were going to be okay. I told the rest of the leadership council how important it was for us to buy in to what the coaches wanted us to do. If we seemed nervous or questioned her decisions, the rest of the team would as well. It was important for us to remain as united as possible.

The game was at 7:30 p.m., and there was a lot of anxious waiting around. We had a strong but small fan section. Family members on the East Coast made the trip to NC that weekend. During warmups, the speaker boomed "Hotel Room Service" by Pitbull, and we danced our way through the passing pattern. We felt loose and ready to go. We had nothing to lose. I don't think Duke expected us to play a 3-5-2 formation. They spent the entire first half trying to figure out what we were doing while we played very fluidly.

We would push into a four-front, but also retreat into a five-back. Halfway through the first half, Lexi played a great pass to Rei, and Reilyn got pulled down in the box and earned a PK. I grabbed the ball and made eye contact with Jayden, our sophomore center back. She walked forward confidently. As Jayden took the ball into her hands, the Duke student section started chanting and banging on the bleachers. We all lined up around the 18-yard box, and I held my breath as JP stepped forward. I knew Jayden was going to hammer it home, and she did. She placed it firmly to the goalkeeper's right and immediately ran near the student section and Duke's bench and jumped in the air. We all ran to her and erupted in cheers.

Bend Never Break

Towards the end of the first half, Michelle Cooper ripped a shot inside the box, and Duke tied it up 1-1. We knew it was going to be a competitive, back and forth game, so we had to remain composed and confident going into the last 45 minutes. At halftime, Quincy, who hurt her ankle early in the first half, was getting tended to and was going to sub back in. This was going to help us add some more speed going forward. We talked about keeping our lines compact and not letting them split us. We stuck with our 3-5-2 formation and took the second half with one goal in mind: getting the second one.

Early in the second half, Quincy, and Lexi combined passes near the endline, and Lex seamlessly slipped a ball to Reilyn. Reilyn, who was at the edge of the left side of the 18-yard box, took a hard touch across her body, beating the defender, and slammed the ball near the post. Her long leg stretched out, and she fell to the ground as the ball hit the inside of the net. It was always a special Reilyn Turner goal whenever she ended up on the ground. 2-1.

She did her signature celebration, flashing a "number one" sign, sticking her tongue out, and running towards us. I knew our defense could shut down their offense for the next 30 minutes. For the remainder of the half, Lauren Brzykcy proved that she was the best goalkeeper in the country. She made sliding 1v1 saves, point blank rebound saves, punched the ball out on wide crosses, and snuffed anything in the 18-yard box. She anchored our backline.

In that game, she made a career-high nine saves that kept us in the game. Our team played a complete performance and took down the second ranked team in the country on the road. We celebrated as the clock counted down, and I ran towards our bench and embraced the girls. This was a huge win for not only our team but for our program as well. We just showed everyone we were not the same team that we were last year.

That Duke game gave us confidence. It highlighted our ability to adapt and display alertness. We were open-minded and trusted our coaches' decisions, and wanted to learn a new system. Despite some hesitancy and only working on the formation for one training session before the game, we believed in ourselves and believed that our coaches had our best interests at heart. Being able to adapt and play different systems proved helpful as the season went on and ultimately separated us from the rest of the country.

We had two days before we played UNC. We were able to spend a lot of time with our families. That year, my parents decided that they, along with my two grandmas, would go to every single game, home and away. I was able to meet them for lunch and tour the campuses with them. Both my parents are big walkers, so they enjoyed touring Duke and UNC. On one of the days, we had lunch after practice together, and then we walked all around UNC. School had just started, so students were out and about, and it was really hot and humid. We walked near their athletic center, and checked out their volleyball arena, and also saw a sneak peak of Dorrance Field. It was the most pristine college soccer stadium I had ever seen. Amazing seating, perfect location, and the pitch was professional. I sent a Snapchat to our group with the caption, "We ride at dawn." We walked to the basketball arena and checked out their Hall of Fame. My dad was in heaven. We saw the letter Michael Jordan wrote to Duke rejecting them. We saw all the trophies and the dynasty of UNC basketball. Being able to spend time with my parents and create those memories was special. That night, our team had dinner in Chapel Hill on the historic Franklin Street. We went to a famous Italian restaurant that was owned by a big UNC fan. We walked around and got ice cream that night, all of us in our team-issued Panda dunks. It was a perfect end-of-the-summer night.

Reilyn Turner

Reilyn Turner is what I call an X-factor. Most teams, irrespective of sport, don't have an X-factor. An X-factor is defined as a noteworthy special talent or quality. An X-factor is a noun – a circumstance, quality, or person that has a strong but unpredictable influence. That is Rei.

Reilyn is unlike any forward that I have ever played with. She's versatile. She's fast. She's dynamic. She can play center forward and lay the ball off, but she can also run in behind. She can play out wide, beat you 1v1, and whip in crosses. She dominates in the air and will put her body on the line. Reilyn can be quiet for 80 minutes and then score the game-winner. She was born for big moments.

During her freshman year, we played in our 2020/21 spring season. Reilyn was the PAC-12 freshman of the year, and we were heading out to North Carolina for the NCAA tournament. The tournament was formatted differently that year; there was an opening round bye and only 36 teams. That year, we won the PAC-12 and earned a first-round bye, so our first game was against Iowa. Within the first 20 minutes, Iowa went up 1-0. We spent the rest of the game trying to find a goal, but it just wasn't happening.

With five minutes left on the clock, Rei tied it up. I vividly remember crying on the sideline. Then, just when I thought the game was headed into overtime, she did it again. With seconds left, Rei's late-game heroics saved us. She scored at the death in regular time, and we moved on to the third round. It was at this point in time that I knew Reilyn was going to have a huge career at UCLA, and it would include some pretty heroic goals. Reilyn was the first collegiate athlete to sign an NIL deal with Nike at the end of 2021.

Throughout 2022, Reilyn showed up time and time again. After never running 40 on the beep test, she showed up in July and pushed through to get 40. She proved to me, our teammates, and our coaches that she meant business that year. Not only was she an offensive heartbeat for us, but she was constantly cracking jokes, dancing to Chris Brown, making everyone laugh, and never stopped being herself. I knew Rei struggled from time to time behind the scenes, but she never let it show.

She was a competitor through and through. Reilyn played for a dominant club team that won many championships, so winning was embedded in her. Even though Rei wasn't a captain or on the leadership council, she led in her own way. There were so many times when she told us older girls to get our shit together, stop crying, and finish the damn job. Her leadership shined in the moments when we were seconds away from losing. I knew she would break her leg for us if it meant scoring a game-winner. Rei was our X-factor and, in more ways than one, I looked up to her.

UNC Game

Going into the game against North Carolina, we knew it was going to be tough. A lot of our players played heavy minutes against Duke, while UNC rested players against Missouri. The day before the game, we walked out on Dorrance Field and did our Match Day -1 meditation. Lexi and I made our TikTok, while other girls did their own rituals, which included handstand competitions, individual meditation, and taking pictures. We were so excited. We decided to stick with the same formation and knew we might have to play a bit more defensively. We were going to shift hard, communicate loudly, make big saves, and score bigger goals. Ultimately, we were going to be ourselves. I told the team, "This game is why we were all here together."

We committed to UCLA to play the best teams in the county. To compete for a National Championship. Playing UNC at UNC is something you dream about. Their program is the winningest program in NCAA history. At that point in time, they had won 22 National Championships and produced players like Mia Hamm, Tobin Heath, Crystal Dunn, Christine Lilly, and so many more. I knew this game meant more than just being a non-conference game.

This game could propel our team and give us the confidence to truly contend for a Championship in December. They had a stadium full of fans, while we had about 50 right above our bench. Our coaches described this game to us as a dress rehearsal. UNC was going to be the best team we would play all year, so it was important for us to learn from this game. Right before the game, they played their hype video. While they watched in awe, our lineup was dancing. We were loose. We felt good.

We started the game on our heels. They pressed us hard and made us uncomfortable. They had a strong midfield that was dictating play. We were not a pressing team, so it was hard for us to get the ball up the field. As the half went on, we created more opportunities and were gaining some momentum. At the very end of the first half, junior Megan Edelman was subbed on. Megan was the teammate you wanted on your team. She was an extremely hard worker, quick with her decisions, had a great shot, and tracked back on defense. The previous two seasons, Megan wasn't valued, but she came in fit, worked hard throughout the spring, and our coaches trusted her.

At the very end of the first half, Megan went up for a header and landed weirdly. She lay on the ground, and our Athletic Trainer ran over to her. She hobbled off the field, crying, clutching her knee. Our hearts were shattered. **Seeing a teammate go down is always heart-breaking. The ref blew their whistle soon after and we went into halftime 0-0.** We really didn't have that many chances, and we were playing in a solid five back formation. We decided at halftime to remain conservative, but when we could push up, we would. At the very beginning of the second half, UNC got a corner. We lined up in our formation, and the ball sailed to the back post. Out of nowhere, a girl flew through and headed the ball in. While she celebrated and ran to the bench, we brought it in. Jackie looked at Bri and said, "That was my mark," and Bri looked at her as calmly as possible and replied, "It's okay Jackie. We're going to come back." And we did.

Some time went by, and we were continuing to push forward. Lauren picked the ball up and quickly tossed it to Jackie, who went on a bit of a dribble. She passed it to Quincy, who combined with Lexi, and all of a sudden Lex broke free. She dribbled hard at the two defenders, cut hard to her right foot, dropped her right shoulder, faked the two defenders out, and pushed the ball to her left. Falling over, she ripped a left footed shot at the far post. The goalkeeper had no chance. We were back in the game. 1-1.

Lauren's highlight reel got added to, as she was making upper 90 saves, flying out on corners, and winning 1v1 duels. We defended hard. Blocked shots, intercepted passes, bumped runners, followed up on rebounds, and sprinted back on defense. The game looked like it was going to end 1-1. But we had Reilyn Turner. While their fans were chanting "TAR…HEELS…" we turned on our Southern California magic. All we needed was one more chance.

With six minutes left, Lex cleared the ball near the bench. As the ball bounced, the UNC defender tried shielding it out of bounds. Right in front of our bench, Rei leaned into her, reaching for the ball, and knocking the defender to the ground. The bench went crazy, the fans went crazy, the players went crazy. Everyone wearing Bruin blue yelling, "GO REI GO, KEEP GOING, YOU GOT THIS!" Her long legs took off, and on the opposite side, Lexi was on a dead sprint, pulling the covering center back out of the play. I was directly behind Rei, watching her run as fast as she could, and right when the UNC defender stepped and covered her goalkeeper's vision, Rei ripped a shot. She sliced it near post and immediately celebrated. She ran across the UNC 18-yard box with a "number one" in the air, all smiles, and we all ran toward her. 2-1.

We needed to hold on for five more minutes, and we would win the game. We subbed in two more defenders and played a six back. We continued to defend with our hearts while UNC sent in cross after cross. It felt as if we were doing a crossing and finishing drill, and the defense was winning every time. At the very end of the game, the ball got sent out to their left back and went underneath her foot. The countdown started at 10, 9, 8, 7, 6… we were all smiles.

We just came back and took down the number one team in the country at their home field. We celebrated, danced, and sang in the locker room. "OLE OLE OLE OLE, UC/LA." Our parents cheered and took pictures from above in the stands. We took a team picture; we were the new number one, and we're going to remain at the top for the next three months.

The New Number One

After we got back from North Carolina, we were celebrities on campus. Everyone knew what we had accomplished. On campus, there was only us, men's soccer, football, and women's volleyball. Out of all the fall sports, we were by far the most successful and were the highest ranked team. Our big weekend, beating the first and second ranked teams in the country, was not only huge for our program, but it was huge for the athletics department as well. We were now first in the country and our egos went through the roof.

That next week, athletics hosted a lunch for us. After practice, we all showered, and those of us who didn't have class right after practice headed to Morgan Center. Morgan Center was where all of the coaches, Athletic Directors, and other members of athletics were. There was also the UCLA Hall of Fame, along with their offices and a conference room. We walked through the Hall of Fame, right by the 119 National Championship trophies, where we were greeted in a tunnel by other coaches, ADs, interns, media, and several UCLA affiliated people.

They cheered, waved flags, and clapped for us as we walked through the tunnel they created. Our videographer, Suzi Mellano, and photographer, Jesus Ramirez, were at the end of the tunnel, capturing us high-fiving and smiling through. We sat down at the many round tables that were scattered in the conference room, and our head Athletic Director brought everyone in. We all looked back at him as he told us how proud he and everyone were of us. We all clapped and cheered and celebrated. It takes a lot to have a perfect team culture. It takes a lot to win big games. It takes a lot to believe in one another. It comes from the top down. Both Martin and Erin loved our program and constantly gave us their time and energy. This lunch was one small example of how they made us feel important.

Chapter 16
Friendship

"Friendship comes from mutual esteem, respect, and devotion. Like marriage, it must not be taken for granted but requires a joint effort."
John Wooden

Growing up, I didn't have any sisters or any girl cousins. My friends meant the world to me. Friendship was also the backbone of our team and one of the main reasons our squad was so successful. After our UNC and Duke weekend, we had one off-day that fell on Kylie's birthday. We all piled in each other's cars, picked up food, and drove to the beach. The entire team met up, and we picked our spot on the beach. We played music, kicked around a soccer ball, and eventually all went into the water. We swam out beyond the waves and floated together. We were the only ones at the beach, and our laughs echoed onto the shore. Soon, a lifeguard came running over and told us that it was not safe for us to be swimming. We laughed at him and told him that we were all athletes and that we would be okay. He blushed but stood firm on his instructions. Before leaving, we took a group picture with the sun setting in the background. We packed up our bags, and everyone carpooled back to Westwood. I'll never forget that memory.

A month into the season, we found out that a teammate's mother had passed away after a battle with breast cancer. It hit our team hard. Our teammate was only 19 at the time and an only child. We had multiple meetings with our coaches and leadership council, making sure we supported her as best as we could. Prior to our San Diego State game, we all bussed down to Orange County to attend the funeral. We all wore our UCLA sweatsuits and showed up for her. Her closest friends showed up for her every day. They made sure she was never sleeping alone, always had dinner planned, and answered whenever she called. Throughout the fall, different people invited her to coffee or grabbed dinner with her. We stayed diligent in checking in on her and making sure she never felt alone. Everyone showed up in their own ways.

Usually, during our season, there was always one weekend where we had Sunday off. This year, it happened to be our PAC-12 opening weekend. We were scheduled to play California Berkeley on Friday. We knew for weeks prior that we could do something on Saturday night. As the obligatory "fun" team amongst the other teams, we decided to host a wig party Saturday night. We invited everyone we knew and told people to all wear wigs. Amazon probably saw a surge in wig sales that week, as dozens of people showed up wearing brightly colored wigs. Our team got a huge win on Friday night against Cal and were beyond excited for Saturday night. This was our first Saturday night free in over a month, and we were looking forward to having a good time. Our team always had fun together.

Mia Fishel, a three-year starter, left UCLA at the end of 2021 and was drafted fifth overall in the NWSL draft by Orlando Pride. Mia decided to turn down the NWSL and Orlando Pride and forge her own path. She made the unique and controversial decision at the time to play for Tigres in Mexico. Earlier in the summer, we saw that Tigres was making a trip to California and was going to play Angel City in August. The coaches knew about this game too, and decided it would be a perfect team bonding experience. On August 11th, we all headed to BMO Stadium to cheer on our former teammate and superstar, Mia Fishel.

Since parking is chaotic and crazy expensive at BMO, we decided it would be best to use public transportation. We all met at the bus stop at UCLA and piled on. The players, coaches, and support staff crammed onto the public bus for the 45-minute drive to BMO. We had all gone out beforehand to pick up food and ate our dinner on the way to the game. This was Angel City's inaugural season, and it was awesome to see the support for women's soccer. Back in the beginning of 2022, Sunshine and I got tickets for their first game ever against North Carolina Courage, where they narrowly lost. It was a sold-out game, and the atmosphere was incredible. We had thousands of people coming to watch us play, so it was amazing to see how many people packed BMO. As the bus pulled up to drop us off, there was already a lively scene around us.

There were Angel City fans decked out in their gear, playing music, drinking, and partying in the parking lot, and there were Tigres fans with their Mexico flags waving in the air. There were close to 40 of us who walked in a massive mob to the entrance of the stadium. Molly checked us all in, and then we walked inside. This was some of the girls' first time at BMO, so it was cool to see them experience the sights and sounds of women's professional soccer in LA. We trekked up to the top of the stadium, where we took over the nosebleed section. The sun glared down on us the entire game, and we cheered on Mia and Tigres for the next 90 minutes. She played great. It was fun to see her in a different environment, playing at a higher level.

As the sun set in LA, we decided to leave the game a little early to beat the foot traffic getting out of BMO. We caught the bus back to Westwood and said goodbye to our coaches and staff as we all walked, scootered, or drove back to our respective apartments. These were the moments that I'll never forget. As I write throughout our story, I have a tab open of UCLA Women's Soccer statistics to help me remember each game, who scored in what game, or how many goals we scored. I'm constantly fact checking to make sure I don't forget anything or texting girls on the team to help me jog my memory. But for these moments, like going to the Angel City game, taking dance classes, going to the beach, or hosting parties and dinners, I don't need to ask anyone. I remember sitting on the bus and laughing or wishing I wore sunscreen because I could feel the sun burning on my face. I remember texting Jackie about what her Chipotle order was, and I remember Molly passing out all our tickets. I remember walking back to the graduate apartments with Lauren and Ally Cook. I remember the funny and inappropriate Snapchats sent in our group chat. The moments off the field are just as important as the moments on the field and sometimes even more memorable.

Ally Cook

When Marg first got to UCLA, she knew she wanted to look in the transfer portal. By the spring of 2022, we had a few girls transfer out, and there was room on our roster to expand. We quickly caught wind that the coaches were interested in pursuing Ally Cook from Oregon. Ally was from Orange County, played club soccer with Maricarmen, and had graduated from Oregon in just three years. She had two years left of eligibility and was looking to move closer to home. Ally was a tenacious, workhorse center forward who left her heart on the field every time she stepped on it. She pressed hard, chased defenders down, and had a wicked shot that she could fire off from any angle.

She was tall, strong, and could hold players off all game long. We could always use more firepower in our attack, and our coaches worked hard to get Ally to come to UCLA. Well, they didn't have to work too hard; it was a slam dunk of a transfer. Ally was from Southern California; she was already friends with several of us, and she still had two years left of eligibility. She had her visit in the spring, and very quickly after she visited, she committed. Everyone was stoked that we got Ally. She was going to help our attack greatly and provide even more leadership and experience.

Ally got to campus in August and immediately fitted in. She quickly bonded with all the girls, and her undying work rate stood out on the pitch. Ally would play a huge role for us down the stretch, and whether she was starting or coming off the bench, she always made an impact. More importantly, her outgoing and kind personality fit in perfectly with our team.

Cal Game

After our clinical 3-0 win over Pepperdine, we finished our non-conference slate on top of the world. We went 8-0-0, scored 23 goals, gave up three goals, and beat three top 10 teams. We were starting to find our groove, and our goal of winning a National Championship seemed possible, something we could see on the horizon. We were scoring goals in different ways, mastering different formations, and showcasing our depth every single game. We were the reigning, back-to-back PAC-12 Champs and wanted to win our threepeat. Our first PAC-12 game was a home game against Cal, which we were all excited about.

It was our first week of school, and we knew it was going to be a packed house. Leading up to the game, we reached out to our Athletic Director, Erin Adkins, to think of ideas to get more students at our games. She set up a meeting with a group of us, herself, and the head of ticketing and marketing. Maricarmen, Bri, Quincy, My, Reilyn, and myself headed over to Morgan Center with our assistant coach, Molly. We gathered around the table and brainstormed ideas. Before PAC-12 home games, we wanted to pass out flyers to students walking to and from class. We wanted to be recognized at pep rallies, Bruin Bash, and other events around campus. Our first PAC-12 game was going to be on Friday, and we wanted to fill Wallis Annenberg.

After training on Wednesday and Thursday, whoever didn't have class was going to pass out flyers on Bruin Walk and all around campus. We had hundreds of blue and gold flyers printed that told the time, date, and location of our game. There were about 20 of us who split up for an hour to pass out flyers. Sometimes, we would simply hand them out. Other times, we would lead with hypothetical questions like, "Do you have Friday night plans?" or "Do you like hot girls?" or "Do you like sports?" and that would usually catch their attention. We would bring our speakers out and blast music. When people excitedly, or reluctantly, took our flyers, we would jump and cheer around them. We would start eight-claps, give out high-fives, and keep the vibes high. Most of the time, we received good vibes back. People would say they were coming, tell us that they had been to games, or say they already got a flyer from one of our teammates. Sometimes, people would hastily walk by with their headphones in, but that was okay too.

At this point in time, we were the number one ranked team in the country, and we used that as our selling point. Being able to have our first PAC-12 game at home was huge, and it put that much more pressure on us to perform. Leading up to that year, the last time we won our PAC-12 home-opener was in 2016. We were able to get the job done on the road, but for some reason, whenever we opened up at home, we struggled. That wasn't going to be the case this year. I called Marg and told her this little stat, which she found shocking. This was going to be our chance to change the narrative and start on the right foot.

I don't miss a lot about college soccer. If anything, I miss the people the most. I am grateful for the pictures, videos, and little mementos that bring me back to such a fun time. Another thing I do miss is the celebrations. Those will always stick with me. Our home opener against Cal was a rollercoaster of a game filled with celebrations that I will never forget.

Going into the game, we were the only NCAA D1 women's soccer team in the county with a perfect record. We walked out to Wally and Whitney Houston's "I Wanna Dance with Somebody" blasted throughout the stadium. You could feel the energy of our sold-out crowd of 2,237 people. Our flyers and obnoxious questions got all the NARPs (Non-Athletic Regular Person) and all the athletes out to our 8 p.m. Friday night game. "The Den," which was the official name of our student-section, all gathered above our bench. The band was across the field getting ready to bring the energy.

We decided to stick with our 3-5-2 formation after finding a lot of success against Pepperdine. Cal was a bit better than Pepperdine and was doing a good job of exploiting us out wide. They struck first in the 21st minute after a defensive breakdown. I lost my cool a bit, and I yelled at my teammates. It wasn't good enough, and we needed to start playing our game. It was our second time all year trailing, and somehow, we were going to have to find an equalizer.

Our worries were short-lived after, you guessed it, Maricarmen came to the rescue minutes after we got scored on. We quickly got control of the ball after kickoff and never gave it up. After maintaining possession for almost 20 passes, Quincy slipped the ball to me on top of the 18-yard box. I dribbled through several defenders, allowing Lexi, Reilyn, and Mari to be wide open in the box. I crossed the ball backward, and Mari was there to slot it in. All 2,000 plus fans erupted, and the bench exploded. We were back in this game.

Eight minutes later, Mari scored again on a pass from Sof Cook. The ball bounced through traffic and into the back of the net with almost 15 minutes left in the half. 2-1. She was relentless. We went into halftime feeling good. As Bri and I walked off the pitch, Gof came up to us and told us how well we were playing. He told us that no one was getting by us, and we were shutting down the right side of the field. Bri and I looked at each other and smiled. Our coaches seldom handed out compliments.

We started off the second half soaring. 10 minutes in, Reilyn reached out with her long legs and intercepted the ball near the bench. She looked up and pinged a pass into Ally Cook, who was on the edge of the box. Ally calmly collected the ball, pushed it to her right foot, and as the defender shifted her weight, Ally struck the ball as hard as she could, and it flew into the back of the net. Her long blonde hair whipped around her face as she pumped her arms and celebrated. The people went crazy in the bleachers, and we erupted on the bench. Our rollercoaster of a game continued when Cal capitalized on a penalty kick in the 61st minute, and then just three minutes later, we missed our own penalty kick.

The score was 3-2, and we needed one more goal for insurance. We moved the ball from side to side, and with eight minutes left, we ping-ponged the ball up the right side of the field, and Mari whipped in a cross. Ally Cook flew out of nowhere and headed the ball hard. The crowd gasped as it dinged off the crossbar and spilled out in the six-yard box. Freshman Bridgette Marin-Valencia bulldozed her way through the defenders and clattered the ball into the goal with her body. Mari jumped, and Ally Cook threw her arms in the air. I sprinted towards my teammates, knowing that we just scored a perfect team goal. Mari and I met halfway, and we collided mid-air. Our teammates were jumping and hugging each other as Wallis Annenberg shook in excitement. Music blasted as we walked back to the midline for the eighth kickoff of the game. The band broke out into our fight song. These are the moments that I remember the most. Celebrating the highs with your people who have seen you at your lowest points. I will never forget standing next to the water cooler as Rei stole the ball and passed it to Ally. I will never forget Quincy running up to me when I crossed the ball to Mari. I will never forget Marg announcing to the team that we had broken the home-opener curse.

In the most dramatic fashion, we won our first PAC-12 home opener in seven years. Maricarmen led the charge, and the best transfer in the country, Ally Cook, put on a show. We proved to ourselves that we could bounce back from being down, score in different ways, and stay resilient as the game went on. We improved to 9-0-0 and continued to show the country that we were really damn good.

Oregon/OSU Weekend

Our first PAC-12 away trip was up to Oregon. We were playing the University of Oregon on Thursday and Oregon State on Sunday. This was the first time in three years that we were playing both Oregon teams away. We left for UO on Wednesday, and after several flight delays, we finally made it up to Eugene. That night, we checked into our hotel, got changed, and headed to UO's practice facility. We were training indoors on their turf field, which was state-of-the art. We did our Match Day –1 training and headed back to the hotel. The next day was game day. We went to their turf home field, which was beautiful, and did our pre-game yoga and stretching. We visualized, walked around the pitch in our socks, and took some pictures. We headed over to their track and field stadium, Hayward Field, and walked around the Hall of Fame.

After a pretty busy morning, we headed back to the hotel to relax and have a pre-game meal. Our game wasn't until 7 p.m., so we had some time to kill. After our meal, we packed up the bus and made our way to the stadium. For the first time in my life, I decided to do my hair in a "slick back" look with a braid. I knew it was going to rain and felt like that would look the best. I fixed my hair in the locker room before going back out to the field.

Before every away match, I would walk the perimeter of our half, listening to music. I would visualize and get a feel for the stadium.

The ref blew the whistle, and we immediately took charge. Sof Cook scored quickly, and the phenom freshman was continuing her special year. Our clean passes skipped on the turf, and we felt comfortable moving the ball back and forth. All of a sudden, in the first half, Reilyn took off on a breakaway and got clobbered by the goalkeeper outside the box. Our bench went crazy as Rei flew through the air and landed hard on the ground. We all rushed to her, and she was already cracking jokes.

The ref pulled out a red card and sent the UO keeper off the field. They now had to play with 10 players, and we got a free kick on top of the 18-yard box. Sunshine stepped up for the free kick. This was her shot, and I knew she was going to slam it in the back of the net. Their wall and their second-choice goalkeeper had no chance of stopping it. The ref blew the whistle, and we all held our breath as Shine stepped up. She hit the ball as hard as she could with her instep and within a millisecond it was in the back of the net. She made it look too easy; she might as well have hit it from the PK spot. We were now up 2-0.

Our game plan going into the second half was to keep our foot on the gas and be relentless in our attack. Despite our aggressive game plan, Oregon scored rather quickly into the second half, and the next thing we knew, it was a one goal game. Their obnoxious coaches and bench hyped them up as they continued to put pressure on us. We eventually turned the second half around, and Kali Trevithick subbed in. Fresh off coming back from her injury, we needed Kali's confidence on the ball and her ability to go 1v1.

Kali received the ball out wide and cut inside, dancing past multiple defenders; she bent the ball around the keeper and scored for us. We quickly silenced Oregon's momentum and were now up 3-1. Rain started to fall as we continued to defend for the rest of the half. Sometimes, wins aren't always pretty, but we got the job done. After greeting our parents, we headed back to the hotel. The hotel had a piano at the entrance and we all gathered around as Neeku Purcell took center stage. She played as we all sang off-pitch to accompany her. Three points down, three more to gain.

The next day, we boarded the bus for our two-hour drive to OSU. Some of us worked on homework, listened to music, or played would you rather. The bus ride went by quickly, and we arrived in Corvallis Friday night. The next day, we had Match Day -1 training. We walked past OSU's home field onto their practice field. We did our normal possession drill and Marg hopped in as usual. She always trained with us on Match Day -1. After training, the sun was setting, and we headed back to the hotel. That night, we all hung out in the team room after dinner to watch UCLA football play. We laughed and joked as they finally got a win. We had our final team meeting that focused on our tactics, lineup, and goals of the game. We wanted to leave Oregon with six points and needed a big team performance on Sunday against the Beavers.

From the first until the last minute, we put on a show. We shut out the Beavers 5-0 and walked away with our six points. Reilyn dropped a first half hat-trick while Sunshine and Sof both scored their second goals of the weekend. We sliced and diced through their defense, and Marg was able to empty the bench, giving everyone substantial minutes. We continued our 2022 campaign with flying colors and felt confident continuing our quest for Back-to-Back-to-Back PAC-12 Championships.

Chapter 17
Team Spirit

"A genuine consideration for others. An eagerness to sacrifice personal interests of glory for the welfare of all." Coach Wooden also liked to quote a passage he'd once read, which stated: "There's a mystical law of nature that the three things that mankind craves most — freedom, happiness, and peace of mind — cannot be attained without giving them to someone else." Team spirit results when the leader inspires those same traits within his or her team, and in so doing, unites all of the members to work towards their shared goal.

Our second game of the year was against CSUN. After coming off a tough performance against Iowa, we wanted to redeem ourselves. We knew we could play sharper and wanted to gain confidence, and luckily, we had the magic of Sunshine Fontes. After not scoring a single goal in 2021, Sunshine propelled us past our weak Iowa performance by scoring a hat trick against CSUN. These weren't just any goals; they were upper-90 bangers, scored with both her left and right foot. After scoring her third and final goal, a beauty of a free kick, we all surrounded her and started bowing down. In typical Shine fashion, she laughed and shook her head as we all were down on one knee, fanning her. Jayden ran up from the back of the field and tipped her hat to Shine. Not only did Shine deserve every ounce of celebration because of her incredible goals, but she deserved to be celebrated because of her commitment to our team. After struggling with her fitness all throughout her career at UCLA, she proved to herself, the coaches, and her teammates that she was going to show up in August ready to go.

One of our very last non-conference games was against San Diego State. There are some games where your "star" players, who are expected to show up and score every game, aren't going to. Not because they're having a bad game, but sometimes the ball just isn't bouncing their way. Our game against SDSU was similar in this aspect; we were "supposed" to win and blow them out of the water, but for some reason, things just weren't clicking. We were dominating on the ball and outshooting the Aztecs 15-2, but the ball wasn't going in the back of the net.

Ellie Walbruch, a true freshman who had enrolled early in January, subbed in at the 38th minute, and two minutes later, making something out of nothing, scored her first career goal and put us up 1-0 in the 40th minute. Ellie hadn't played many minutes leading up to this game, but she made the most of her opportunity and capitalized when we needed it the most. Sofia Cook, another true freshman, came off the bench for us in the second half and doubled our lead on a header. As the second half went on, Marg cleared the bench, and everyone was subbing in. I think our team demonstrated team spirit in moments like this; we all worked towards a common goal, and everyone was aware of their role. Ellie and Sof weren't starters, but when our starters weren't getting the job done, they filled that role perfectly.

One of the highlights of 2022 was Kali Trevithick's comeback. Kali was a senior and had been injured for most of her career at UCLA. I grew up going to national team camps with Kali since we were 13, so I knew Kali before she got to UCLA. Kali was an unconventional player. The ball was always connected to her feet. She shimmied and scissored her way through defenders and could shoot with both feet. Kali had great vision and could play any attacking position. When Kali came in as a freshman, she had a big future at UCLA. Towards the end of her freshman year, Kali hurt her knee. This would start the two-and-a-half-year journey of her many ups and downs battling injuries.

She had plenty of injections, MRIs, and scopes. Kali ended up having cartilage surgery, and we all crossed our fingers that her body would take the donor cartilage. She spent the next two years fighting through pain, and by the time Spring 2022 rolled around, Kali was getting back into training and hoping to be healthy enough to play in the fall. She hadn't played in a UCLA soccer game since the 2021 Covid spring season, where she only played in the two tournament games.

Right before our game against Fullerton in September, Kali was waiting to get the clearance from our team's orthopedic surgeon, Dr. Jones, who was busy all day. Finally, he was able to respond and gave Kali the green light in the second half. It was something out of a movie. We were literally in the tent when Nikki, our athletic trainer, got a text saying Kali could play 10 minutes. She warmed up and got ready to sub in.

It was like everything was happening in slow motion. Marg subbed Kali in, and within nine minutes, she scored two goals. Her first touch of the game, Kali ran hard near post and finished off a cross. The bench erupted. Kali threw her arms in the air, and everyone ran to her. She was smiling from ear to ear, and everyone was going crazy. Her boyfriend was in the stands, and he put his hands on his head, shocked. Within minutes, she did it again. She didn't give up on the play and threw herself towards the ball as it bounced off of her into the goal.

The bench started chanting, "KALI! KALI! KALI!" and soon the entire stadium joined in. There wasn't a dry eye in the stadium, and soon, the ref blew the whistle to end the game. Every person in a UCLA jersey ran towards Kali, and we all jumped and cheered around her. With tears glistening in her eyes, Kali smiled back, and we all celebrated together. The coaches were crying as we all came together. The older girls on the team all hugged each other. We had all seen Kali battle back time after time, and I was so happy for her. Our team came together, and we took a picture. There was a beautiful sunset over Wallis Annenberg, and we all pointed to Kali. It was truly a night to remember, and everyone was so incredibly happy for Kali. She deserved that moment more than anyone else.

In that moment, everyone put their own agenda and thoughts aside and celebrated Kali. Our team did a really good job of that. We were able to separate teammates from friends from competitors. Every week we competed against each other for starting spots and playing time, and every weekend, we celebrated each other's wins. An individual win was a team win.

ASU/UofA Weekend

We were excited to play at home against Arizona and Arizona State. After being in Oregon the previous weekend, we were excited to play at home. We were 3-0-0 in conference play and 11-0-0 overall. We were one game away from setting the program record for the best start in the school's history. We all knew we were on the edge of record-breaking, but we remained focused and just wanted to play our style of soccer. The year prior, we clawed out wins against them on the road. It wasn't easy, but we had gotten the job done and knew it would be a similar task this time around. Our first challenge was ASU. The game was Thursday night under the lights, and we were excited.

Thursday night rolled around, and we went through our normal warmups. I had planned what I was going to say to the team, and it reminded me of Maricarmen, who was in Mexico for a national team camp. We finished warmups, changed into our jerseys, and huddled together. I said, "We aren't giving this sorry ass team any hope." I remember Bri hiding her laugh, and some people probably rolled their eyes. But it was true. Too often in the past, we let teams who had no business hanging with us, hang.

Within five minutes, we were up 2-0. As she did the weekend prior, Reilyn scored on an Ally Lemos corner kick for her seventh goal of the year. It was a classic Reilyn Turner goal. Somehow, she ended up on the ground, and the ball ended up in the net. Three minutes later, Sunshine and Lexi combined with each other to find Ally Cook, her third goal of the year.

We started off strong in the second half when Bri found Ally Lemos in the middle of the field. Within five minutes of the second half, Ally hit a banger outside the box for her first collegiate goal. Everyone went crazy as the Assist Queen, and true freshman, finally got herself a goal. I started the second half on the bench, and I had a fire in me when I got subbed on. They subbed me in as left back, a position I primarily played in 2021, but for 2022, I had been only playing on the right. My goal was to finish the half strong. Connect my passes, make smart plays, and make an impact in our attack.

I felt confident and poised out there. Around the 70th minute, Sunshine played the ball out to Lexi. Lexi started to dribble, and I took off running. I overlapped her, and said, "Yeah Lex," and as I got closer to her my voice quickened as I said, "Yeah Lex!" She cut inside and laid the ball off to me. Her pass was in front of me, so I could run onto it. I was at the edge of the 18 and started to turn my hips a bit and, I looked up and saw the keeper out of position. I hit the ball with the inside of my foot, and it curled up and around the diving keeper.

Before the ball hit the back of the net, I was already celebrating. This was my first collegiate goal and a moment I will never ever forget. Reilyn and Lexi jumped on me as Jackie and Sunshine threw their arms in the air. It's such a sweet moment celebrating with people who have been there at such different points in your life. I ran to them, and we jumped up and down. I looked to my left and saw the bench on the field. I ran with my arms out wide and jumped into Jayden and Quincy's arms as the bench collapsed together. Jen looked at me with tears in her eyes as I hugged her tightly. I broke from the group and ran back to the middle of the field. I pointed up to my parents as Sunshine ran towards me to give me a hug. Finally, I could leave

UCLA with a goal, something I always dreamed about. We won 4-0 and set the record for the best start in the program's history. 12-0-0.

Sunshine Fontes

Sunshine Fontes. What a name. What a person. What a teammate. What a soccer player. One of my very best friends, Sunshine, and I, went through high highs and low lows together. We both recovered from our ACLs at the same time and would fight our way back onto the pitch together for the next two years.

Sunshine is a player that you can't emulate. Her raw talent is something you can't coach. Her incredible strength allowed her to score bangers. All she needed was a tiny bit of space to rip a shot from inside the box or outside the box. One of my favorite memories of Sunshine was in 2019. We were both red-shirting that fall and during warmups before games, our coach would let Shine and I each hit one volley. Shine passed the ball to Amanda, and behind her, I was videotaping. Amanda tossed the ball in the air, and Shine put her head down, and her high pony flew in the air as she released a half-volley into the top right corner. She threw her arms in the air, and I went ballistic. We ran around the field together, screaming and yelling. Later that year, during the College Cup, Shine and I sat next to each other during the semifinal. We wondered if we would ever get to play with each other in the Final Four.

Sunshine recovered from her ACL injury slowly but surely. Her first game back in the spring of 2021 was against Pepperdine, which was one of my fondest memories. We all cheered for her as she ran onto the field during the first half. Watching Shine battle back from her ACL tear was inspiring. We woke up early to go to the 7 a.m. lifts together. Our strength coach, Joe, put us through some of the most grueling lifts ever. We spent hours in the Acosta Center doing rehab together. From calf raises to BFR split squats, I saw Shine put in the work every single day to get back to doing her thing. That spring season in 2021, Shine started one game against Oregon State and tallied five goals and three assists.

Going into fall 2021, our previous coaches used her fitness against her instead of motivating her. That season, her minutes were inconsistent. She started five out of 20 games and had one assist and zero goals the whole season. As the season went on, her minutes dwindled, and she only played 16 minutes against UCI in the first-round tournament game. Her confidence was rocked from that season. When the new coaches came in, they looked at Shine with such admiration and hope. They looked past her fitness and saw her talent. Her vision, passes, and intelligence set her apart from the other girls. Instead of using her fitness against her, they encouraged her that it would only help the other parts of her game.

Shine scored her best beep test score ever in 2022. She came into pre-season in shape and ready to go. Throughout non-conference play, Shine scored six goals for us, including the crucial game-winner against Santa Clara. As PAC-12 play went on, Shine's minutes increased. She went from playing 45-50 minutes to now playing 65-70 minutes. Sunshine controlled the midfield for us, and since Mari was gone for National team duty, we needed Shine to come up big for us against Arizona.

Arizona was a tough team. They had a lot of local So Cal talent, and they always played aggressively and hard against us. They pressed us hard in the first half, and we were unable to generate any offense. As the game went on, the clock ticked down and all of a sudden there were 10 minutes left. We pushed to try and score as our defense continued to play steadily. I was on the bench for most of the second half, crossing my fingers that my teammates could get the job done. All of a sudden, Ally Cook picked the ball off and passed it to Shine.

She looked up and nailed the ball low and hard on the ground. The keeper was slow to react as the ball slid into the bottom right corner. With seven minutes left, Shine scored the game-winner and our streak continued to 13-0-0. The bench exploded, and she ran to the girls on the field with her arms in the air. You could see her smile from the top of the stands. Shine was a big-time player. She made plays when the team needed her most. She slipped passes through the midfield and backline, sprinted back on defense, and organized everyone around her. She was the voice of reason for us and would play a huge role for us during our playoff run.

Chapter 18
Self-Control

"Practice self-discipline and keep emotions under control. Good judgment and common sense are essential."
John Wooden

In 2021, we went the entire regular season undefeated. We tied plenty of games, and went into overtime, but we never lost a game. This loomed over us in 2022 as we continued undefeated. We didn't know how our team would respond to a loss. Would we come together and rise to the occasion? Would we crumble? A loss forced you to look inward. Change things up. Reflect on what is working and what needs to be fixed. A loss humbles you. Unfortunately, in 2021, we never found out how we would react. Our season ended abruptly with our first and only loss in the first round of the tournament.

Our team continued to have a dream season. We cruised through PAC-12 play and set a new program record, 13-0-0, for the best start of the season. We swept the Arizona schools and were now heading up to play Stanford for our single-game weekend. This was Marg's homecoming, and it was also their Mental Health night. The Stanford team, coaches, and community had gone through a hard year, and this was the game they planned to honor Katie. Our team spent that week preparing for Stanford. Marg ran the scout, gave us insight into individual players, and told us where we could expose them. We headed up to Palo Alto and hoped to continue our undefeated streak. I was a bit nervous about this game because it was our first true test since being in North Carolina in early September.

We started the game off flat. They passed around us, and we struggled to generate any attack. They intercepted passes and pressed us harder than we had been pressed before, while we continued to sit in our mid block, inviting pressure. In the first five minutes, Stanford ripped out four shots. Lauren Brzykcy made two crucial saves in the 36th minute to keep the game scoreless.

With a few minutes left in the first half, Allie Montoya served in a corner for Stanford, and we were unable to clear it. The ball took a bounce off Elise Evans, and she turned and fired to the right post for the game's only goal. We quickly sent the ball up for kickoff, and I took off running up the sideline. I whipped in a cross to Mari, and she took a shot that was saved by the Stanford keeper. We finished off the first half with a little bit more momentum.

At halftime, Marg admitted that we started off the game too conservatively. We changed the formation to a 3-5-2 in hopes of generating more offense. As we flew numbers forward, pressed harder, forced Stanford into mistakes, and took shots from everywhere on the field, we could not find the equalizer. We out-shot Stanford 12-4 in the second half and 17-8 overall. It was our first loss of the season, and it stung. We gave up a soft goal and then played an outstanding second half, but it just wasn't enough. Stanford's backline and goalkeeper played a hell of a game, and we just couldn't get through them.

As the final whistle blew, we high-fived the Stanford girls and came together as a team. Tears brimmed my teammate's eyes. Not because the world was ending or because we were sad to lose, but out of frustration. We didn't get broken down and exposed through the run of play; we got scored on by a lame corner kick. We gave everything we had in the second half but fell short. Marg pulled us together and told us she was proud of our fight in the second half, and now it was important for us to focus on the future. This was her first loss as a head coach, coincidentally right back where her coaching career started. As we gathered our stuff and headed to see our families, Marg was standing next to Molly, quietly crying. I know how badly she wanted to beat Stanford. I went up to her, put my hand on her shoulder, and told her, "Marg we're going to be okay." We were going to be just fine.

Later that night, we went back to our hotel and had a post-game meal. Half the team was in the meal room, and we were just goofing around. Reilyn and Emma started doing stand-up comedy; people were singing karaoke, and we were all laughing our asses off. The Daily Bruin wanted a quote from me, so I left the team room to take the call. As our music and laughter carried through the hotel, I called the reporter from the Daily Bruin. As they talked in a somber voice, they asked me how the girls on the team were doing and what the vibes were. I tried not to smile when I lied a little bit back to him.

I told him we were all very upset, but we were focused on our games against Colorado and Utah. I told him I was proud of the team's performance and knew we gave everything we had in the second half. I hung up with the reporter and went back to the team room, where I laughed and smiled for the rest of the night. I wasn't worried for us. Our team knew this loss was necessary. It stung, it hurt, it was frustrating, but in order for us to play even better, we needed to be tested. We needed to experience the feeling of losing. It was only going to make us stronger.

The next week of training was essential. We locked down more on set plays, worked on winning the ball higher up the field, and got ready to fly to Colorado and Utah. These were big games for us. It was imperative that we bounce back and show the country that we might bend, but we will Never Break. Our coaches were never rattled and never showed any signs of desperation or blame. They cut film for us, prepared us for the Colorado game, and moved on as well. We all knew that one loss wasn't going to kill us, and to fight for our third PAC-12 title in three years, every game was just as important as the last. Having this level of common sense and not getting wrapped up in results was important for our ability to deal with adversity.

Our game against Colorado was exactly what we needed. We started the game off on our front foot and applied pressure from the start. Playing in Colorado always posed a challenge because of the altitude, but that didn't bother us. We had spent the last nine months flying at sea level, and we were going to fly through the mountains as well. We put on a clinic, defeating Colorado 6-0. We were just six days removed from our first loss of the season, and we bounced back in a big way. We outshot Colorado, 20-6, and had 11 shots on goal to the Buffs' two. We improved to 14-1 and 6-1 in the PAC-12 standings.

Within six days, our team displayed self-control. From our coaches to us as players, we learned from the Stanford game and moved on. We didn't point fingers, dwell on any mistakes, or crumble. We didn't self-sabotage or play the "what if" game. We honestly didn't have time for it. The second the whistle blew to end the Stanford game, we wanted to play again. We wanted to redeem ourselves and get back in the win column.

Colorado Dinner with Marg's Mom

After the game, we had a team dinner planned. Marg's mom recently moved to Colorado and was going to host a dinner for us at the YMCA Boys' and Girls' Club space. Very rarely on our away trips did we have families host us, but for both Colorado and Utah, we had family and friends that hosted us throughout the weekend. We showered and changed, and everyone boarded the bus to dinner. Our families and friends who traveled were all invited as well, so they made their way to dinner.

We got to the YMCA Club, and they had pushed all the tables to one side to make room for the long table of catered Mexican food. Now, my team could eat. We piled our plates with taco salads, guacamole, and chips. I sat next to my family, who made the trip out to watch our game. We were all tuned in to the PAC-12 games that were still going on and we desperately needed USC and Stanford to drop points. We huddled around each other's phones, watching and trying not to show any indication if someone scored or not in case someone was behind. Music played throughout the room as we continued to shout at Utah in hopes they would score against USC.

We finished up dinner and thanked Marg's mom for hosting, and I said goodbye to my parents and grandmas. They were staying in Colorado with my mom's college roommate and had a whole day planned to see the Red Rocks and explore Boulder. As we were herded onto the bus, we looked at each other, and all silently planned on trekking to Cold Stone later that night. Once we got back to our hotel, we piled on more layers and went out to get ice cream. There was a whole group that went, and we sat outside together.

This was also the trip where Taylor Swift dropped her Midnights album. I was roommates with Brianne, and we stayed up until 10 p.m. for her newest album to hit Apple Music. My fellow Swiftie, Lexi, came by and we sat in my bed dissecting each song and lyric. I immediately fell in love with Maroon. I played it on repeat throughout the entire trip and soon learned every single lyric. Beating CU 6-0 was a memorable moment and game; assisting Lex was also awesome, but the moments that I miss the most are staying up late and yapping away with my roommate, team dinners, as well as going and getting ice cream.

Utah Game/Walbruchs

Feeling good after our big win against Colorado, we now took a quick flight down to Salt Lake City. This PAC-12 trip was always a bit taxing, given the extra flight in between games. As we landed at the Salt Lake City airport, the cold air hit us like a truck. We trained on Friday and Saturday afternoons and explored SLC. Our hotel was located downtown, and of course, we hit up the nearest Starbies. Right after training at Utah's field, we ate lunch, showered, and put on layers of clothes to make the trek in the rain to Starbucks.

Ellie Walbruch, a true freshman, was from Utah. She enrolled early in January and had almost been at UCLA for a year now. She was a strong, dynamic center forward who had the best shot we had seen from a freshman in a long time. She was quick with her feet and played confidently. I was super excited for her to return home and play in front of all her family and friends. Her family graciously offered to host a meal for us on Friday night. We bussed down to Ellie's home, where her family had a cute set-up in front of her house.

Her family had a "Welcome Bruins" sign on their front lawn, and their house was decked out in blue and gold. Her parents and family waited in the driveway and said hello to all of us as we gathered in their living room. Her parents catered from Costa Vida, which is a Mexican grill restaurant, and her mom had these cute UCLA cookies made for dessert. It was warm enough to sit outside, so we all sat side by side and had dinner together. After dinner, we explored Ellie's house. In her backyard, there was a basketball court. Girls started playing Horse and Lightning. Another group went down to the basement and played around the world on their ping pong table. I had a good conversation with Ellie's dad, who played soccer professionally in Europe, and he told me how much I would enjoy playing soccer abroad. This was probably the first conversation I had regarding "what's next" for me. I'll never forget how much fun we had at the Walbruchs. They are good people.

Before our game against Utah, our jack-of-all-trades Team Manager/Director of Operations/Content creator, Anish, sent us our pre-game hype video. Before every game, Anish made us the most incredible videos compiled of all our highlights from the game before. Anish had been with our team since 2019 and had been with us through all the ups and downs over the years. Throughout his four years with us, he had made us highlight videos and Instagram reels, and helped drive up our engagement on social media. With the help of his entertaining videos and graphics, our Instagram account hit 100K followers and became the most followed NCAA college soccer account at the time, men's, or women's.

He was also a loyal friend and always invited us over for dinner. He didn't always travel with us, so he messaged our hype video in the GroupMe called "Je M'appelle," otherwise known as "My Name Is." He compiled all our highlights from the 6-0 against Colorado and mirrored them with professional players, set to the tune of "Je M'appelle" by Benzz ft. Tion Wayne. Mackenzee's banger was followed by a banger by David Beckham. Reilyn's goals were side by side with Ronaldinho's. It was some of his best work.

As we got ready to play Utah, the snow started to come down on us. We all bundled in layers with leggings, long-sleeves, gloves, headbands on, while the Utah girls only wore long-sleeves. We definitely looked like we were from California. Trying to warm up in our warmup, we took the field feeling frozen but brought the heat. We recorded our 10th shutout of the season, beating Utah 3-0. Lexi and Sof had two first half goals, with Ally Cook putting the finishing touch on the game in the second half to make it 3-0.

With this win, we improved to 15-1 overall and 7-1 in PAC-12 Play. Coming to the Rockies and getting six points on the road is not easy, especially given that we had just suffered our first loss of the season; on top of the weather and altitude, we came together and got the job done. We didn't have time to let the Stanford game affect us more than it already did. Our focus now shifted to the next weekend, where we met Washington State and UW at home.

Jackie Gilday

A lot of our seniors were having dream senior years. Jackie Gilday was having one herself. One of my best friends, Jackie's career at UCLA was nothing short of smooth. She enrolled early in the winter of 2019, and me and my friends immediately welcomed her into our friend group. She played for Nicaragua and represented her heritage with pride and love. We would gather around my laptop and watch Jackie and her team crush a small CONCACAF team 19-0. During her freshman year, she remained fairly healthy and got to play limited minutes in 2019. She was down on the sideline during our College Cup semifinal loss to Stanford.

That winter in 2020, she represented Nicaragua at the U20 qualifiers. For the next two years, she was constantly in pain. During the fall of 2020, Jackie started having knee pain, and since we didn't have a season that fall, they tried different remedies to help fix the problem. The surgery was intensive and required cartilage replacement. Finally, before Thanksgiving, they went ahead and did the surgery. She came down to San Clemente and spent Thanksgiving with me and my family.

Jackie continued to rehab her knee that spring and missed out on our spring Covid season. She worked hard to come back and be ready for our 2021 season. That summer, Jen and I visited Jackie at her hometown in Florida. We met her parents and brother for the first time and had a ton of fun surfing, kayaking, and exploring NSB. We would run at the track together, and Jackie looked fit going into the season. She made it through pre-season, played in our exhibition game, and Nicaragua had just announced the World Cup qualifiers would be in February of 2022.

As our 2021 season continued, she started having hip pain that was not going away with injections or physical therapy. Exactly a year after she had knee surgery, she was now going to have labrum surgery in October. There was still hope for her to come back for qualifiers, which were a few months out. Somehow, a few weeks later, we were in New York, and Jackie ran for the first time. We returned to Westwood to start the "New Era" with Marg, and Jackie slowly started coming back. She crushed the first beep test, beating out girls who had never been injured a day in their lives, and got the clearance to go to the World Cup qualifiers. It was inspirational watching her come back.

During the spring of 2022, Jackie managed her injuries. She knew her body well and wanted to do everything in her power to play that fall. Coming into the fall, her motto was "One day, one practice, one game at a time". She was going to make the most of every time she got to play soccer because she didn't know how much more she got to play. The coaches loved Jackie. Her midfield mind was exactly what they wanted.

She had great feet, could get out of sticky situations, was calm and composed under pressure, and defensively set our mid-block next to Sunshine. They also believed in her. She pushed through her first full pre-season in three years and earned her way onto the starting lineup. I'll never forget sitting in the San Jose hotel and seeing her name in the starting lineup. I turned all the way back and smiled at her. She had the biggest smile on her face. Jackie played her first 90 minutes ever at UCLA against Santa Clara, and then continued starting and playing heavy minutes against UNC and

Duke. After being injured year after year, watching hundreds of practices from the sideline, and going through multiple surgeries, MRIs, and injections, she got to start and play on the biggest stage.

Senior Day

Cue the waterworks. Senior Day was fast approaching, and I couldn't believe it. I had two more regular-season games left at Wallis Annenberg. Two more games left to go undefeated at home and fight for the top spot in the PAC-12 standings. There were eight of us being honored this weekend: Kylie Kerr, Brianne Riley, Jackie Gilday, Kali Trevithick, Sunshine Fontes, the two fifth years: me, Maricarmen, and sixth year Lauren. The senior day festivities were happening against UW on Sunday, but we first had to take care of business against WSU on Thursday night. The race to first place was tight. There were only three games left, and it was essential that we got six points leading up to our big clash against USC.

    For the past year, Sunshine and I coached a youth team at the club Autobahn. Twice a week, we drove to Santa Monica and coached the U17 girls' team and helped out with the baby group filled with 3-and-4-year-olds. We ran them through passing patterns, rondo drills, and small-sided games. We worked on their first touch, being aggressive, and learning to use both feet. It was a highlight of our week and also the extra time that Sunshine and I got to spend with each other. The club decided to buy block tickets to our game against Washington State. There were dozens of young girls in the stands who looked up to us and we wanted to make them proud.

    We always struggled against WSU. They were always a physical test for us. They were aggressive in their defending and matched up with us athletically. We tied them in Pullman the year before and were looking for revenge in Westwood. Leading up to the game, one of our starting center-backs got hurt and wasn't able to play. We quickly adapted, and Maya Evans was going to start in lieu of Jayden. Our starting 9, Reilyn Turner, was also out for the game. We were at the point of the season where we needed our starters ready for playoffs, and we had a deep enough bench and trusted teammates to fill those roles.

    I loved Thursday night games. We got a good crowd of students, the lights were bright, and a good performance was going to set us up well for

Sunday. Marg's plan for this weekend was to get the seniors as many minutes as possible. Thursday rolled around, and we went through our normal pre-game routine. I switched up my hair and decided to wear it in a high ponytail. I was excited for that weekend. I felt like I needed a turning point that season and felt confident that it was going to happen that weekend.

We kicked off, and our late-night match with WSU was underway. We took control of the game early on and set the tempo. Mackenzee Vance, who struggled with injury after injury, earned the start and was playing in front of me. Mac is a very technical, dynamic winger who was confident going 1v1 and loved to create going forward. We formed a good partnership, and from the start we were combining up the field. Maricarmen was everywhere in the midfield and was pushing to get a goal. She hit the post twice in the first half as the crowd roared with excitement. We made changes throughout the first half in hopes of wearing and tearing on WSU's steady defense. We just couldn't get the ball in the back of the net. As we went into halftime, there was an unspoken understanding that we had to win this game. We needed to find a way to score one goal.

We started the second half strong. We controlled the tempo and continued to fight for a goal. As we neared the 60th minute mark, I threw the ball into Ally Cook right by the bench in WSU's half. She held onto the ball strong, and somehow, the ball found its way back to me. I attracted two defenders and went on a little dribble, and then quickly dished the ball out to Sunshine. Shine, in two touches, looked up and pinged the ball to our center back, Lilly Reale.

Lilly burst into the midfield and took a commanding touch forward. The WSU defense stayed back as Lilly dribbled forward. She was about 30 yards out when she let it rip with her left foot. The stadium went quiet as the ball shot hard at the keeper. The keeper fumbled with the ball and somehow, it ended up in the back of the net. We had found our way. It was Lilly's first goal of the season, and it couldn't have come at a more perfect time. We ran to her and celebrated as the crowd went crazy. For the next 30 minutes, Marg emptied the bench. We continued to tire out WSU and all our available seniors got to play. We played committed defense and worked hard to earn our shutout.

The whistle blew to end the game, and we hugged each other. Every point mattered. There were games where our defense was struggling, and our offense showed up. There were games where our offense was struggling. Games where we missed Reilyn and Lex due to injury, and our defense stepped up. We maintained the shutout and the game winning goal came from our center-back. We had the depth, the talent, and the belief to pull through even when we weren't 100%. After the game, Sunshine and I saw all our Autobahn girls. They swarmed around us, asking for selfies and autographs. I hugged and kissed my family, and all eyes turned to our very last regular-season game against the University of Washington on Sunday.

As Friday and Saturday rolled through, the anticipation for Senior Day was at an all-time high. We had special traditions to uphold, and after four and a half years, it was my turn to feel the love and joy that encompassed Senior Day. Anish put together the best video ever of alumni wishing us a happy Senior Day. It was so special seeing all of our past teammates and friends and we all were teary-eyed when it ended. The traditions continued throughout Sunday, and everyone on the team was involved.

Since it was the coaches' first Senior Day with us, they had no idea what any of the traditions were. They texted the underclassmen, asking them how much time they needed and what the vibes were going to be. While the freshmen flocked down to Target and CVS to create heartfelt and special posters for us, the sophomores decorated the locker room with streamers, signs, and balloons. We walked into the locker room the morning of Senior Day in awe. They did such a good job. Cori James, a freshman, made my poster. She included pictures of me when I was younger and decked it out with glitter. The Juniors rallied together the week prior to come up with a hilarious and touching skit that imitated the seniors.

They dressed up in costumes, memorized their lines, and put together a full-on skit that poked fun at each of us. Each Junior (with some help from the sophomores) acted out each senior. Whether it had to do with boys, embarrassing moments, or certain quirks, they nailed it. We all sat in front of them as they performed, spilling out secrets and off-the-pitch moments that had us crying and laughing. Our coaches shook their heads during the stories of us at the bars and clubs. We all laughed with each other. They did a great job and accurately described all of us.

After the skits, each Junior lined up and shared a meaningful message to each Senior they acted out. We all sat in front of them; Seniors on the ground all huddled together. Mac spoke about me. From the day she stepped foot on campus, Mac had something special. I took her under my wing and supported her through her laundry list of injuries. I backed her to the coaches and to our teammates in times when she didn't have the best of attitudes. She teared up, talking about the impact I had on our program and how much she and the team would miss me. I smiled back at her and got up to give her a hug. The Juniors continued to spill their hearts out to the seniors, and people all over the locker room were holding back tears. After the festivities, we all had to lock in and get ready for our last PAC-12 game at Wallis Annenberg.

 I sat at my locker one more time. The next thing I knew, Quincy barged through the locker. In her hand was a pink sparkly headband. All throughout club soccer and my youth national team days, I wore a hot pink sparkly headband. It was the dancer in me. My youth national team coaches would call me "sparkles." Once I got to UCLA, to my mom's disappointment, I decided to retire sparkles. It was time for me to move on. I hadn't worn it since my very last club soccer game in December 2017, and now Quincy was standing in front of me holding it. She told me that my mom had given it to her to give to me. Maricarmen saw what was going on, and next thing you know, she was hugging me, and we were both crying. At some point, someone whipped out their phone and captured this whole moment. I put the headband on and decided that I would wear it one last time. I headed downstairs as the entire team gathered. With the IM field on our left and Pauley Pavilion on our right, we headed out to our matinee clash against UW.

 Once we got to the stadium, our jerseys were framed with flowers placed in front of them. There was a huge poster hung over the bench reading THANK YOU SENIORS. I had seen the last four senior days unfold, and I was so excited to experience mine. On the huge scoreboard, a slideshow of pictures played of all of us seniors when we were little youth players. As warmups commenced, we all would stop and watch videos of our families wishing us "Good Luck and Happy Senior Day!"

 As warmups came to an end, all the seniors lined up with their families by the bench. The announcer read out each name and the family members who were walking with us. I quickly ran to Bri and told her to put her earrings on. Priorities! My mom, dad, and brother walked out with me. My cousins, family, and friends in the stands were cheering and yelling for me when my name was announced. We hugged our coaches, and Mac walked out to give me my flowers and framed jersey. All the seniors and our families stood together, and we took a group shot. I hugged my family goodbye, and they headed up to the stands. Our team came together and huddled one more time. I thanked our team for such an amazing day. It was now time to get three more points and finish our regular season at Wally undefeated.

The ref blew the whistle to start the game, and it was *déjà vu* from Thursday's first half. Nothing was going in. Marg did her usual subs, and one by one, all the seniors got on the pitch. We pushed and pushed to get a goal, but we ended the first half 0-0. Just like Thursday's game, the coaches were calm and composed at halftime. We knew a goal was going to come; it was just a matter of who and when.

The second half started, and we immediately took control of the game. Within four minutes, Ally Lemos played a perfect pass to Ally Cook, and we went up 1-0.

2,500 fans went crazy. It was a packed Sunday game, and we could feel the energy. 10 minutes later, our reigning PAC-12 defender of the week, Quincy, rifled a shot from 25 yards out. Our dynamic leftback cut in on her right foot and let it rip. The ball ricocheted off the net, and the stadium erupted. We all ran to Q and celebrated. Marg continued to sub in the seniors, and we continued playing great soccer. We had one more goal in us.

The weeks leading up to Senior Day were hard for Jackie. Her opposite knee started bothering her, and it was the same pain the other one had before the cartilage replacement. She limited herself to the games and trainings leading up to Senior Day and didn't play in our Thursday game against Washington State. Her family flew in from Florida, and she was slated to get limited minutes against UW. After not playing much in the first half, she was subbed late into the second half. She was about 20 yards out when she faked a left footed shot and put the ball on her right. Everyone in the stadium and bench held their breath as she curled a shot around the keeper and into the back of the net. It was her first career goal. On Senior Day. After she just found out she would eventually need knee surgery. The bench exploded and as the clock ticked down, we all ran out on the field to celebrate Jackie. It was her moment, and you could feel the joy and love in the air. She had gone through so much adversity to get to this point, and her dream senior year was continuing. We were witnessing a full-circle moment come together.

After the game, my family came down and we took pictures together. I had a whole group come for Senior Day, and I felt the love and support from everyone. I hugged and kissed them all, and we walked over to Acosta for our post-game meal. Our moms had set up a whole photo booth spot with decorations and signs. Sunshine had a million leis on her, and we all got together and took more pictures. It was the end to the most perfect day.

Chapter 19
Enthusiasm

"Enthusiasm brushes off upon those with whom you come in contact. You must truly enjoy what you're doing."
John Wooden

John Wooden describes that enthusiasm "brushes upon those with whom you come in contact." I describe enthusiasm as Gof Boyoko. When Gof was hired at the beginning of the year, Marg wanted a coach who was different from her. Marg was steady. She never got too high and never got too low, either. She sat with her arms crossed and backward hat on during games. She never yelled, and she rarely stood up and applauded when she was impressed. Marg knew she needed a sidekick that was the opposite of her. Someone who was incredibly soccer smart, emotional, and motivated us through their personality. She found the perfect guy when she hired her long-time friend and UCSB associate head coach, Gof Boyoko.

Gof came to UCLA from UC Santa Barbara, where he served as the associate head coach and recruiting coordinator of the women's team from 2017-2021. He helped guide the Gauchos to Big West Tournament appearances in 2017, 2018, and 2021, along with an appearance in the 2018 Big West final.

Gof was from Paris. He grew up playing football and was surrounded by European football. He brought that flair and style of play to our team. In one of our very first practices with him in the spring, he introduced a complicated passing pattern to us. Our team rarely did passing patterns with our old coaches, so this was different from us. There were no defenders, no pressure, and the patterns ranged from three to four passes up to however many you wanted. Maybe it was all one touch, or one pass was with your left foot, and the next one you collected with your right and passed with your right, or maybe the same pattern got more complicated as it went on. The point of passing patterns is to get your brain working and to create pictures.

Gof's favorite passing pattern was challenging. Our starting positions were in a diamond with two people in the middle. We moved counterclockwise while playing the ball into the middle and then outside. There was a pass between the people in the middle and a one-two out wide. The hard part was the rotation. There were different variations of the pattern, and they got harder as we went. It took all spring for every person on the team to 100% understand what each pattern was and to switch from variation to variation without any hesitation.

It was complicated, but when it clicked, we moved the ball so fluidly. When it clicked, it was fun. Gof was patient with all of us. We worked on it until we got it right. He told us, "If you don't get it, step out and watch for a bit." Once the freshman came in, they had to learn the passing pattern, and it was a learning curve for a lot of us. The majority of the team wanted to fly through it, but there were seven or eight girls who couldn't get it. By the time games started, we had the pattern down pat for warmups.

Gof loved our game-day warm-ups. He loved setting up the passing patterns by the away team's fans. We bounced the ball so complicatedly and so fast back and forth to each other. We moved off each other and communicated with ease. He would say, "Two!" and we would immediately do the second variation. We pinged the ball around the diamond while he clapped and hyped us all up. I'll never forget the semifinal game in the College Cup; we started our warmup on the practice field a little too early. Once we moved into the stadium, he quickly re-set up the diamonds near the Alabama bench, near all the fans, and we did the pattern again.

Gof loved his routine. He was beyond superstitious. He wore the same sneakers, the same outfit, the same hat every single game. He always showered before our games. He was particular about our Match Day -1 training. We always warmed up on our IM turf field with our strength coach, Paige. He would walk over from Drake Stadium, which was right next to IM, with two different pinnies, and he would split the teams up during the warmup, so when we walked over to training, we all knew what teams we were on and could get started right away.

He made sure our pre-game meal was always the same. During our tournament run, we had four home games in a row. He ordered from the same chicken place every single game. By the Sweet 16 game, we asked to change locations, and he refused. Everything had to be the same. The two games we lost, Stanford and USC, he didn't follow the same routine. Before one of the games, he didn't shower and before another one he wore a different hat. After the losses, he switched up his game-day outfits to something else.

Gof loved what he was doing. He loved coaching us. He loved celebrating our goals. He loved celebrating our wins. And it influenced us. He believed in every single one of us, and he looked straight into our eyes every single day and told us how good we were. He said that he believed, to his core, that we were the best team in the country, and it brushed up on us. He was constantly amping us up in training. If our passes were off or things would get messy, he would pause us and tell us how good we were and how we needed to be better. Gof brought joy every single day to training. He made me want to win for him. I knew how much he cared for our team, and we appreciated it so much. He brought enthusiasm to our team.

Halloween

We played UW on October 30th, so the next day was Halloween. We had our normal schedule of film and training. In the past, sometimes, each class dressed up together, people paired up, or we were put in specific groups. This year, each class planned to dress up. The seniors went back and forth trying to figure out what to dress up as. There were eight of us. We waited until the last minute and decided to go with "Holidays."

Each of us was decked out in a costume that represented the holiday we were dressing up as. I was dressed up as New Year's Eve, Shine was the Grinch, Bri was Santa, Lauren was Mardi Gras, Kali was Valentine's Day, Jackie was Easter, and Kylie was Labor Day. The juniors were dressed up as "red flags," the sophomores dressed up as "fight night," and the freshmen broke up into groups to dress up. The coaches took first place as they dressed up as the softball coaching staff. They went to our equipment manager before training and put on the softball uniform. Gof put a long wig on and tied the hair back into a bubble braid. They had cleats, hats, gloves, and bats all out. We took pictures, voted on who was best dressed, and stripped back down into our practice kit. We continued on with training and laughed at the sophomores as they had fake tattoos on their neck and face.

USC Loss

"Losing is only temporary and not encompassing. You must simply study it, learn from it, and try hard not to lose the same way again. Then you must have the self-control to forget about it." - John Wooden

In 1974, USC football was playing Notre Dame, and Anthony Davis ran back the 2nd half kickoff. USC came back to win after being down 24-0. My dad was seven years old and instantly became a USC fan for life. He supported the Trojans through the Pete Carroll era from 2001 to 2009, where they went 97-19 and won two National Championships. I was born into a USC supporting family. We took trips up to the Colosseum and the Galen Center to watch USC basketball. I wore the SC cheerleader outfits and grew up supporting cardinal and gold. It was my dad's dream for me or my brother to attend USC.

During the recruiting process, he pushed me to talk to the SC coaches and saw me representing USC on the national stage. I'll never forget driving back from a club practice in 2015 and talking to the assistant coach, where she told me they "weren't interested in recruiting defenders." I thought to myself, "Okay, I'll just commit to your rival school." My dad said he would wear a UCLA Soccer shirt, and his first post ever on Facebook was announcing my commitment to play soccer at UCLA. He was a proud dad, and he still is. While my dad was a huge USC fan, he also was a basketball player and coach at heart. He obviously admired legendary basketball coach John Wooden and ingrained in my head the importance of "hard work beats talent when talent doesn't work hard." I was going to write my own story, and despite my dad's buddies giving him a hard time supporting UCLA, he was excited to take the trip up to Westwood.

Leading up to our match-up this fall, we hadn't lost to USC since 2015. We had dramatic wins in overtime and clawed out ties, but we hadn't lost to them in nearly seven years. This game was huge nonetheless for several reasons. First, the PAC-12 title was on the line. If we won, we won the title outright. If we tied, we clinched a share with Stanford. If we lost, we would get second place, and Stanford would win. Secondly, our old assistant coach, Jane Alukonis, was now the head coach at USC. There was an extra edge to this game, knowing her ties with UCLA. Thirdly, it was a rivalry, and we didn't want to lose. This was the first time in a long time we weren't playing in a big stadium.

We were playing at USC's home field, and usually, when USC hosted us, we either played them in Carson or in the Colosseum. USC's home field is up against the street near the fire station in South Central LA. The stands were small, and they couldn't fit a lot of people. We played them in the early afternoon, and we believed Jane wanted to take away the hype of the game. She knew we rose to the occasion whenever the spotlight was on, so we guessed that for this game, she tried to remove any outside factors that would help us.

Leading up to our game against USC, we knew it was going to be a challenge. USC was unlike the other PAC-12 teams we faced. They matched our athleticism out wide, and their midfield was dynamic and creative on the ball. They were talented and had a knack for scoring. Their best player, Croix Bethune had just torn her ACL and was out for the rest of the season. Even without her though, they were still a dangerous team, and we knew we were going to have to play really well to get our result.

I felt really confident going into that game. I was going to be matched up against Simone Jackson and knew I needed to be on my A-game. Since she was so dangerous on the attack, I knew I wasn't going to be able to make a ton of runs going forward. Every time we played USC, they came out hot in the first 10 minutes. They would press us hard, run at our back line, and create chances fast. We knew they would do the same this year and were somewhat prepared.

As we took the field and the ref blew the whistle, the game started exactly how we thought it would. SC put pressure on us from the jump and started the game out on the front foot. We struggled to figure out their midfield and played so far back that we weren't able to get pressure out on the ball. We gave up a weak foul, and USC went up 1-0 off a set piece. The ball sailed as if it was going out of bounds, and we didn't communicate well. It bounced in the box, and USC capitalized. There was just something in the air.

A few minutes later, off a corner, we had a handball in the box, and USC went up 2-0 off a penalty kick. This was the first time we went down since the Stanford game and the first time we ever were down 2-0.

Throughout the first half, we struggled to adapt and find solutions. We resulted in playing individually, and USC was able to hang with us athletically. Going into halftime, we needed to change things around. Marg admitted, for the second time this season, that we came out too conservatively. We allowed them to eat up space and put so much pressure on us that we eventually gave up poor fouls and corners that resulted in them scoring. We needed to start the second half on the front foot and turn this game around.

We decided we would switch to a 3-5-2 and provide some more attack. We knew this would be dangerous because USC had fast and strong wingers who could take advantage of the space out wide, but we also knew we had to go for the win. We needed to find a way to score two or three goals in the next 45 minutes. Right before we took the field, I looked over and saw Lilly start to cry. She gave up the handball and felt the weight of the game on her shoulders. I grabbed her and told her everything was going to be alright. We had her back, and that I wasn't worried. I told the group to scratch the first half and focus on the next 45 minutes. We scored goals every day in training, and 45 minutes was plenty to find a way to score a few more.

As the second half started, we just couldn't get into the game. Our aggressive formation going forward left us vulnerable in the back, and Lauren had to make three big saves right from the start. We were able to create a bit more up the field, but overall, we were playing flat. Individuals struggled, and it's hard to win a game against a good team when more than half your lineup isn't playing well.

Marg continued to make subs and adjust things, but we were unable to create any sort of attack. Our best chance of the game came in the 80th minute when I stole the ball from their center back and dribbled up the field. I looked to my left and passed the ball squarely to Sunshine seven yards out from the goal. She hit it the first time with her left foot right to the keeper, and the defender recovered to clear it off the line. I put my hands on my knees and looked down, frustrated. I knew deep down we weren't going to win this game. It just wasn't in the cards.

With seven minutes left in the game, Marg subbed me out. I was so tired. It was probably one of my best games all season. As I walked down the bench, I sat down with my water in my hands and started to cry a little bit. I wasn't sad. I didn't necessarily care about losing the PAC-12 title, I had done that twice, but I was more pissed off that we lost to USC for the first time in seven years.

Erin Adkins, our Athletic Director, was at the end of the bench, and she came up and gave me a big hug. She told me, "That's the last game you guys are losing. Don't let them see your tears." I wiped back my tears and stood next to my teammates, and cheered them on for the next five minutes.

Marg came down the bench and told us that we were class, and that we would go and high-five every player on their team. While they celebrated like they won the NCAA tournament, we held our heads high, but knew we could play better. That was the first game all year where we couldn't figure it out. We pointed fingers, yelled at each other, and played selfishly for stretches of the game. We tried to adapt and change formations and personnel, but nothing seemed to work. Against Stanford, we outplayed them and fought back the second half, but there was little fight in this game. That was a hard pill to swallow because now we had to change our focus and get ready for the NCAA tournament.

As we pulled in together as a group, Jayden showed her leadership in that moment. She told us that we had to take accountability and we couldn't resort to yelling at each other and not being good teammates. We had to shift our focus for this next week, and we would learn from this game and move on. I had nothing to say and was grateful that Jayden, a sophomore, stepped up when some of us older girls couldn't. She wasn't a captain or a leader but truly was the unsung leader of that year.

We had six days to re-group and come together. Six days to get our shit together. That loss exposed us more than any other game, and it was a little nerve-racking knowing that the Selection Show was a few days away. This game was a turning point for our team. We never wanted to feel like that again. After the game, Marg told us that there were going to be moments throughout the tournament that we would be down a goal or maybe down two goals. We would have to find a way and dig deep. She was right.

After the USC game, I went into the coach's office for a meeting before the tournament started. Up until our USC game, I really didn't know what the future held for me. I had a pretty good season, individually.

I had plenty of film. I had produced for our team. But I didn't have years and years of standout soccer. I didn't have an "automatic" name. I still had the option to take my sixth year; whether that was at UCLA or somewhere else, I could still play one more year of college soccer. I didn't put too much thought into playing pro. I believed in myself but didn't think I had the resume to make it into the NWSL.

After the USC game, something switched. I had a really good game. I knew I needed to move on. Something clicked within me, and I knew I was ready for what was next. I told my parents after that game I wanted to play pro. They looked back, wide-eyed, and quietly said, "We think you can too." I walked into Marg's office, knowing I would probably cry.

There were a lot of emotions. Leaving. Tournament play. The USC loss. The coaches complimented me for the last few weeks of play. Said the WSU/UW weekend was a breakout weekend for me. I teared up a little bit and told them I was ready to move on. Obviously, I had my eyes set on the NCAA tournament, and I wanted to win so badly, but it kind of hit me that this was the end of my career at UCLA. I cried harder when I thought about my parents watching me for the last few times. Marg handed me tissues. The coaches told me how excited they were for me.

Chapter 20
Initiative

"Cultivate the ability to make decisions and think alone. Do not be afraid of failure, but learn from it."
John Wooden

There were times throughout our season when I was just so tired. Tired of being a leader. Tired of always showing up. Tired of talking about soccer, watching film, and thinking of solutions. Tired of knowing this would be my last year. I was having so much fun, and this year was truly a dream year for me, but I was also really stressed. Deep down, I knew what we were capable of doing, so I wanted to protect us. I didn't want us to fall short. It would be a disservice to us, our coaches, our program, and everyone who has poured all their time and energy into us. So, I kept going. Kept being the leader I was meant to be. Our USC loss was a turning point for our team. While the UNC and Duke games showed us that we could win a National Championship, the USC loss showed us we could lose it as well. The playoff draw was Monday, so that morning, I had called a player-only meeting before practice.

I went back and forth on what I wanted to say. How did I want to approach our vulnerable team right now? We didn't have much time. Our first game was in four days, and we needed to move on from our loss Friday. I didn't want to act like it didn't happen, but I didn't want to dwell on the past. So, I decided to do some research.

The last time UCLA Women's Soccer won a National Championship was in 2013. That team included stars like Sam Mewis, Abby Dahlkemper, Caprice Dydasco, Katelyn Rowland, and so many more. I actually DM'ed all of them on Instagram, asking for help (no one responded). From the top down, they were stacked. Their playoff run included beating San Diego State, Kentucky, and Stanford at home. Beating UNC 1-0 in the Elite Eight in Chapel Hill. Beating UVA in penalties in the College Cup semifinal, and then finally beating Florida State in the final 1-0. They beat three powerhouse ACC opponents on the road while winning games in overtime and penalties. Their journey to winning UCLA Women's Soccer's first National Championship wasn't easy. And us winning our second wasn't going to be any easier.

We were going to have a hard path regardless of who we were slated to play.

We played our best soccer when we played free. When we played possession-based soccer with our outside backs bombing forward, nines finishing, midfield creating chances, and back-line shutting teams out, we were unbeatable. We knew what we struggled against, and we knew how to fix our problems. The USC loss exposed a lot of our vulnerabilities. We were unable to adapt to being down 2-0. We couldn't figure out how to play against a team just as athletic as us. We mentally shut down, and our communication became desperate and unhelpful.

We didn't play our game at all. USC outplayed us for 90 minutes, and that was going to be the last time that ever happened. I decided to be as motivating and inspirational as possible.

I told our captains, Lilly, and Mari, that I was going to call a meeting for just the players. I let them know what I was going to touch on. That morning, we met in our locker room, and I sat and faced the team. I told everyone that I didn't care what happened on Friday. We learn from it and move on. Use the next few days to do what you need to do. Talk to the players around you, go to therapy, talk to the coaches; do whatever you need to do to prepare you mentally and emotionally for Friday. I told them that later that day, we would find out who we would play and how important it would be for us to stay focused one game at a time. I also said it doesn't matter who we play or our route to the final four.

I used the 2013 team as an example; they beat powerhouse programs and stayed true to their style of play and who they were. We could do the same thing. I told them there would be moments where we would be 10 seconds away from losing. Moments in overtime and during PKs where things are left up to fate. Moments when someone was going to sub on and make a big play for us. I told them there wasn't a better team in the country; I would take our locker room over anyone. There wasn't a doubt in my mind that we could win this thing. I told our team that everything was written. We are supposed to win, and if we internalize this tournament and make it about us, everything would play out how it was supposed to. The room was extremely quiet as the girls looked back at me. My voice started to crack a little bit as I told them I wouldn't be up here saying all this if I really didn't believe we could.

Bend Never Break

I told them that we would be better than every team we played. I said that we respect them and welcome them to Wally, but the second the whistle blows, we send them back to wherever they came from. We kick their ass from minute one to 90 and make them wish they never flew out to Westwood. I told them that we earn the right to have this mindset. It's not cockiness or arrogance; it's knowing that when we look across the field at our opponent, we will beat them. We watch film, study our opponents, respect them, but we never fear them. There is nothing to be scared of when you're the best team in the country. They all looked back, and I could see the light in their eyes. I knew they believed me. To be completely honest, I played into the bit. I knew our team was capable, but I needed them to 100% believe. So when we went into overtime, PKs, or when we would be down 2-0, we were never worried.

Throughout my career at UCLA, I took initiative a lot. I was our team BAC rep when no one volunteered. I was our team rep during the 2020 election, making sure everyone was registered to vote. I suggested we wear "Katie's Saves" patches on our shirts to show support for Katie and her family. I didn't do it for recognition or praise; I knew I wouldn't get any. I did it because I wanted to. I wanted our team to be on the right side of history. Being inclusive, being welcoming, being a team that led other teams to achieve excellence on and off the playing field.

Now, there were definitely moments where I said the wrong thing. Moments when I told our team we didn't have high soccer IQ (yikes) or dropped a few F bombs during the game or argued with Gof about set pieces. Clearly, I still think about those times. Those weren't my finest moments, but I really tried to be the best leader I could be. Whether that was in the locker room, answering panicked FaceTimes, sending motivating text messages, or comforting someone when they were down.

I wouldn't be able to do any of this without the support of my girls. My teammates allowed me to be the outgoing, honest, and passionate person and teammate I was. They looked at me with inspiration and motivation. I wasn't afraid of failing. I was afraid of not doing everything in my power to help our team achieve greatness. I knew this meant taking the initiative at every corner.

Later that day, we gathered in the Acosta film room to watch the selection show. We had a feeling deep down we would be a number one seed.

There were four number one seeds, and they all got to host up until the Final Four. Up until the tournament, we were undefeated at Wallis Annenberg, and it would be really special for us seniors to get to host four more games. We projected the selection show on the big projector and sat down. The NCAA selection show is exactly what it sounds like. All around the country, most teams waited anxiously to hear their names called. There were 30 automatic bids, all given to one team in each conference, and then 34 at-large bids. Stanford was the PAC-12 automatic bid because they won our conference. We had our phones out, getting ready to videotape every time a seed was announced. Florida State was the first number one seed announced. As the announcer went through each team, we waited on the edge of our seats to see where we were going to end up.

UNC was named the number two seed, and then Alabama and Notre Dame were named number one seeds. There was one more number one seed up for grabs sitting in the bottom right quadrant. Finally, the TV showed our highlights, and the announcer called us "Big, bad UCLA!" as our name popped up next to the number one seed. We cheered and clapped and were all smiles. This was the first time we were a number one seed since 2014. We were going to have four more opportunities to play in front of our families, friends, students, and the LA community. We quickly scanned our potential path to the College Cup and were slated to play teams we hadn't played before. Our first opponent was NAU. Liza, our media SID, quickly called me over for an interview with the Daily Bruin. I ducked into an office next to our film room and logged onto the Zoom. The student-interviewer was watching the selection show as well and asked me how I was feeling, and I responded enthusiastically, "We're just going to internalize this tournament and make it about us, the only team we have to worry about – the only team we have to focus on – is ourselves, and if we do that, we're going to play our style of soccer. We'll play for each other, and we'll win a National Championship."

Going into the tournament, Melinda suggested we do something before the game that brought us all together. With the extra dose of nerves and anxiety that playoffs brought, we needed a moment of calmness. She brought up the idea of a "power pose." Basically, right after warmups, before we all changed into our jerseys, every member- player, coach, support staff, doctor, Athletic Director, student-intern, and anyone else who was down on the field-would all form a big circle. This was the first year where everyone was allowed down on the bench.

In the past, only the players rostered were allowed to be on the bench, and everyone else would have to sit in the stands behind us. This was huge for us because we had four more home games and needed every ounce of energy and home field advantage that we could have. As we would all finish up our warmups and gather around the bench, we would spend a few extra minutes doing our new tradition. All 50 of us would link arms, and we would all close our eyes and take a deep breath. After a moment of solitude, we would stretch out the circle, and all do a "power pose." We would make ourselves big, stretching our arms out to the sky, and hold our pose for a few seconds.

From the stands or from across the field, we probably looked ridiculous, but we didn't care. I thought it would look intimidating. I was linking arms with our team doctor to my left and Reilyn Turner to my right. Everyone who put their time, energy, and heart into our program felt like they had something worth playing, supporting, and cheering for.

Leading up to the tournament, our program had a tradition that had been in place for as long as I was at UCLA. We would write anonymous compliments to each other, and everyone would get a paper with 34 different compliments written about them. In the past, we did it via Google Docs, and one girl would coordinate copying and pasting each compliment for each person. They would be taped in our locker room before the first round game, and we would all sit there reading really special words from our teammates.

This year, we did it a little differently. After practice one day, we were sitting on the IM turf in a circle. We all had a single piece of paper and a pen. We all wrote our name on our sheet of paper and passed it to our right. We would all spend 30 seconds to a minute writing a compliment for our teammate. You could sign your name or leave it anonymous; it was up to you. At the end, you would get your paper back, and it was filled with the sweetest messages from your teammates that you could cherish forever. I still have my compliments in my drawer at home. The compliments could be about anything. Who you are as a person, leader, friend, or soccer player. Sometimes, they were filled with inside jokes and little sayings that you knew came from a specific person.

Bend Never Break

    The compliments were such a small action that we did to help lift each other up. We don't always tell each other how much we all mean to each other. What we were trying to do, pursue greatness, is not easy, and a lot of the time, it's mentally draining. I knew my teammates cared because they put in the work every single day, but these compliments showed me that they listened and bought in more than I thought they had.

Chapter 21
Confidence

"Respect without fear may come from being prepared and keeping all things in proper perspective."
John Wooden

I believe confidence is a part of you. People often mistake confidence as a feeling, as in, "I feel like I've lost confidence." However, confidence is innate, and it stems from preparation. Our confidence also came from our carefree and funny attitude. Our team had big personalities, and the jokes were always flowing. I will never forget the day we played Stanford; we were walking to pre-game lunch, and we were talking about the party we were going to throw when we won the National Championship. We said we were going to raid Wasserman Football Center and set it on fire (cue the dramatics). We said we were going to call Drake and Chris Brown up. We were going to rent a stage on Wallis Annenberg and sleep over on the field.

Seven hours later, we lost to Stanford. An hour after the loss, we were singing karaoke and Reilyn, and Emma were doing improv. We always had a good time. At the Oregon airport, on our way home, we were sitting eating dinner, talking about winning the National Championship. Quincy said we all have to give up our first-born child if we didn't make it to the Final Four. It was truly do or die for us.

Going into our first playoff game, we needed to prepare as much as we could. The most successful teams that compete for National Championships every year know what their weaknesses are. They are able to evaluate, adapt, and fix their "holes" within the season. Teams that compete for the Sweet 16s have a few holes, teams that reach the College Cup have one or two, and teams that win have none. They had filled their holes at the point and now check every single box off. "Holes" can be anything. They can be having a weak goalkeeper, a young backline, a lack of leadership, or a toxic team culture. Maybe your star forward gets hurt, or maybe your left side is weaker than your right side. Maybe you don't have a deep bench, or maybe the weakness is you, the coach. Unable to make critical decisions, or maybe you're blinded by your own ego. It's the coaches' job to understand what your team's holes are and find solutions for how to fill them.

Sometimes, your holes are unfillable, and therefore, you have to get creative. Can we move player X to a new position to give us speed up top? Should we play with two 9s instead of one because we don't have strong wingers? Do I tell the toxic Drama Queen that it's time to hit the transfer portal? How do I bring out leadership from our center backs? The best teams and the best coaches spend all year thinking about their possible holes. During the off-season, are you in the transfer portal trying to recruit a new holding midfielder because your starter tore her ACL? Are you preparing your freshman during spring games, getting them ready for heavy minutes in the fall? Are you using 10-hour weeks to hone your team culture?

Our team didn't have any glaring holes. We didn't have a problem scoring; we had quick and dynamic wingers and strong nines. Our defense was solid. Lauren was our anchor, and the rest of the backline had pace, leadership, and experience. Our midfield was smart. They set the tempo and dictated what shape we were going to play. Our bench was deep. Up until the tournament, we had 19 different goal-scorers, and we were unpredictable in our attack. The girls who subbed on ranged from seniors to freshmen. We had a great team culture that was put into place months ago. We spent all spring having meetings and workshops focused on mental health, communication, and getting to know each other personally. We didn't have a laundry list of injuries that brought down morale.

Marg coached with such freedom. She coached fearlessly. She made decisions on the fly and trusted her gut. She took risks. We switched formations at halftime, made subs when necessary, changed strategy based on our opponent's strengths, and she listened to Gof, Molly, and us players. Marg coached every game like it was her last.

Before she was hired, I told our head Athletic Director, Martin, that we needed a coach who would coach with no regrets. As players, we were expected to step on the field and play with no regrets, and we needed a coach who would do the same. Marg had only been our coach for six months; she had no ego, no favorites, and no reason not to trust herself. She was still finding out what her coaching philosophy was and what type of coach she wanted to be, so in the meantime, she just went with what she felt right in the moment. Whether she felt like this or not, every game, she showed us that she was coaching to win. This is something I really appreciated and admired about her. She wasn't coaching like a rookie. Our one potentially harmful hole was set pieces.

Leading up to the tournament, our record was 17-2. We scored 53 goals and were scored against nine times. Six of the 53 goals we scored were via set pieces. Six of the nine goals scored against us were via set plays.

66% of our goals given up were on set plays. This was our hole. Since teams struggled to break us down in the run of play, they were extra efficient with their set plays. Going into the playoffs, we knew we had to fix this problem. We were vulnerable both in scoring set pieces and giving up goals on set pieces. Our lack of intensity and effort to score on set plays showed on the defensive side as well. Our view on set pieces, led by the coaches, was "The best way to defend a corner is to not give one up." This created a fear in fouling and fear of defending corners. It was almost this automatic panic when the ball went out for a corner or feeling stressed when you committed a foul. We needed to change our mentality.

Leading up to our first tournament game, we practiced set plays every day. We watched film and wanted to solve the problem from the root. We needed to embrace set pieces. We needed to treat them as a worthy challenge, not as something to be afraid of. We had long discussions about our set-up. Should we have more people man-marking? Should we keep two post-players? Should we add a zonal person? We ran drills in practice that focused on set plays. We would do situational 11s, where there would be a random free-kick, and we had five seconds to get organized and set. We did competitive set-piece games, where teams had to come up with their own corners to attack and defend.

For every goal scored or for every clearance, there would be some sort of reward. We went over how to man-mark. We paired up and stood across from a teammate and practiced how to bump your runner. We got physical. We worked on our clearances. We would chuck unpredictable balls at each other to work on making clean contact and clearing the ball as far as possible. We did everything we could to fill our hole before our first NCAA tournament game.

My club coach, Tad Bobak, had a saying about confidence. He would always tell our team, "The best way to respect your opponent is to destroy them." We were all around 11 years old at the time and probably didn't process it as having confidence but as the art of never backing down to any team. It didn't matter if the team we were playing had the best 12-year-old in the country, or if they had never won a game all year, we were going to respect them by putting them in their place. Destroying them.

That year, our first-round matchup was against Northern Arizona University (NAU). We spent the week preparing against them. We knew player-for-player we were better, but it was imperative that we didn't come out flat and scared. By Thursday night, we had completely moved on from the loss against USC and were fully focused and ready to go for our game against NAU. That week, Sunshine and I got dinner at a local spot in Westwood. We pulled out our phones and watched all of NAU's positive actions from their conference tournament. They fought through games to make the NCAA tournament.

I was nervous. I think out of all the playoff games, even including the National Championship, I was most nervous for the first game because of how we finished last year. I could sense a wave of nervousness from the girls but remained calm and composed. The day before the game, a Tweet popped up on my timeline,

"I'm pretty tired of hearing UCLA being upset in last year's NCAAs, and so are they in all likelihood. NAU has done well to get here, but they also won 0 non-conference games, which makes an upset for them highly unlikely." (Chris Henderson, 11/10/2022).

He was right; we were over it. After warmups, we all came together for our first power pose of the season. Melinda was right; in the midst of chaos and nerves, our little moment of togetherness went a long way. It was a chance for us to all catch our breath and remind ourselves that this was just another soccer game. This was something to be grateful for, not anxious for.

We scored in 35 seconds. 1-0. Lexi ran back on defense, stripped the ball from the midfielder, and ran hard at the center back. She took a commanding touch wide on to her left foot and fired it near post. Wally erupted. Lex sailed her arms in the air and embraced Mari. We ran over to her like it was the most important goal Lexi had ever scored. The bench went crazy. My nerves and anxiety immediately subsided, and we started to play loose and free. We knew we were going to win this game. Seven minutes later, Lex did it again. 2-0.

We were feeling good now. Marg made changes throughout the first half, and with about five minutes left in the half, Emma Egizii, or who we liked to call "Lil Cheerio," scored her first collegiate goal. Sidelined in her freshman year due to a second ACL tear, Emma was finally healthy during her sophomore year. Her hips swiveled as she dribbled hard at the defenders, squeezing between them, and went 1v1 with the keeper. She blasted it hard past the keeper and celebrated accordingly.

We went into halftime feeling great. We wanted more goals. NAU didn't have any opportunities as the game went on, and with about eight minutes left in the game, we earned a corner kick. Sunshine was standing outside the box, and the ball got cleared out to her. As calmly as possible, she collected the ball with her left foot and smacked a half-volley with her right foot on the ground. We went up 4-0 with minutes to spare. At the very end of the game, we gave up a foul pretty far out. We were prepared for these moments. We worked on them all week. Yet, we were unable to produce. The ball sailed far post, and we couldn't clear it. A NAU player came flying in and volleyed it in the goal during the chaos. They celebrated like they won the National Championship. Their goalkeeper ran from her goal to celebrate with them. There were 90 seconds left. Back to the drawing board we went. Even though getting scored on from a set piece was frustrating at the end, we knew we could continue to hone the details. From a positive perspective, we scored our first set-piece goal of the tournament. One game down, five to go.

Lauren/Jackie's Birthday

Amidst all the soccer, we still had birthdays to celebrate. My Scorpio queens, Lauren, and Jackie, both had birthdays during playoffs, and we had to make time to celebrate them. For Lauren's 23rd, a group of us went to dinner at a restaurant in West Hollywood. It was vegan and very bougie. Lauren was good friends with some of the girls in our master's program, so it was fun getting to hang out with them. Lauren and I have been friends forever, and it was special getting to celebrate her with all of our teammates and friends. Jackie's birthday was a few days later after our first playoff game. We went back and forth trying to decide what to do, and landed on Catalina. We packed up and drove down to Long Beach to catch the ferry over to Catalina Island. We put wet suits on, went snorkeling, and laid out on the beach. We rented a golf cart, and explored the island, and finished the day with Mexican food and hot chocolate. It was a perfect day and fun to escape soccer for a little bit.

Lilly Reale/Quincy McMahon/Jayden Perry

As the starting right back, I was a fifth-year senior, and Lauren was a sixth year senior. The other three starters in the back were Lilly, Jayden, and Quincy. Three absolute studs and three people who carried me through the National Championship. All three of them were Sophomores, and all played minutes during their freshman year. Lilly and Quincy were returning starters, while Jayden earned her starting spot for this fall.

They all brought unique strengths to the backline. Quincy brought her speed and quickness. She jolted into the attack, whipping crosses endline or cutting inside on her right foot and cracking a shot. She worked incredibly hard, tracking back on defense, and covering for those around her. Quincy was the ultimate teammate who was going to work until she dropped dead for you. Lilly brought leadership, communication, and cleaned up everything. She could send left footed diagonals with her eyes closed, threaded passes into the midfield, and defended the box with her life. Lilly was a true leader in the back line and organized those in front of her. Lilly was a strong 1v1 defender who always made the last-ditch effort to save a goal.

Jayden was a force to be reckoned with. She provided us with physicality, winning every aerial duel, putting in hard tackles, bumping runners, and stepping into the midfield. She provided a calmness to the backline. Her, Lilly, and Lauren anchored our back line and gave Quincy and I the freedom to go forward. Our backline was experienced, fast, and tenacious, with 1v1 defenders that could provide help in the attack. During our playoff run, both Quincy and I scored two goals while Jayden and Lilly scored crucial PKs for us. They all played with such maturity and were wise beyond their years. They were only sophomores at the time, but they played like they were well-seasoned seniors. I constantly told them that defense wins championships, and we needed to continue playing our stellar defense into the tournament.

Chapter 22
Condition

"Success is never final; failure is never fatal. It's courage that counts."
John Wooden

All throughout high school, I loved PKs. I would put the ball low and hard into the corners every time. I walked up confidently and knew that I was going to put the ball in the back of the net. In our spring 2021 season, we went to penalties against Clemson in the second round of the NCAA tournament. All week, I had been solid in training. I hit every rep to the same spot. I felt confident and knew that I would be in the potential lineup. After regulation and both overtime periods, it was tied 1-1. After a long lighting delay, we listened to music and got ready to take to the field on the bus. Amanda asked, "Who wants to take a penalty?"

I volunteered confidently. I knew that I had trained them well during the week and wanted to step up and help our team out. I hadn't played in the game at all, so I warmed up and got ready. My mom had flown in the night before and was watching from the stands. Up until I went to kick, both teams had made every penalty kick, and we were now entering sudden death. Clemson made their kick, and then it was time for me to take mine. I stepped up, knew where I was going to go, and did my routine. My legs felt like jello in the moment. I ran up and kicked it softly to my left. The goalkeeper made the save. We lost the game. My soft PK decided our season. I never wanted to feel like that again, and I never wanted to lose in penalties ever again.

As we started to prepare for our second-round NCAA tournament game against UCF, we took penalties every day. Whether it was in training or on our own, we got as many reps in as possible. I practiced going both ways, had new run-ups, and then perfected how I was going to shoot. I knew I would most likely be in the lineup because I would have played the full game, and I was a 5th year senior.

UCF's two games prior went to penalties: they lost to Memphis in the AAC tournament in PKs and beat North Carolina State in the first round of the tournament. Lauren and Molly went over their penalties all week and felt prepared going into Friday's game. We studied the keeper's tendencies – did she guess? Did she favor diving one side or the other? Was she decisive?

From the start of the tournament, I knew one of our games would be decided by penalties. The odds were too high. It was imperative that we prepared as much as we could, regardless of which round of the tournament we were playing in. After watching the scout and some of UCF's games, I realized that they reminded me a lot of USC. I knew it was going to be a hard match-up for us. They were well coached, had tons of senior leadership, a strong backline, and dynamic fast forwards.

Since we were hosting the next two rounds, there was a different feeling in the air. Knowing teams were coming and playing at our stadium provided an extra sense of competition and edge. That week, Northwestern, Vanderbilt, and UCF all flew out to Los Angeles. All four of us hailed from different conferences and had different styles of play. Since every team was to be treated equally, we had allotted training times, and any UCLA banners or posters were removed from Wallis Annenberg. Friday rolled around, and it was time to take on the Knights.

We were the second game of the night, so first, we watched Northwestern beat Vanderbilt and then took the field after them. The game started off great for us. We applied pressure, had chances, and kept the ball well. They definitely could keep up with our pace, but we were still able to create overloads and run in behind. Mid-way through the first half, they crossed the ball, and one of their players finished it with one touch. She ran to the bench, and they celebrated loudly after taking the lead. We were down 1-0.

Usually, our team struggled when we got scored on but there was plenty of time left. Five minutes later, we earned back-to-back corner kicks. Against her "home-town" team, and with plenty of her friends wearing Knight's jerseys, Jackie flew out of nowhere and headed the ball in the back of the net, the game now tied 1-1. This was now our second set-piece goal in two weeks, and we were back in the game. With a few minutes left in the first half, Sunshine ripped a volley from outside the box and just missed – we felt the energy going into halftime. The next 45 minutes were like a chess match. We created chances and continued to run at them. Their defense held strong though, and we just couldn't get a clean look on goal. 90 minutes came and went, and we were now headed to overtime.

The NCAA decided that year there wouldn't be overtime in regular season matches. Since we didn't have a conference tournament, we hadn't gone into overtime at all. We continued to put pressure and run at them throughout overtime. I had a feeling that the game was heading to penalties. They defended hard all game, and their goalkeeper was playing lights out. I knew they weren't going to give up a goal that late into the game. 20 minutes went by, and the ref blew the whistle. It was time to head to the spot.

We had spent the entire week preparing. Preparation equals confidence. Lauren was ready. Our lineup was ready. The fans were ready. Personally, I was going through an emotional rollercoaster. I was holding back tears, and Reilyn told me to "Stop crying." Our first five kickers were decided right away. There wasn't any "who wants to take one." We had a lineup that was prepared and confident. Our first five were Jayden, Sunshine, Lilly, Ally Lemos, and Ally Cook.

All five of those girls were very calm and composed people. I had also seen them smash the ball in the back of the net throughout the week. I felt confident in our kickers and knew all we needed was for Lauren to make one save. As we lined up for the spot, Lilly and Mari went to the referee. They lost the coin toss, and we were slated to kick second. That comforted me because the pressure immediately went to UCF, who had spent the last three weekends on the road. The first kicker started her walk-up, and Wally erupted in chants. The bench led the fans to "UC…LA" that rang throughout campus. The kicker took the ball from her keeper and walked wobbly to her spot. I knew Lauren had this. The fans continued to yell and bang on the bleachers as she gingerly walked up and kicked it softly to her right. Lauren barely dove and stopped it. The stadium went crazy.

A rush of confidence ran through me as I watched Jayden walk up. Our center-back stud made every single PK the last two weeks, going either way with her eyes closed. The stadium went quiet as Jayden did her little point. She ran up and smacked the ball with her left foot to the right corner. The keeper dived the other way, and we were up 1-0. JP ran to Lauren and gave her a fist-bump as the UCF second kicker ran up. The stadium erupted again in chants. She banged the ball off the crossbar, and now UCF had missed two penalties in a row. We celebrated from the halfway line like we had just won the National Championship. This was huge.

Sunshine stepped up, her long ponytail bobbing up and down as she trotted to the penalty spot. She spun the ball around to her preferred spot and took her steps back. She took a quick breath as her shoulders dropped, and then she took three powerful steps. She hit the ball as hard as she could to the top left corner. It hits the net so hard that it came spitting back out. We all went wild. We were hugging, jumping, and screaming. Shine ran back to us, throwing her arms in the air. The third UCF kicker collected the ball and set it up. To keep her team's confidence alive, she had to make that kick. She lined up, and as the ball sailed to her left, Lauren dived to her right. Lauren's fingertip brushed off the ball as it hit off the post. We erupted again. All we needed was one more goal.

Lilly was up next, our left-footed center back, who had spent all week smacking the ball to the right corner. Lilly set the ball up, and the stadium went quiet again. I was clutching Reilyn and JP's hands. We decided that when Lilly scored, we would all run to Lauren and celebrate together. The ref blew the whistle, and Lilly automatically ran up and hit the ball with such power. The second the ball left her foot, we were already running to Lauren. Wally erupted as we all ran, arms open, to Lauren. The girls on the bench rushed the field, and we met Lilly halfway. She turned around to Lauren and jumped into her arms. I was sobbing as we all came together. Sunshine wrapped her arms around me as Jackie bear-hugged us.

We continued to jump up and down, and everyone took turns hugging. Not only did we go three for three, but Lauren also made two huge saves. As I walked over to the stands, Mari hugged me, and we were both in tears. There was no way our dream season was going to end in a penalty kick shootout. John Wooden said, "Success is never final; failure is never fatal, it's courage that counts."

Penalties come down to courage. The courage to step up when no one else wants to. The courage to prepare every day. Make them. Miss them. Change it up. Study the kicker. It all takes courage, and this game showed us that we were capable of being clutch under pressure.

Ally Lemos and Sofia Cook

There aren't too many automatic freshmen. Freshmen that come in and immediately make a difference for an entire team. More than just playing for themselves or being really good on a poor team. I am talking about really good 18-year-olds who play for the best teams in the country and still can make an impact beyond their years. Most teams have none. Some teams had one. We had two. At the start of 2022, there were three incoming freshmen who came in early. Ellie Walbruch, Sofia Cook, and Ally Lemos. All three of them excelled, and from Day One, showed that they could hang.

They crushed the fitness tests, played with confidence and ease, and were really good people. They weren't egotistical or bratty, and they didn't have smart mouths on them. They listened to the older girls, learned from the coaches, and grew a lot within the first few months. We had just graduated two starting midfielders, so our midfield was going to be a question mark. When she first came in, Ally Lemos wasn't a holding midfielder. She was an attacking midfielder who scored tons of goals and had great vision. We desperately needed a six (holding midfield), so our coaches started playing her there in the spring. She worked through some kinks and was eager to learn how to play the six in her own way. We wanted Lemos to bring her attacking flair and still create going forward for us.

Sof was also a midfielder. Sof was a magician with the ball at her feet. She was great at dribbling at players, slipping forwards through, and was composed in front of goal. Both Lemos and Sof were projected to play big roles for us during the fall.

Lemos, from the jump, was a starter for us. Her calm demeanor and ability to set the tempo for us was invaluable. She stopped counterattacks, organized people in front of her, and was just such a staple in our midfield. She immediately took over the starting six spot for us and never looked back. Lemos led our team and tied for the PAC-12 lead with nine assists and had one goal.

She was one of two Bruins who started every single game, 25, and played the third highest minutes on our team with 1,958. She was named to the College Cup All-Tournament team and was selected to the PAC-12 all-freshman team. But most importantly, she delivered the most historic assist in NCAA history.

Sof Cook had her own magical season. Sof was a player that produced behind the scenes for us. While Reilyn, Lexi, Sunshine, and Ally Cook scored and assisted time and time again, Sof led the team with goals per minute. While only starting seven games and averaging 45 minutes a game, Sof had seven goals and four assists for us. She ranked fourth on the team and wasn't even playing heavy minutes. She just got the job done. She could play in the midfield and out wide for us. She connected her passes, dribbled out of pressure, and had a nose for the goal.

Bend Never Break

She was named to the Top Drawer Soccer Best XI Freshman second team, selected to the PAC-12 all-freshman team, and ended the year ranked 19th in the Top Drawer Soccer's Freshman 100. Like Lemos, Sof delivered her own heroic moment for us in our quarter-final game against Virginia.

Despite not starting and producing more than girls who played more, Sof never complained. She shined every time she stepped on the field and executed her role perfectly. We needed our bench to elevate the game when they stepped on the field. We needed our bench to produce when our starters couldn't. We needed our bench just as much as they wanted to be on the field. It's imperative for winning teams to have a bench that was bought in. Sof showed that.

Chapter 23
Skill

"A knowledge of and the ability to properly and quickly execute the fundamentals. Be prepared and cover every little detail."
John Wooden

In soccer, there are no timeouts. There are no "plays." With the coaches being on the sideline, it's hard enough to get a message across from the right side of the field to the left side. The players on the field have to be able to adapt to what the game presents. After our dramatic finish to the UCF game, our next opponent was Northwestern in the Sweet 16. Our program hadn't made it past the Sweet 16 since 2019, and we wanted to change that. This was our second game in two days, and most of the starters had just played 110 minutes on Friday night. We recovered as much as we could on Saturday and got ready to take the field again on Sunday night. We decided that we were going to bring out the 3-5-2 again. The last time we started in a 3-5-2 was weeks ago. Since our offense started out a bit slower against UCF, we thought this would help us generate some offense from the kickoff. We went over the rotations and patterns in training on Saturday and felt prepared to go into the game.

Usually, my pre-game talks weren't planned; they mostly came from the heart. One "planned" one that I remember, that was especially funny, was before we played Northwestern. The night before our game, UCLA was playing USC in football and lost dramatically at the end. The game went back and forth with a lot of touchdowns. One of the commentators said that at this point of the season when wins were vital, there was no such thing as an ugly win or a pretty win; a win is a win.

I was watching the game with Jackie and My, and I told them – I'm telling that to the team tomorrow. They both laughed and said they couldn't wait to hear it. 24 hours later, we were tightly huddled up before we were about to take the field. I told the team, "At this point in November, there is no such thing as an ugly win or a pretty win, a win is a win. We leave everything out on the field and get this win." I looked down and My smiled up at me. As we took the field, the starting 11 came together, and I looked everyone in the eyes and told them that we were going to finish our chances today. And we did exactly that.

Within five minutes, Sunshine slipped me a ball through the back line, right inside the 18-yard box. I bodied off my defender and drew the goalkeeper out. I heard Reilyn yell at me, so I passed the ball off squarely in front of the open net. Reilyn contested for the pass, and the ball hit off the Northwestern defender and went in. I was credited with the goal, my second of the year. As the first half went on, our 3-5-2 was starting to crack. We couldn't figure out how to get pressure out on the ball, and our midfield was being split. After a few scary moments where Lauren and our back line had to make a play, Marg switched the formation on the fly within 20 minutes. She made a few subs, and the information was passed along. She put in our most defensive midfield with Ally Lemos, Sunshine, and Jackie.

We sat in our organized mid-block and adapted quickly. We got to halftime and felt good about our performance. It was comforting to know that we were able to figure things out on the fly. Only being up 1-0, we knew we had to continue to play strong defense and keep our attack going. We wanted to get one more goal to put the game away. We started off the second half on the front foot, and our 4-1-4-1 was the best it ever looked. We shifted hard from side to side, communicated when runners came flying, and kept their offense in front of us. Our backline kept everything out, and our midfield did a fantastic job screening players and intercepting passes.

Despite just playing a heavy game on Friday, we all looked fresh. During the middle of the second half, Quincy provided an insurance goal for us. After combining through the midfield, Sofia Cook went on a dribble and slipped Q a perfect pass. Taking a confident touch, Quincy made the goalkeeper come out as she dribbled around her. She passed the ball into the net, and we went up 2-0. We all ran towards her and celebrated, as we all knew deep down that we were moving onto the Elite Eight for the 17th time in the school's history. This win was huge for us.

After the win, Marg said, "Tonight was really important for us; it was kind of a statement win…I thought our team executed really well, and at the end of the day, that's what it's all about. I was really proud of them." Our team showed once again that we were able to adapt on the fly. Marg trusted us to change formations and play a different style of soccer, all within the first half.

We were able to execute and score by playing our attacking 3-5-2 while also executing our more defensive 4-1-4-1. Our team had the ability to do it all.

Our Northwestern masterclass of the 4-1-4-1 was just the dress rehearsal for our big Elite Eight game against Virginia. This was our first trip to the Elite Eight since 2019. That year, our team flew to Tallahassee over Thanksgiving break to beat FSU and move on to the College Cup. That week, I focused on gratitude. I was so thankful that we got one more game playing at Wally together. I was grateful that I got to drive down to San Clemente and spend Thanksgiving with my family. I was grateful that my body felt strong, and I was healthy to play in our 23rd game of the season. I played my "grateful" playlist during practice that week, filled with songs such as "Lean on Me," "God's Plan," "Live Your Life," and "Rather Be."

That week, we got ready to meet the Cavaliers. We were going to switch back and start in our 4-3-3. We knew UVA was going to have the ball more this game. They were notorious for playing slow, possession-based soccer. They were used to ACC teams pressing them and being able to break lines through pressure. We trusted our disciplined block and were okay with not having the ball. We continued to hammer down on set pieces and spent the week going over different scenarios. We practiced being down 2-0 with 10 minutes left. We practiced being down a player and maintaining a 1-0 lead. We practiced changing shapes and formations while playing 11s. We practiced set pieces while we played 11s. We prepared for every scenario possible.

One of the forwards, Alexa Spaanstra, was a fifth-year star who I had played with and against for years. In the 2015 ECNL Finals, Lauren and I played Alexa, who was on the Michigan Hawks. We were roommates at our national team camp in China and played together for years. I knew what type of player Alexa was. Leading up to our game, Molly sent me a whole PDF with links to Alexa's film and her tendencies. UVA beat Penn State in the Sweet 16 in Happy Valley. They came from behind and showed that they could get the job done on the road.

Going into the Elite Eight game, I felt at peace. Our team always found a way at Wally. There wasn't a doubt in my mind that we weren't going to find goals. Our team scored goals all yearlong, and that mentality wasn't going to go away any time soon. Fans began piling into Wallis Annenberg stadium as warmups got started. It was the perfect fall night, and I could feel the intensity in the air.

As we huddled up, I told the team to enjoy playing at Wally one last time. "We've all, at one point in our career, had everything on the line in this field. We've run our asses off here, cried, laughed, scored bangers, and shut teams out, but most importantly, we have had so much fun together. Enjoy the next 90 minutes because it's time to go to the big dance." We did our walkout and got ready to take the field. As we ran out there, I remember taking a deep breath as I looked up into the stands to see my family and friends sitting up there. This would be their last time watching me play at Wally, too.

The ref blew the whistle and unleashed two heavyweight teams to battle against each other. UVA sustained possession for the first 10 minutes as we were back on our heels a bit. They quickly earned two corners in the first couple of minutes, and I knew we needed some type of energy change. As UVA set up for their corner kick, I called over to Lauren and gave her a head nod. I tilted my head up the field, and she nodded. The ball got cleared out, and the UVA defender sent it back into the box. As the ball floated in, I yelled, "Lauren!" and took off on a dead sprint up the field. Lauren scanned the field and jumped up to catch the ball before quickly running towards the edge of the box to punt it.

I kept my head down and continued to sprint hard as she punted the ball in my direction. I slowed down a bit and looked where the ball was; I was about 60 yards up the field as the ball bounced in front of me. As I went up to head it, the UVA defender shoved me and headed the ball out of bounds. I hit the ground hard and rolled a few times. I quickly grabbed the ball, and as everyone else on the field moved up the field, I threw the ball into Bridgette, and she went on a little dribble and took a shot. We finally had some momentum going for us. Over the next 10 minutes, we took control of the game.

At about 15 minutes in, the ball popped out wide to Sunshine. She took a controlling touch forward and dribbled at pace towards Lexi. Lex checked off the center back as Shine chipped a ball to her. With one touch, Lex laid it off as Sunshine ran around the defender. She dribbled inside the box and chipped it over the keeper with her left foot. The crowd went crazy. She threw her arms in the air, and we ran towards her. The bench exploded off the sideline, and our coaches jumped up and down. Shine ran with her arms out towards the bench as I ran on the other side of her. We embraced the girls on the bench and celebrated all together. 1-0.

We finished the first half strong and re-grouped at halftime. We knew Virginia could come back. They had proven that throughout their season. They came back from behind and won several games, being the "underdog". It was important for us to stay focused and to continue playing our game. From the start of the second half, we started back on our heels. They threw numbers forward and eventually earned a corner kick in the 75th minute.

Their best aerial threat got on the end of the corner, and they tied it up 1-1. We finally pulled it together and generated some offense towards the end of the game. We stopped sitting back and got our attacking players on the ball a bit more. Again, we never lost a game where we scored a goal. I knew we would pull one back. Regulation time ended, and we huddled up. This was our second overtime game, and we knew we had 20 more minutes left to finish it. We only had a few minutes together. Our coaches quickly decided we were going to change shape into a 4-4-2. We had never played in a 4-4-2 the entire year, so within minutes, they pulled the huddle in tight and went over tactics. All 35 of us hovered around while they told the midfield what they needed to do.

We hoped that adding another midfielder would out-match Virginia, and having two center forwards would help with pressing. From day one, our coaches wanted us to think like coaches. They wanted us to understand why we were switching formations and how this was going to affect our opponent. As we broke it down, Gof pulled the four midfielders together: Sunshine, Jackie, Sof, and Ally Lemos. Two freshmen and two seniors. He went over the final points with them, and the ref blew the whistle for both teams to take the field. Danza Kuduro blasted through Wally, and our whole team started dancing.

I danced as we ran out to the field, and the first overtime started. Both teams pressed for the go-ahead goal, and both teams had shots blocked at the very beginning. In the 98th minute, with two minutes left in the first overtime, Jackie nutmegged a Virginia defender, picked her head up, and with her left foot, crossed the ball to the other side of the field. A Virginia defender headed the ball backward, and it landed right outside the 18-yard box. Sof Cook ran hard, and with the outside of her right foot, volleyed it around their defense and goalkeeper for her seventh goal of the year and to make it 2-1. The place went nuts. I stood behind Sof and watched the ball curve into the corner as I threw my arms in the air and sprinted toward her and my friends.

    I thought, "We are going to win this freaking game." We changed formations, learned how to play a diamond midfield, and executed with a goal within eight minutes. Sof had played beyond her years the entire fall, but that moment from her was big-time. In an Elite Eight game, she came off the bench and produced for us when we needed it most. I've dreamed about that moment. There were two minutes left in the first overtime, and we continued to defend hard. The ref blew their whistle, and we had 10 more minutes left in this game.

    I went to every player and gave them a high five and some words of encouragement. We had done this in practice time and time again. A scenario where we were up by one goal with minutes left. We huddled back up for the fourth time in the game, and we switched formations once again to a 5-3-2. After being cold for 100 minutes, Bri was told to warm up and get ready. She was going to play another center back, and we were going to sit in our mid-block. The next 10 minutes were complete chaos. We sat back and defended the entire time. They sent long crosses in, went 1v1 against our tired legs, and took shots left and right.

    We worked hard to stay organized, mark up in the box, and not give up any stupid fouls or corner kicks. We remained disciplined in our defense. "Preparation equals confidence. We've done this before." Earlier in the year, we defended with our hearts against UNC as they peppered in crosses and shots. It felt like the longest 10 minutes of my life. The crowd and the bench cheered as we all watched the clock tick down on the big screen. Marg continued to make tactical subs throughout the second overtime. Subbing in and out Ally Cook, Lexi, and Rei. Whoever wasn't cramping was in the game. She subbed in another defender, Maya, as we needed more reinforcements in the back. We had zero offense in those 10 minutes, but that was okay. In the last 30 seconds, I cleared the ball out of bounds as the announcer started counting down from 10. The crowd yelled with her,
"Ten! Nine! Eight! Seven! Six! Five! Four! Three! Two! One!"

    I put my hands on my knees and leaned over. I looked up and locked eyes with Sunshine as we ran towards each other. Her arms were up in the sky, and mine were out wide. Ally Lemos walked towards us as we hugged each other. Our team ran from the bench, and everyone was hugging, crying, and cheering. Last year, our final countdown was a dagger. The crowd was silent. We were silent. We weren't crying tears of joy. There was no happiness. One year later, our final countdown was to send us to the Final Four. We continued to write our story, and there was one final chapter left to be told.

We came together one last time, and everyone was hugging. Marg pulled us in and told us how proud she was. We adapted on the fly, and now it was time for us to go to the big dance. Lexi and I had learned a dance we were doing all season and pulled the videographer aside as we danced side by side together. We were going to dance all the way to Cary, North Carolina. "One of the things we asked of our team was to be super-disciplined defensively, and I thought we did that," said Marg, "It wasn't until very late in the game that we allowed a goal. Although they had a lot of possession, we were limiting dangerous chances. Attacking-wise, I'm really proud of the group because we asked them to be adaptable, and we played three or four different shapes in this game based on tactics, and everyone delivered, and everyone executed. I couldn't be prouder of the team."

John Wooden describes skill as "A knowledge of and the ability to properly and quickly execute the fundamentals. Be prepared and cover every little detail." Our team, without a doubt, showed skill. We showed skill all yearlong, but it shined through during the Northwestern and Virginia games. We played multiple formations on the fly, adapted seamlessly, and then executed and won games. We went undefeated at home the entire year. That was one of our goals earlier in the year, and we did it. We made playing at Wally scary. We welcomed our opponents, respected them, and then kicked their ass. We played with confidence, creativity, and teeth. Most importantly, we played freely.

After the game, the seniors came together and took a picture in front of the scoreboard. It was our last game playing at Wally, and what a way to end it. We walked back to Acosta Training Center, where our families were setting up our last post-game meal. Some of our moms were outside looking at flights to Cary and planning our hotels. We went upstairs to our locker room, where the lights were turned off, the disco was going on, and WIN by Jay Rock was blaring. We screamed-sang and danced our hearts out. Those are the moments I miss the most. I showered, changed, and went downstairs where my family was.

We recapped the game together and talked in circles. This was our last team dinner together. My wet hair hung down, and mascara was under my eyes as we took a family picture. We walked to the car: me, my mom, my dad, my two grandmas, and Jackie. We squished in the car, and my parents hyped Jackie up after her huge performance and assist. We said goodbye and dropped her off at her apartment while my parents took me to mine. They told me how proud they were of me and how special this year was. I told them we still had two big games left, but I was so happy. My dream of a fifth year continued.

Final Four

Not only was this my final hurrah with UCLA Women's Soccer, but it was also my final hurrah with school. After five years and an undergraduate degree in Political Science with a Master's in Transformative Coaching and Leadership almost completed, I was close to the finish line. In typical Maddi Desiano fashion, I waited until the last minute to write my capstone. My capstone was a 34-page paper focusing on three famous coaches, John Wooden, Pete Carroll, and Vince Lombardi, and their coaching philosophies. My paper was called "How to Build a Championship Legacy." The last two pages were dedicated to my own coaching philosophy.

When writing about Pete Carroll, you could feel his love for his players and USC football. He led USC to two National Championships and cemented USC into College Football history. When researching him and reading his book, "Win Forever," I came across a YouTube video from August 2009. I encourage you all to watch it right now. During a team meeting, freshman linebacker Marquis Simmons leads his team to a rendition of Bill Withers' "Lean on Me," with Pete Carroll taking over on the piano.

At first, the team stays sitting down, singing along, then they start clapping, and some guys stand up, and at the end, the entire room erupts. Every player is on his feet, arm in arm, swaying side to side, clapping along and singing as if no one was watching. Two weeks later, Bill Withers attends a USC Football meeting, pranking the players by telling them he's there to sell them a shower shoe for a foot fungus that is popping up in locker rooms.

After going with the bit for a few minutes, he tells them they had been pranked and he saw the video of them singing a few weeks back. He brings Marquis to the front of the room, and they all sing "Lean on Me," one more time. Side by side, they sing and sway, and afterward, they coined "Lean on Me," as their team mantra that year. Watching these videos always puts a smile on my face because it reminds me of my team. Always leaning on each other. Always singing with each other. When we weren't strong, we always had a friend to help us carry on.

One year ago, we met with our head Athletic Director, Martin Jarmond, on December 1st in his office to go over what we wanted in a head coach. I told him that I had one more year left, and I wanted to win a National Championship. We didn't need a rebuilding year. We didn't need time. We could do it immediately. I was finishing up writing my last political science paper to finish my undergraduate degree. I sat in Starbucks with Sunshine for hours, and we "did homework" while ordering peppermint mochas and talking about the same things over and over. Both of us had up and down 2021 seasons, and we wanted to turn things around the next year. In December of 2019, I sat next to her in the stands of the College Cup, and we watched from above. Sunshine and I will always be bonded with our "full circle" moments. In 2019, we boarded the "injured" flight and met our team on the day of the semifinal in San Jose. Three years later, our flight to Cary was a bit different.

We woke up at the crack of dawn on Tuesday morning to make our way to the Acosta Training Center for our flight to Cary. We reached out to our professors, scheduled early finals, and finished assignments that weekend. I walked from my apartment to Acosta with my suitcase in tow. I would meet Sunshine at 7/11, and we would walk together. As we walked side by side, girls on the team scooted by on the street with their suitcases attached to the bottom. Kylie and Bri sat in Kylie's moped and waved to us as they pulled into Mo Ostin. We walked up the little hill onto campus, pressed our finger on the security system to allow us into Acosta, and walked upstairs to our locker room.

I had sent out our packing list two days prior and had everything packed and ready to go. I had my laptop and charger ready to tackle my capstone and a Lululemon bag filled with gluten-free snacks. Whenever we left before a trip, there was always chaos. People throwing in laundry from their lockers, deciding what sneakers to bring, forgetting, and then remembering shin guards. People had their own recovery tools, pillows, and water bottles that they carried in their arms. The bright light in our locker room was always blinding at 5 a.m.

Normally, there would have been some type of "going away," party filled with student-athletes, coaches, and members of the athletic department, all saying goodbye and good luck. Since our flight was so early though, there was no one. No one to take pictures or post on Instagram. Just us as we walked in small groups towards the bus. It was dark out, with only the streetlight shining down on us. The air was cold and sharp, and we knew it was going to be worse in Cary. I wrapped my jacket tighter around me and rubbed my eyes. We boarded the bus, which was waiting for us between Mo Ostin and Wasserman Football Center. I put my suitcase underneath the bus and walked to the back where I usually sat near Sunshine and Maricarmen. Everyone boarded, and Marg passed out her "snack bags" that she made for all of us. We were also given per diem for breakfast, so we were set when it came to fueling. I put my air pods in, listening to Taylor Swift's new album, "Midnights," and closed my eyes.

As we pulled into LAX, I opened my eyes again, and we pulled off to the side. We exited one by one off the bus and started to help unload the bus. We called off to each other when we saw one another's suitcases, helped Nikki with the equipment, and helped Molly with passing out the boarding passes. Once everyone was distributed their boarding pass, had their suitcases, and the equipment was all taken care of, we walked into the airport. At this point in the year, we had our "away trip" routine down.

Once we got through TSA, everyone split up and did their own thing. Some of us went to Starbucks; others got breakfast, and others went and waited at the gate. I got something to eat, and a coffee and I made my way over to our gate.

I opened up my laptop and made sure it was completely charged. I spent the next 45 minutes downloading my documents so I could work on my capstone during our flight. I had procrastinated the entire fall and waited until the last two weeks to finish it. I knew I had the material and research already organized because of my years' worth of course homework and papers, but I needed to assemble my paper.

I had spent the entire year dissecting my three chosen coaching philosophies, reading their books, and breaking down what made them successful. I had to define their philosophies, compare them to one another, and provide my own commentary on them. At the end of the paper, I had to write my own coaching philosophy. I decided I would tackle the last part first. I figured it would be easier to reflect, criticize, and commentate on the coaches if I knew where I stood.

As our team stood in our grey sweatsuits, we filed onto the plane one by one and sat on the plane. I immediately got out my laptop and got to work. I had six uninterrupted hours to get as much as I could done. I pulled up a fresh document and copied and pasted my old coaching philosophy into it. I got to work editing it. I decided it would be easiest if I took the role of Marg, a young, ambitious rookie head coach who landed the job of her dreams. I had a front row viewing of how she handled her first year, and I could pull inspiration from it. I decided to start the paper as if we already won the National Championship. I also thought this would help manifest in us winning. This was part of my paper:

DESIANO COACHING PHILOSOPHY

I am the UCLA Women's Soccer Head Coach. I was a part of the 2022 NCAA Championship-winning team and helped lead the team to our second ever National Title. I went on to play in NWSL and professionally in Europe. After my career playing, I was the assistant coach at Boston College, where I helped lead the program to their first-ever ACC Championship and Elite Eight appearances. After coaching at BC for four years, I landed the head coaching job after my former head coach, Margueritte Aozasa, left to coach professionally.

This is my first year with the Bruins, and I hope to lead us to our 3rd national title. I was a part of the Transformative Coaching and Leadership Master's program at UCLA. From the program, as well as from my lived experiences playing and coaching, I created my coaching philosophy. The most important principles in my philosophy are preparation, the importance of team culture, using intangibles to create a competitive environment, communication, and success is having no regrets. I believe that preparation builds confidence, team culture wins championships, and the intangibles like work, grit, and character create a competitive environment. This allows my players to play freely and be themselves on the pitch.

Bend Never Break

My coaching philosophy is to help uplift and champion my student-athletes in becoming the best people, students, and soccer players they can become. By coaching at a school like UCLA, I am aware that I can attract the top talent in the country, and it is my job to foster that talent and not become complacent or reliant on it. Yet, regardless of if my student-athlete is a highly-recruited national team player or a walk-on, they are people before they are soccer players. I believe in the powers of connection, empathy, and love. By creating a safe and motivating environment, I hope my student-athletes feel free. Playing with freedom opens doors to championships and winning. Everything we do in practice, meetings, the weight room, and on and off the pitch is to be the best team in the country. Mentality matters. Attention to detail matters. The intangibles like grit, heart, and hard work all matter. By cultivating an environment where preparation equals confidence, not only can we be the best, but we can play with no regrets. Knowing we left everything out on the pitch means we can never fail.

Real Time

I took a step back and re-read my work. I smiled as I re-read the first bit about winning the National Championship. I paused for a while and listened to music while looking out the window. I thought about how I wanted to tackle the rest of my paper. I scooched past the two other people in my row and walked to the back of the plane to use the restroom. I passed my teammates, who were mostly all working on schoolwork. I passed my coaches, who had their laptops out, cutting film of Alabama, and got to the back of the plane.

We soon landed, and I turned on my personal hotspot for my computer, and I quickly finished my last paragraph. I downloaded it into a PDF and emailed it to my advisor. Once the email was sent off, I closed my laptop and got my things together to get off the plane.

It was a bit like *deja vu* being back at the RDU airport. We picked up our bags at the same baggage claim from a few months ago. We waited around, some of us sitting on the ground, others walking to the bathroom, and most of us sitting on our carry-on suitcases, waiting for our bags to come up. Nikki, our athletic trainer, pulled out the massage gun and began giving me treatment on my upper back and lower neck. We waited probably 10 minutes, and the bags soon came around. We pulled the bags off the baggage carousel, and all grabbed our things as we made our way to the bus. Waiting at the same spot the bus was a few months ago, we helped pull the bags underneath the bus and all piled on.

The bus drive to our hotel was about fifteen minutes. The sun had already set, and it was a bit chilly out as we pulled up to our hotel. As Gof and our managers got out and went inside to check in, they quickly realized we were at the wrong hotel. The Florida State University signs and yellow and red balloons were a clear indicator that we were at the wrong place. We got back on the bus and drove another five minutes down the road to our hotel.

Gof got out one more time to double check and confirmed that we were at the right hotel. We got off the bus and unloaded from underneath. On the bus, we found out who our roommates were. My roommate for this trip was Kylie. I was so excited because Kylie was one of my closest friends and an easy roommate to have. I was also glad because Kylie and I understood each other on a deeper level, so I knew I could count on her during this weekend. As we started to walk into the hotel, Suzi was standing at the entrance with her fancy camera out.

Suzi Mellano was a videographer and photographer for UCLA Athletics. She put together the most incredible content for all our sports, and we were so lucky she was traveling with us the entire week. Her, Jesus, and Liza were in charge of putting out content throughout the entire week and had the brilliant idea to post a mini-series documenting our weekend. Suzi was really creative and always knew how to get the right shot. As she stood at the entrance of the hotel, she crouched down and began snapping shots of us walking into the hotel.

She got this picture of me that was so pure and just captured the moment. It was a solo shot of me looking to the right at one of my teammates, and I had the biggest smile on my face. I already had our big UCLA puffy on, you could see my gluten-free bagels poking out of the Lululemon bag, and even though I was walking alone, you could tell how happy I was to be there with my team. The next picture she captured of me was with Lilly, Lauren, Shine, Lexi, and Jackie, and we were standing in front of a "Welcome!" sign inside the hotel lobby.

There was a big balloon arch in the background, decked out with blue and yellow balloons and soccer balls. Our tired faces grinned into the camera, and we were ready for things to get started. As we put all the equipment bags into the team room, Kylie and I headed up to our room to drop our stuff off quickly. Usually, after these long travel trips, all you wanted to do was shower and get to bed. We still needed to eat, and we had a team meeting that night.

We walked back downstairs to have dinner, and after, our team had a quick recovery session. Our strength and conditioning coach, Paige, guided us through yoga and meditation. We laid down on the gross hotel carpet while she walked us through a yoga session. After almost falling asleep, we went upstairs to finally rewind from our long travel day. Kylie and I showered and got ready to go to bed. I took a selfie of us and sent it to our moms, and we got ready to go to bed.

The next morning, we woke up early for practice. Being three hours ahead, it was a little hard to wake up and get ready. We walked down to the meal room and stood in the buffet line for breakfast. After breakfast, we had a quick team meeting where we watched film on Alabama.

Alabama was having a dream season. It was the season of "firsts." They were 23-2-1 and had just won their 20th straight home game against Duke in a thrilling 3-2 quarterfinal match up. It was their first trip to the round of 32, round of 16, Elite Eight, and now Final Four. Their playoff run was both exciting and commanding. They beat Jackson State in the first round 9-0, Portland 2-1 in the round of 32, UCI 3-1 in the Sweet 16, and Duke in overtime in the Elite Eight. They were a number one seed as well, so they hosted the first four rounds. They went undefeated in SEC play, while their last loss was in the SEC tournament final to South Carolina. We both had that in common: losing our last game before the NCAA tournament.

Alabama was also known for their press. They pressed all game long. They suffocated their opponents and tried to make it impossible to build out. They scored dozens of goals off their press, forcing turnovers and capitalizing on their opponent's mistakes. They played in a 4-4-2 with a diamond in the midfield. This meant they had four defenders, four people shaped like a diamond in the midfield, and two forwards up top. They had two strong 9s up top, and their midfield was the heartbeat of their team. Gof turned on his laptop and played their scout. We had played against a 4-4-2 formation multiple times and knew where the spaces were to exploit them. Since they didn't play with any wingers or any wide forwards, it was imperative for us to keep our width and expose them out wide. Our wide players were impactful as it was, so we knew this game would be huge for us, especially for our outside backs, Quincy, and me.

Our job was to pull their midfield out. Make their "wide" part of the diamond step out to us. This would open up their midfield, and we could find Sunshine or Ally Lemos. Gof played a "lowlight" (opposite of highlight) reel of their back line and how poor they were at passing and breaking pressure. He encouraged us to be relentless in attacking them and putting as much pressure on them as possible. We talked about how we would break their press and the multiple patterns we would train at practice. Leaving scout, I felt confident in our game plan.

We boarded the bus to practice, and it was a quick 15-minute drive to NC State. While the other teams were training at WakeMed, where we were going to play, Marg used her connections so we could train more privately. It was a perfect fall day. The leaves were all falling to the ground; it was chilly out, and there was something in the air. I'll never forget the long walk to the field. I walked alongside my friends as we passed the recreational fields, immersed in the colorful trees, as we made it to the field in the back. The countdown for my last week of training at UCLA had started.

The NC State coach stood at the entrance and hugged our coaches. We thanked him for letting us train on their field, and he waved goodbye. We started off training in all our layers. Marg always started training out with something fun. Today, it was juggling with a partner. We always did some sort of technical work to get our feet going. As training continued, we took our layers off one by one and eventually, I was playing in my tank top. Yep. It was December 1st in Raleigh, North Carolina, and most of the team were in tank tops. Gof broke us into two groups, and you could start to see lineups forming.

Throughout the tournament, we had a similar lineup in almost every game. It looked like the group that started against Virginia. As we knocked the ball around in our possession game, we were moving quickly. Bouncing the ball from side to side. Checking in hard, asking for the ball. Defending in unison. We looked sharp.

Practice continued, and we went on to the next drill. We did our 11's. This was our starting 11 vs. "Alabama". Gof pulled together the reserves and told them how to press. They set up in Alabama's 4-4-2 diamond and got organized in their shape. We set up in our 4-3-3 formation and tried to break their press.

The starting lineup was primarily the same group from the last playoff games, but there was one switch: senior captain Maricarmen wasn't starting. It wasn't set in stone, but she was getting less and less reps with the starting group as the training went on. Jackie was getting more reps starting in the midfield with Sunshine and Ally Lemos. Our starting group began finding more success breaking "Alabama's" press. We knew which pockets would be open and where we could expose them the best. We stretched the field and were patient in our buildup.

Since "Alabama" was playing with four people in the midfield, we moved the ball side to side and used Quincy and me to break their press. Our starting wide positions allowed our wingers to get even higher and force their midfielders to make a quick decision. Do they stay inside and worry about Sunshine, Lemos, Reilyn, and Jackie? Or do they step out wide to Quincy and me? It was a game of cat and mouse. Our reserves worked hard to be like Alabama. In fact, they were better than Alabama. They pressed us hard. They gave us different problems to solve. They communicated effectively and did their best to replicate what Alabama did.

Several times, they punished us for mistakes and made it hard for us to pass out of their press. They scored on us. They intercepted passes. They listened to Gof and Marg and emulated how the Alabama center back would overstep or how their two 9s worked in tandem with each other. After all of this, we were beyond prepared for this game. Even though we hadn't met a team like Alabama yet, I knew we could handle anything they threw at us, especially because our teammates prepared us so well.

We headed back to the hotel and had lunch. We didn't have anything else planned for the day, so everyone was free to do whatever they wanted. Since we had finals coming up, our coaches gave us a lot of free time throughout the trip. People got treatment, studied, hung out in their rooms, or went to the mall that was across the street. I went with Sunshine and a few other girls to the mall, where we sat at Starbucks for a while. The rest of the day was ours to kill.

That night, we had team dinner, and then everyone headed to bed. I raided the snack room and got some snacks for later, and Kylie and I searched Netflix for a movie to watch. We both wanted something intense and exciting, so we landed on Captain Phillips. I'll never forget us watching on her iPad and staring wide-eyed at the screen. The next day was a busy schedule; we had a walk-through at the stadium, media, training, and then a team dinner with everyone. The rest of the team, injured girls and support staff were flying in, and we all were going to be reunited. I set out my makeup and curling iron for the next day and said goodnight to Kylie.

The next morning, I woke up and touched up my hair, then applied some makeup. Lauren came over, and I fixed her hair, something I had been doing for years. We all headed down for breakfast, and I went and picked up my jersey for our media day. After breakfast, we took the short bus ride over to WakeMed Soccer Park. As we walked through the tunnel out to the field, you could feel the magnitude of the moment. You could feel the history that radiated off the pitch and surrounded the stadium. All four teams had dedicated time slots for their walk-through, so we all took our time taking pictures, walking around the field, and getting out all our pre-game rituals, such as meditating and handstands. The pitch was beautiful. I had watched many NWSL games and College Cup games played here, and it always felt surreal to be walking out on such a storied pitch. As I watched my teammates dance around the field, I just kept picturing us winning the next night and heading to the final. *It is going to happen.*

After about 45 minutes at the field, we said goodbye to the girls heading back to the hotel, and the group of us who were doing media headed to the back side of the stadium. We looked out and saw UNC training down on the practice fields and were thankful that we were training at NC State, where no one could watch us. We all changed into our classic blue jerseys, with the freshly printed College Cup patch proudly on the side, and broke up into groups. Quincy, Lexi, and Sofia headed to take pictures, while Lilly, Lauren, Sunshine, Ally Lemos, Reilyn, and I headed to do an interview with analysts Julie Foudy and Jenn Hildreth. Julie was actually my parents' neighbor in San Clemente, so I was familiar with her.

We all sat next to each other and answered their questions. Julie asked us how we were going to defend Alabama's "two-front," and asked Lilly if she was ready to mark their star forward, Riley Parker. Lilly responded confidently that she and our defense had been tested all year and were ready for anyone. Julie asked us for a special story about our season, and I spoke about our New Era with Marg and how much she had taught us about being adaptable and versatile.

Jenn brought up Sunshine and the superstar season she was having. Shine spoke about her journey at UCLA and how things were coming "full circle." We talked about our pre-season games back in North Carolina and how those prepared us for the tournament despite them being the first few games of the year. The interview was in-depth, and everyone had a chance to answer questions about their experiences. After the interview, we met up with the other three girls and took some more pictures. Sunshine and Ally Lemos took some shots together, same with Reilyn and Lexi, foreshadowing all four of their impacts throughout the weekend. Suzi was working her magic with her camera, capturing all the fun moments in between. All the laughs, hair flips, dancing, and smiles when we thought no one was noticing, she got. Things were starting to feel real. Besides the seniors, no one else on the team had been to a College Cup, and even with us seniors, Mari was the only one who played in that semifinal game against Stanford. This was new for all of us.

Match Day -1 training was ordinary. We did our same warmup, same possession drill, and the same crossing and shooting drill that we had been doing all year. You could feel the elevated energy compared to the day before, and there was an extra sharpness from everyone. At the end of training, we worked on our penalties and figured out any last-minute tactics. I think that in the back of our heads, we knew this could be our last training together, but none of us treated it with a sense of sadness or anxiety. Despite the edge and intensity, we still laughed and danced our way through training. Rihanna and Drake still played in the background during warmups, and Reilyn was still doing her impersonations during penalties.

The rest of the team and staff arrived in the afternoon, and it felt right that we all were reunited. We all got glammed up, put on our best outfits, and headed down to the lobby to take pictures. I had on sparkly silver pants and a black top, and Kylie wore a longer brown dress with gold jewelry. We had spent 20 minutes taking mirror pictures together, and now it was time for us to pose and smile with our friends. Everyone looked amazing. After a photo session, we boarded the bus and headed to the steak dinner put on by the NCAA.

Bend Never Break

As we piled off the bus and all sat down, we were served a perfect Match Day -1 meal. The director of WakeMed Soccer Park stopped by and told us that our semifinal against Alabama was the 50th NCAA Women's Soccer match played at WakeMed. We all let out some "*ooh*"s and "*aah*"s as we knew we had a chance to make history with a special win. It was funny; Alabama was in the room next to us having dinner, so of course, we were cracking jokes, and the Snapchat group chat was going off. After dinner, we all headed back to the hotel. We all went into the team room to pick up extra electrolytes, water, and snacks. Our coaches stopped us before heading back upstairs, and they passed out letters to each of us from our parents. We all sat down on the circular tables and smiled, laughed, and cried while reading the heartfelt messages from our families.

I wiped away tears as I read mine and folded it to take upstairs. Our journey was so much more than just winning soccer games. Our journey was our parents' too, and we all wanted to make them proud. I headed upstairs, and our long, eventful day came to an end in Cary. I closed my eyes, picturing moments of glory and celebrations with my best friends.

We punched our ticket to compete for a championship. In five years, I had witnessed our program lose in the College Cup semifinal, Elite Eight game, Sweet 16 in penalties, and the first round of the tournament. I watched us win two PAC-12 titles, graduate All-Americans and Olympic gold medalists, change coaches, build a new culture, take down the top two teams in the country back-to-back, and now I was witnessing us heading to the College Cup semifinal. I had one more shot at writing my name in UCLA Women's Soccer history.

I woke up on the day of our Alabama game feeling extremely thankful. There wasn't an ounce of nerves or anxiety in my body. It was a weird feeling. I had been so nervous for our Elite Eight game against Virginia, but for some reason, I was so at peace going into our semifinal. We had our normal game-day routine that day. We woke up, had breakfast, and ventured out on our team walk around the hotel. I walked towards the back with Sunshine and Marg.

I told them that I dreamed we won 2-0. I vividly remember us getting a shutout and moving on to the final. Marg looked at me sideways and said she dreamed we won 2-0 as well. Sunshine and I looked at each other with wide eyes. This was a sign. Our day continued as normal. Half the team walked to Starbucks at the nearby strip ball. This is usually how our team traveled. Whether it was watching a basketball game, going to a party, or getting coffee, we moved in a flock. We mobile-ordered our drinks and claimed the biggest table Starbucks had to offer. With Lexi to my left and Ally Cook and Brianne across from me, the table was filled with our Grande Coffees and Powerade bottles filled with water and electrolytes alternated in between them. We sat around the table joking about the girls on Alabama and playing would-you-rather. The vibes were light, but you could sense we were all counting down the hours until kickoff.

All throughout high school, I practiced my shooting over and over. Even though I was a defender, I wanted to have a powerful and dynamic shot. One of my coaches taught me how to curl the ball around the defenders into the far post. I would be at the edge of the 18-yard box, dribble inside a few yards, and wrap my big toe around the ball. I would keep my head down and land hard on my kicking foot. When I would hit it perfectly, the ball would sail into the top corner. When I would be off-balance, the ball would shank out wide or roll into the net. I would practice on both sides. Rep after rep.

As Match Day continued, we all continued with our routine. Kylie went downstairs to the lobby to visit her family, so I took advantage of the silence and tried to take a nap. I tossed and turned, trying to get comfortable. I was just too excited. I kept envisioning us winning. I would picture myself running forward and connecting my crosses. I pictured Lauren getting a shutout. I pictured myself scoring. I pictured the bench rushing the field after we won. I pictured us training throughout the weekend. I sat up in my hotel bed and started putting together a collage of pictures together for my Instagram story.

I copied and pasted pictures from the media day photoshoot, celebrations after our UVA game, and other pictures from throughout our season onto an Instagram story. I captioned it, "One more opportunity to play with my best friends." I sat there and thought about what song to put behind it. I opened up my music app and searched through my playlists. I was looking through my Oldies playlist and came across Phil Collins's "In the Air Tonight." I pressed play, and the long intro started. As the song continued to build up, memories flooded in from the last time we played in the College Cup semifinal. I was sitting, injured, in a San Jose hotel room, getting ready to watch my friends play. This time, things were very different. I had been waiting for this moment all my life. I added the song behind my Instagram story and posted it. There was something definitely in the air.

Soon, we had our pre-game meal. As we sat around the tables, our coaches started their pre-game talk. Gof usually led these. He replayed Alabama's scout, emphasizing their weakness and the keys to our game plan.

We nodded back at him, locked in and ready for the challenge. After our pre-game meal and meeting, we had about 30 minutes to get ready before we left for the game. I went upstairs to our room and started to braid my hair. Throughout the tournament, I wore my hair the same every game. Two small Dutch braids pulled back into a bun on top of my head. After we won our first-round game, I knew I had to keep my hair the same. I parted my hair and started to braid my hair back. As the games went on, I got less anal about what my hair looked like. We didn't have a ton of time, so I got to work. It was a good braid day. I tied each braid with a small elastic and left the rest of my hair down. I washed my face and put on waterproof mascara. We were going to be on live TV, and it was imperative that I still looked cute.

I packed my bag, which included my shin guards, cleats, headband and gloves, water bottle, snacks, leftover food, hair ties, hair spray, and my air pods. I put on my black UCLA sweatpants and our white UCLA quarter zip. We could hear our families downstairs gathering around the entrance. We had about 75 to 100 people travel to North Carolina, and they were ready to scream and cheer all game long. As I went down the elevator, the cheers got louder. Our families stood alongside both sides with loud clappers, signs, and pom-poms. They erupted in cheers as we walked through the "tunnel." I high fived everyone as I went through and got to my parents, who were at the end of the line. I hugged and kissed them, and they wished me good luck and told me to have fun out there. As I boarded the bus, and I headed to the back, as tears glistened in my eyes. I was so excited to play in the game. The car ride to the game was quick. Our police escort got us past the long line of cars waiting to turn into WakeMed Soccer Park. My AirPods blasted "Keeping Your Head Up," by Birdy. I just kept replaying us winning in my mind over and over again.

Once we got to the field, ESPN cameras were outside our bus, waiting for us to walk out. The sun had already set, and the first semifinal between UNC and FSU had started. It was tied 0-0. Up until that moment, I truly hadn't thought about the final at all. I hadn't thought about who I would rather play or anything like that. I don't think any of us had. As we walked to the locker room, cheers echoed throughout WakeMed. UNC took the lead 1-0.

Once we got to the locker room, it was surreal. Our College Cup jerseys hung under our name tags. I pulled on my Under Armor and leggings and sat at my locker to eat my final snack before we started warmups. Before every game, Bri and I would have peanut butter and a banana. Faith had her mini camera out, taking pictures of everyone before warmups. The other semifinal continued on as UNC doubled their lead. It was starting to look like we would have a potential rematch with UNC. We went down to the practice field to start our warmup.

We overestimated our time and spent a little too much time outside. I went over to Jackie, who looked really nervous, and asked her how she was feeling. She told me she was anxious about how athletic Alabama was going to be. I told her she had nothing to worry about and that our style of play would cause problems for them. We heard another loud roar from the stadium, and UNC was now up 3-0.

We started our warmups as the wind whipped around us. I took off my headband and gloves as they kept sliding off. Everyone looked very locked in. Usually, warmups had a playful feel to them. Usually Whitney Houston's "I Wanna Dance with Somebody," would be blaring at our home field. This time, Nicki Minaj was playing from our portable speaker. The next thing we knew, FSU started to claw back. They found two goals to keep the game 3-2. You could tell we were all not trying to worry about that game, but we also were giving each other glances left and right.

As we continued with our warmups, the first semifinal was nearing the end. We had gotten through half our warmup and had about 20 more minutes before we walked out for the national anthem. Our coaches and managers ran onto the field as soon as the final whistle blew, amidst UNC's celebrations and FSU tears, to set up the warmup. I ran to one of my lifelong friends who played for FSU. I hugged Jenna as tears fell down her cheeks. She kept saying, "You guys need to beat UNC and do it for the first-time coaches." She had a brand-new head coach, and we did as well. She hugged me and wished me good luck as I consoled her. Her college career came to an end. I looked at my teammates who were watching our interaction, and there was a common understanding that none of us were going to feel how Jenna felt at the end of our game.

Drake blared through the stadium speakers as our families made their way down behind our bench. Alabama's section nearly doubled ours. The wind was cold, and the air was wet. Everything was heightened. We pinged balls back and forth to each other during warmup, and our coaches yelled out instructions. It was almost impossible to hear over the music and crowd. Everyone looked so serious. Amidst the chaos, our team never felt closer. I felt like I was about to explode. My heart was pounding so hard, and I was so anxious to start the game. We continued throughout the warmup, encouraging each other with every pass and every movement. We looked loose in warmup, but I could tell some of the younger girls were fighting every emotion possible.

Our lineup was filled with experience and leadership. Our back line consisted of two fifth year leaders and three mature sophomores. Our midfield was anchored by a steady freshman with two seasoned seniors flanked on either side of her. Our front line was mixed between a sophomore, a junior, and a freshman. Our bench had seniors, fifth years, and freshmen ready to come on and make a difference. We were fucking ready.

Our warmups came to an end, and we went to the bench to change into our jerseys and put on our shin guards. We did our power pose before all coming together. Everyone's rosy cheeks looked back at me as I spoke with passion and heart. I told our team that it took every single one of us to get to this moment, and we were exactly where we were supposed to be. Lean on each other and play for the person next to you.

All my friends looked at me in admiration while I tried my hardest to connect with both the 90-minute starter and the injured freshmen. We finished our cheer and broke our huddle. The starters went inside the tunnel as we got ready to walk onto the beautiful pitch. I grabbed the ball girl's hand, who was standing next to me, and smiled down at her. We walked out to midfield, and the introduction began. I stepped forward and beamed up to my family and friends and waved when my name was announced. We put our hands over our pounding hearts and listened to the National Anthem.

Our team high-fived Alabama, and we ran to our teammates on the sideline. As our final words were said, I went through and made eye contact and high-fived my girls. The starters came together, and we all spoke with such love and anticipation. I fist-bumped Lauren, Jayden, Lilly, and Quincy. I trusted every single one of them with my life and knew this game was going to go our way.

Chapter 24
Poise

On the fourth tier of Coach Wooden's Pyramid of Success are Poise and Confidence. Poise is defined as: "Just being yourself. Being at ease in any situation. Never fighting yourself."

John Wooden describes poise as "Just being yourself. Being at ease in any situation. Never fighting yourself." I describe it as December 2nd, 2022. At the very beginning of the fall, our equipment manager let the seniors design their own cleats. This was the first time we'd ever been allowed to do something like this. I picked a pink and white design and decided to put the word "Free" on the back of the heel. I knew I wanted my very last season at UCLA to be special and memorable. I knew that in order for that to happen, I needed to play free. I couldn't worry about lineups, minutes, or politics. I couldn't dread mistakes and bad games. I couldn't become too content with the good games. I had to become secure in myself, physically and mentally, so that I could play free. I could make mistakes. I could play bravely. I could play risky passes. I could test the limits and run miles and miles and miles. In order for me to leave UCLA with no regrets, I needed to play free.

The whistle blew to start the game, and we immediately started on the front foot. As the first half went on, we were dribbling out of pressure like we were in a telephone booth. We passed side to side as Alabama relentlessly pressured. Within the first 15 minutes Lexi got the most perfect look on goal. Bridgette played a through ball between the outside back and center back onto Lex running onto it. She collected it and let a shot rip with her left foot. The goalkeeper saved it, diving to the ground, and Lex attacked the rebound. She was a few feet from the goal and kicked it right at the goalkeeper, who was still on the ground. Lex's hands flew to her head in disbelief. We were so close.

As the first half went on, Reilyn was relentlessly shooting. She was taking every opportunity she got in front of the net. Since Alabama played with no wingers, Quincy and I were on every single time. We continued putting on the pressure offensively, and defensively, we covered for each other and tracked back on defense. About 20 minutes in, Alabama scored, but the goal quickly got called offsides, and I think it was a reality check for all of us to get one in the back of the net. We were dominating the half and needed to score going into the second half.

With 15 minutes left in the first half, we finally put it away. Ally Lemos broke from the pressure on the dribble and played a blind ball to her left. Unmarked with yards of space in front of her, Quincy was on her horse, chasing the ball down. She collected it cleanly and started dribbling hard at her defender. It was outside back vs. outside back. Q scissored with her right foot over the ball and took a long touch with her left foot. Two defenders collapsed on her, and as the ball was about to roll out of bounce, she cut it back hard with her left foot. Lexi darted to the near post, dragging defenders with her, which left Reilyn wide open in the middle of the goal. She calmly tapped it in with her left foot, and the stadium erupted. We all threw our hands to the sky as Rei jumped onto Ally Cook. We finally got the breakthrough we desperately needed. The whistle blew to signal the end of the half as we made our way into the locker room.

As we high-fived each other and passed along the "good jobs," we knew we needed to take over the second half. Alabama had weapons of their own and experienced seniors who didn't want their season to end. We talked about what was working for us. It was important for us not to sit back and play for a 1-0 win. We needed to continue scoring and put this game to rest. During halftime, the Alabama head coach was interviewed and asked what his team needed to do better in the second half. He agreed that when our midfield got a hold of the ball and was able to switch the point of attack, they were in trouble. I pulled Rei aside and told her to keep playing Q and me out wide. As we huddled up, Q was helping Lexi breathe. Lex blamed herself for not scoring earlier in the first half, but we encouraged her that everything was going to be okay and we would win this game no matter what.

To start the second half, Marg put Maricarmen in. Mari was our captain and leader and had gotten limited minutes at the end of the season. We still needed Mari in the game, but it wasn't going to be in the midfield. Mari and I play really well together. We read each other well. We were also best friends and roommates. Marg decided to play Mari at right forward, right in front of me. I told Mari we were going to dominate this game and the right side of the field together. And we did exactly that.

That second half was one of the best performances we ever played. We played with poise. With every minute we got stronger, Alabama got weaker. Within the first five minutes of the second half, we created multiple goal-scoring opportunities. Mari played a perfect ball to Reilyn, and we created a great chance on goal. We earned back-to-back corner kicks, and Sunshine found herself in a 1v1 situation. You could feel a goal coming.

Hustling back on defense, Mari slid, won the ball, and it popped out for Jackie. They connected a pass, and Jackie laid the ball off to me. I looked up and saw Ally Lemos in a sea of red and white. I threaded a ball through multiple Alabama players, and Ally turned in one touch. She looked up, saw Lex on her horse, and played a perfect 50-yard diagonal ball over the top of Alabama's defense. Lex received the ball in front of our bench, nearing the corner of the 18. She cut left and right and eventually played Quincy, who was streaking up the left flank. In one touch, Q nutmegged the defender, took another commanding touch, and curled the ball with her right foot into the back of the net. The ball slid past the keeper, who dived hard to try and stop it. The crowd went crazy. The bench went crazy. Our equipment manager bear hugged our Athletic Director as we all jumped on Quincy. After a few moments, she ran with her hands out wide with the biggest smile on her face. The bench engulfed her; we all knew this game was going our way. Quincy now had an assist and a goal for us, playing left back. A few minutes later, we did it again.

Jackie stripped the ball from Alabama's midfielder, pushed her way through, and somehow got the ball to Rei. As this was unfolding, I was now the highest player on the field, and I took off running. Rei received the ball in one touch, and without even looking at me, she played the ball out wide as I took off running hard. The ball was a bit wider than I anticipated, so while I was running, I looked to my left to see if there was anyone to cross to. Usually, my girl Lexi was on the opposite side, getting ready for my early cross, but this time, it was just me. I continued to dribble with my head up and thinking, "Shit, I am getting pretty close to the goal." It felt like it was happening in slow motion. I hear Maricarmen from behind me yell, "Keep going!" I took her advice and took a touch inside. I was now on the edge of the 18-yard box in the middle of the field. Soon, I was running out of space, and the defender was closing in on me. With no one to pass to, I got closer to the goal, put my head down and shot the ball as hard as I could with my left foot. You know those feelings you never want to forget? This was one of those moments. My eyes stayed on the ball, and my heart raced as I watched the ball slightly curve into the corner. I don't know how I did it, but I did.

I was parallel to the ground when I shot it, and I ended up on my side, lying on the field, watching the ball soar into the back of the net. My head hit the ground as the ball hit the net. I couldn't believe it. The ball went in the back of the net so fast it bounced out. Everything after that was pure adrenaline and excitement. I stood up so fast and let out a "Let's go!" I started to tear up a little bit and looked to my left. Jackie had her hands out, and we started running towards the bench. I looked up, and the bench was on the field; the crowd was in a complete frenzy, and the girls on the field followed me to the bench. I did a "Mario jump" and embraced the first person I saw. The bench ran out to meet us, and all 35 of us celebrated that moment together. My teammates jumped on me, hugged me, cried with me, and together we celebrated that moment. There are truly not enough words to describe that moment. Everything I had dreamed about was coming true. I manifested that shot for weeks. I knew eventually it would go in. That knee that gave me so much heartbreak and trauma just helped me take a rocket of a shot while falling over. Tears welled up while I ran back for kickoff, and I just couldn't believe it. The announcer said "GOAL! By Madelyn Desiano!" The crowd let out another cheer. You honestly couldn't have written it any better.

I ended up subbing off with about 15 minutes left. I ran towards the bench and put my hands up in the air as I smiled and looked up at my parents and grandmas in the stands. Brianne, who was subbing in for me, gave me a hug and said, "I'm so happy for you." All of our fans were on their feet, cheering for me. I gave my coaches the biggest hugs and went down the line of my friends. I hugged my strength coach, our sports psychologist, our team doctor, everyone who had helped me get through the last four and a half years. I cheered my team on for the remainder of the half, and it hit me that we were going to play for a National Championship.

A year ago, I dreaded the 10 second countdown as it signaled our season being done, but this time, happy tears welled up. I counted down with my team and ran on the field with my hands in the air. One more game. Poise. Being yourself. Never fighting yourself. Being at ease. All things that, given the circumstances, are hard to do. My team exemplified poise in our semifinal game. As the match went on, we continued being composed under pressure, played hard defense, and kept a 3-0 lead for 36 minutes. We never sacrificed our style of play and high expectations. The National Final would be another animal we would have to tackle, but for the next 24 hours we soaked our dominating win in together.

After the game, we led our fan section to an Eight-Clap. We started our "OLE OLE OLE OLE, UC…LA" chant that rang throughout WakeMed Soccer Park. I continued to celebrate with my friends down on the field and eventually made my way to the stands where my parents and grandmas were. They were hugging and crying as they just kept telling me how proud they were. After I said hello to my family, I headed to answer media questions with Reilyn, Quincy, and Marg. We put on our black College Cup hoodies, and all sat next to each other. We sat in front of a sea of journalists and interviewers, and they went one by one, asking us questions. One guy asked me if that was my favorite goal I had ever scored, and I laughed and said, "Well, I don't get to score many, so that one was the most special for sure." One journalist commented that we were the most communicative team she'd ever watched play, and we all laughed a little bit and looked side to side at each other. We told her that we had focused on communication this whole year, and it was something that we took pride in. We laughed when we all followed up with more commentary, proving how much communication was important to our team and culture. When asked about playing UNC again, we responded that we were a different team back in September and that game was a dress rehearsal. We were excited for the challenge to play UNC at home once again.

While we were interviewing, our team was going crazy in the lockerroom. Music blasted as they were singing and dancing to WIN by Jay Rock. On the bus, our strength coach was walking up and down the aisle screamsinging as we shined our flashlights up to her. We partied on the way back to the hotel, and we continued the good vibes that night. Our families all gathered in the hotel lobby, and we all sat and ate dinner with them. We went over every play, every goal, every celebration from all our different perspectives. Texts, calls, and social media mentions were blowing up my phone. Family, friends, old teammates and coaches, all reached out to tell me how happy they were for me. My heart was full.

The next two days were a blur. Thankfully, we had two full days to recover for the final, and we used every bit of free time to reset mentally and physically. The day after our Alabama game, our coaches wanted to set up a team building activity, so they set up a game of Jeopardy for us. We all got into teams, and our coaches put up the categories on the board. The categories were sound, 80s/90s slang, staff, World Cups, and UCLA History. The staff had collectively come up with the answers, and Erin Adkins, our Athletic Director, was the referee. Unfortunately for Erin, she was being screamed at and taunted the whole time.

Our competitive nature rang true even off the pitch, and a friendly game of Jeopardy got heated really fast. We tried to keep the vibes light throughout those 48 hours leading up to the final. Our trainings were still intense and sharp, but we wanted everything to feel natural. Our scout was short and simple; since starting the NCAA tournament, UNC changed its system from a 4-3-3 to a 3-5-2. This meant that our three forwards would be matched up with their three defenders. We thought this would help us since the first time we played them, we exploited them athletically and in transition. Regardless, we were going to prepare for whatever they threw out our way. Our coaches decided to stick with our conservative, defensive style of play. I was a little wary because in every game that we started off super defensive against a really good team, we didn't do well. In both the Stanford and USC losses, Marg apologized at halftime for us starting off too conservative. Once is a lesson, twice is a coincidence, but three times is a pattern, and I was nervous that this game plan wouldn't bode well for us. Either way, this was the game plan, and we were going to execute it.

Chapter 25
Loyalty

"A trait one owes to yourself and to all those depending upon you. Keep your self-respect."
John Wooden

Maricarmen Reyes

Loyalty can be defined in many different ways. Some see loyalty as the undying desire to help those they love. Others see it as backing up their friend in a room they aren't in. Others see it as devotion to time spent. Maricarmen Reyes was the most loyal friend and teammate I know. She exemplified true loyalty on our championship weekend and showed the soccer world what it means to be a true competitor. Mari was our captain and one of our fearless leaders. She was tenacious and aggressive on the field, fighting for her teammates and never backing down from a challenge. She loved her family and her hometown Santa Ana, and wore her heart on her sleeve.

Mari was our team's heartbeat. She scored big goals throughout her entire career. Her first career goal at UCLA was against FSU in her freshman year. She scored game-winners against Stanford, UW, and in our first game of 2022, against Iowa. Mari showed up when the lights were bright, and we needed to win.

Throughout the tournament, Mari's minutes dwindled. She brought something different to our midfield: creativity, flair, a bite. Yet, against some of the teams we played, we needed a steadier midfield. We had our mid-block down to a tee, and Sunshine, Lemos, and Jackie perfected it for us. Against UVA, Mari had the flu and barely played for us. The other trio held it down in the midfield, and all three of them played huge roles for us in winning those home playoff games. Sunshine and Jackie both had huge goals for us, as well as Lemos, who had played every minute up to that point.

Before the UVA game, Mari woke up with the flu and spent the entire day in bed sick. She loaded up on medication so she could push through our Elite Eight matchup. One year prior, Mari was sick before our first-round game at UCI and decided to sit out that game. She wasn't about to do that again. Mari started and played 22 minutes in our quarterfinal game. She was subbed out in the first half and never went back in. As we got to North Carolina, lineups started to form, and it became obvious that Mari wasn't going to be starting in our semifinal game.

I noticed something was up, and I decided that it would be best if I didn't say anything to her about the elephant in the room. Her mom and boyfriend flew in, and she was spending a lot of time with them. She wasn't her normal bubbly self, wasn't socializing, and spent a lot of time by herself. We had worked so hard to be there, and it wouldn't be doing anyone justice to dwell and bring the vibes down. I decided I would text Mari the night before our Alabama game. I texted her, ***"You're going to score tonight, I feel it."*** She never responded to me, and I didn't take it personally. I knew, no matter what, that Mari would put the team first.

Mari still led throughout the weekend. Even though she wasn't starting, she still cheered on her teammates, gave pointers, and when her name was called upon, she made a huge impact once she stepped on the field. Against Alabama, she subbed on late in the first half and played out of position in the second half, yet still helped us in so many aspects. She connected her cheeky passes, moved off the ball well, and helped double-teamed on defense. She created goal-scoring chances and was the voice behind my goal, encouraging me to keep dribbling. She never complained, brought the vibes down, or was a shitty teammate. We didn't have any other player like her, and we knew we were going to need her going into the final.

John Wooden said, "I do not see how anyone can attain true peace of mind without having something to which they must show loyalty; someone to whom they must express loyalty at all times." As we were gearing up for our final against UNC, the coaches decided to go with the same lineup that we had against Alabama. They stuck with the same midfield that handled business against UNC the first time we played them. Mari and I were on slightly better terms, and I think we both had a common understanding that we would just focus on the final. The night before our final game, I texted Mari one more time,

"Don't let the coaches or anything get in ur head or ruin this moment for u. Not saying they will but I know its annoying. This is our time and its going to be awesome tomorrow."

I know it was hard for Mari, but she never stopped being the loyal leader, teammate, and friend that she was. What we couldn't have known then was that Mari was going to be our hero.

The night before the final, I sent out a few more texts. I texted Reilyn:

"Let's do this thing. You are meant to be here and have been such a light to our team. This is OUR MOMENT and we are going to finish this game in 90 and walk out as champions. PLAY FREE and have fun!!! Lets go."

She responded,

"Yes mam!!! We know exactly what to do and I'm so confident in all of us. Play your heart out and leave it all on the field because that's what's got us here in the first place goddamnit!!! Sleep good and lets get this natty."

I texted Lauren, Jayden, Quincy, and Lilly. We had been playing stellar defense the entire year, and now we had one more performance in us.

Match Day was a blur. We had our usual team breakfast and then a team walk. A big group of us went to Starbucks, and we all sat around the table. I was fairly calm throughout the day. I had felt a lot more nervous in the earlier rounds of the tournament; now I was just so excited to play. Marg had the most perfect pre-game speech. She reminded us to be grateful. We had already done the work, and now it was time to have fun. Anish put together the perfect hype video, ending with a video of our alumni all wishing us "good luck." We felt the tightness of the Bruin Bubble, and I sat there knowing that the next time I would be in the team room was when we were celebrating. I vividly remember sitting there thinking, there is no way I am coming back to this hotel as a loser. Our families were outside in the lobby, lining up to wish us good luck like they did in the semifinal. They took a huge group picture in the lobby, and we could feel their support and love. We were going to need every bit of energy we could get.

As I stared out the bus into the darkness, I kept repeating Marg's words over and over. *I am grateful to be here. I am grateful to be healthy. I am grateful to get one last opportunity to play with my best friends.* "Keeping my Head Up" blasted in my air pods as I ate my last snack of the night. I reminisced on a crazy year filled with so much growth, determination, and love. Through a coaching change, a mental health crisis, and a chaotic college season, my teammates stood strong, side by side, as we faced adversity. I went on my phone, and my mom had added to her Instagram story. It was a collage of all the teams I had ever played for, and she captioned it, "Regardless of the jersey, the goal remained the same." Pictures of me in my So Cal Blues jersey, Aliso Niguel High School jersey, So Cal ODP jersey, USYNT jersey, and finally, my UCLA jersey all together. The last picture was me, eight years old, in my bright green AYSO jersey. I had a goofy smile on my face and was kicking the ball. I decided that was who I was going to play for. As our bus pulled up to the stadium, our parents were in the parking lot pregaming with fireball shots. They were ready.

    As we got off the bus, ESPN was waiting outside with their cameras out. We walked into the locker room, and I remember being in the back corner. The last picture I have on my camera roll is my College Cup jersey. This would be the last time I would ever put on my UCLA jersey. We dropped off our stuff and then headed out to the field for our normal walk-through. Quincy was standing alone on the left side of the field. Sof Cook was meditating. Lauren was standing in between the posts.

    Our coaches were sitting in their seats. Kylie and Lilly were doing their ritual handstands. UCLA alum Sydney Leroux flew out with her son Cassius, and she was taking pictures with Reilyn. I did my normal lap around the field and then visualized celebrating with my team. I visualized running towards the bench and jumping in their arms. There's this great picture of me with my hands in the air, looking up to the sky. After a few minutes, we all went back into the locker room to get ready.

    Music played as we danced, sang, meditated, fixed our hair, and did everything we usually did for game days. For the very last time, I flipped my hair over and tied it into a bun on the top of my head. I sprayed hair spray and applied my waterproof mascara. I had my very last pre-game snack – banana and peanut butter. Faith was taking pictures with her mini-cam, and I posed next to Emma. ESPN came in 10 minutes before we went out to warm up to get some pre-game footage and filmed Lauren and Sunshine putting on their cleats. It was finally time to take the field, and we walked out.

Similarly, to the semifinal, there was something in the air. Our game was earlier than Friday's, but it was just as dark out. The wind whipped around us, and the music played so loud you couldn't hear anything. As warmups went on, thousands and thousands of people, mostly Tar Heel fans, filled the stadium. It felt like an away game, and we were greatly outnumbered. Every time I looked up into the stands, powder blue stared back at me. I was grateful that we played at Dorrance Field a few months ago; I knew it was going to prepare us well for this moment. I remember our warmup not being our best. We looked a bit tight during our possession game, and I remember telling our group that we have to want to be on the ball; we weren't going to be able to hide today. Everything seemed really rushed. We jogged from our dynamic warmup to our passing drill to the possession drill and then to crossing and finishing. In the chaos, there was a moment while I was hitting long balls to Brianne that I looked up at the jumbotron. Our school's logo flashed on the screen, and I remember thinking, "I can't believe we're here." It truly felt like everything was finally connecting. People say that everything happens for a reason, and for the first time in a very long time, I was seeing the "reason" in real time.

After warmup, we all put on our jerseys and huddled up. I don't remember exactly what I said, but I remember it was short because UNC was already lined up and ready to walk out. The starters made their way over to the tunnel, and I held out my hand for the ball girl to grab. We walked out and stood at center field facing away from our team. I remember fireworks blasting right after the National Anthem and looking up at them. The stadium erupted when UNC was announced, and you could feel the energy for them. We were going to have to make our own energy. We wished the UNC girls good luck and ran to our team, who was running on the field to meet us.

For the very last time in 2022, we did our "Bruins on three!" I will never forget taking the field and "Nice for What" by Drake blaring in the background. This was one of our team's songs, and I remember thinking, "We are winning this game." I looked at the bench, and they were all looking at me, and we were all dancing and singing along. I glanced over to Jayden, and she was dancing like no one was watching. The ref finally blew her whistle, and it was time to do the damn thing.

Chapter 26
Competitive Greatness

At the top block on Coach Wooden's Pyramid of Success is Competitive Greatness. "Be at your best when your best is needed. Enjoyment of a difficult challenge."

The first half was rough. They pressed hard at us, and we were turning the ball over left and right. You could tell we were nervous and weren't feeling totally like ourselves. 10 minutes into the first half, they set a dangerous cross, and I was covering the back post. Unbalanced, facing my own goal, with a UNC player running at me, I back-heeled the ball out of the six-yard box. We also could not stop fouling. In the first half, we were called for 10 fouls to UNC's one, and at halftime, Marg went up to the ref and made a point that the game was not being called evenly. We struggled to get pressure out on UNC's wide players, and I remember looking exasperated to the sideline and telling the coaches we needed to get some pressure out on the ball.

They had a close call for a goal on a set play. Lauren made a great save, and I think that woke all of us up. Our defense held on strong, doing everything we could to win our 1v1 battles and making last-ditch defensive efforts. The girls on the sideline were yelling at me to get the team up, and I agreed with them that we needed to step up. As the half went on, we started to create more chances. Bridgette played a great ball to Sunshine, who was busting ass up the field. Her shot slammed into the side netting and was our best chance of the half. With two minutes left in the first half, we earned a corner kick, and you could feel the momentum start to shift. Despite the half feeling lopsided, UNC generated five shots to our three, and we had two corners to their one. By the end of the first half, we had a bit more control, but the ref quickly blew her whistle to end the first 45 minutes.

We walked off the field and headed into the locker room. Things were fairly quiet. I remember standing up towards the side of the room, facing everyone. The coaches usually waited a few minutes before coming in. I remember telling everyone that we didn't need to "go" every time we got the ball. Our chances would come. We would find a way to score. It didn't need to be rushed. Marg and the coaches then came in. She apologized for coming out too conservative. I knew it wasn't time to be petty, but I was also visibly frustrated because this was the third time, in a big game, that she told us that at halftime.

She also said Shine's shot was the best chance of the game, which we all agreed with. We knew we could get in behind them and expose their three-back formation. In the corner, Maricarmen was talking to Bridgette and giving her pointers. Marg also noted that their goalkeeper was suspect on set plays. She struggled to command her box, and she felt that we were going to score off a set piece. I agreed. We had been generating a lot of corner kicks throughout the tournament, and our services had been great. As the time dwindled down, we headed back out to the field. It was time to turn this game around.

We started the second half as a different team. Sunshine was all over the field, causing trouble, and Reilyn was now playing out wide. Between the two of them, we were getting more crosses and shots on goal than the entire first half. We swarmed around the UNC midfield, breaking up their rhythm and doing our best not to give up any more fouls. Jayden was on a yellow card, and we needed her to stay on the pitch. We started using their formation against them and forced them to mark either our outside back or forward. They were used to Reilyn playing center forward, and since she was out wide now, they started dropping a lot earlier. This allowed us to have more space and attack them with more numbers. We had complete control of the first 15 minutes, but eventually, the chess match broke, and UNC went up.

Their right forward whipped in a high cross in, and my mark jumped in the air and headed the ball straight into the back of the net. The entire stadium erupted, and my hands went to my head; I was distraught. Up until that moment, I had defended the back post perfectly but couldn't do enough that time. We quickly re-grouped while UNC celebrated on the sideline, and all agreed that we were still in this game. We had been playing a great second half so far and needed to continue playing with momentum. I told Reilyn to keep dribbling at her defender and to trust her instincts. I told her I was going to keep playing her the ball since we were gaining so much momentum on our side.

Sunshine kept encouraging her and Ally Cook to continue taking shots. We spent the next 10 minutes on top of them. We were earning corners, sending in dangerous crosses, and getting good shots on goal. The unbelievable effort from our team to get forward and support each other was inspiring. I was watching my teammates sprint 40 yards to get on the end of the crosses. We started to feel UNC weather a little bit and felt that we could tie it up at any second.

The game continued to be physical, and bodies were flying left and right. Just when things started going our way, UNC doubled their lead, with almost a mirror goal from their first. A high ball sails from the right side of the field, and the same player heads it in the back of the net. Unlike the first goal, the second one was a weaker header, but nonetheless, with 15 minutes left in the game, we were down 2-0. We came together again and knew it was going to take everything and more for us to come back. We changed formations to a 3-4-3, and I was now playing center back with Jayden and Lilly. We were pushing forward, trying to create anything.

With about 12 minutes left in the game, the announcer boasts over the loudspeaker, "Tar Heel fans, you cannot rush the field when the game is over!"

I looked to my left at Jayden in absolute shock. There's no way this man actually said that. I thought to myself, *there is plenty of time left in the game, and nothing is over until it's* over. We had been playing so well throughout the second half, and you could still feel a glimmer of hope. The UNC girls looked at each other and smiled as the stadium erupted. I just kept thinking I had to do something. I had to contribute in some way. I was blaming myself for the goals against us, and I needed to do something to change this game. Score, assist, create, it didn't matter. Whatever I had to do in the next 15 minutes, it needed to help us win this damn game.

In every game that we scored, we won. Every single game in the fall, whether we were down, tied, or winning, if we scored, we won. In the two games we lost, USC and Stanford, we were shutout. Everyone on our team knew this. Our coaches, players on the field, and players on the bench were all aware that if we could score one goal, we could find a way to score another. We had practiced this scenario in training. We had trained being down 1-0, being down 2-0, switching formations, being down a player, and capitalizing and defending on set plays. We were prepared for everything.

On the contrary, this was UNC's biggest weakness. UNC's record going into the National Championship game was 20-4-1. All four losses were games where they gave up a lead. We started their curse back on Labor Day Weekend where we came back and beat them 2-1 at Dorrance Field. Since that game, their next three losses in ACC play and in the ACC championship were all a result of them not being able to defend a lead. Even in the College Cup semifinal against FSU, UNC almost gave up their 3-0 lead when FSU rallied back to score two goals in nine minutes. This wasn't some crazy secret. We were definitely aware of this hole for them. Ultimately, every single person in that stadium who was familiar with the Tar Heels knew that they couldn't defend a lead. Their coaches knew it, their bench knew it, and the girls on the field knew it.

We joked about this after, but that announcer really jinxed the game. Minutes after he essentially called the game for UNC, we found a way. With about 11 minutes left, we earned a free kick around the top of the circle, about 45 yards away from the goal. Jayden set the ball up, and everyone else was running in the box to try and score. JP had a great left foot and could smash this free kick 50+ yards.

She signaled to everyone to back up and get the hell in the box. She put her hand in the air and lined up to take it. The ball sailed into the box. Reilyn jumped up and contested for the header, but the UNC girl behind her headed the ball out. Sunshine, who was standing on top of the box, reacted quickly, and as the ball was bouncing out of the 18-yard box, Sunshine darted around the UNC defender. The ball took two bounces, and the second it popped up from the second bounce, Shine put her head down and smacked the ball with her laces. You could hear the contact of her foot hitting the ball, shooting toward the goal. The UNC goalkeeper reacted to the point-blank volley and hit the ball straight out in front of her. Lexi, who was inside the 18-yard box, watched Shine unleash her shot and started to move towards the keeper. As the keeper saved the ball directly out in front of her, Lexi read the rebound perfectly. As the ball hung in the air, she ran towards it and smacked it straight out of the air into the goal. The UNC defenders stuck their feet out, trying to block the shot, but it rolled right past them to the corner of the goal. 2-1.

All of us jumped in the air and had a moment of celebration before we locked in. Sunshine, Reilyn, and Quincy sprinted toward the goal to get the ball, which the UNC defender was holding protectively. I was running back to our side of the field. JP was on the verge of tears, and Lexi ran back and let out a "Let's go!" to all of us. The bench exploded, and now there was hope in all of us. Our fans were starting a "UC…LA!" chant and we all looked at each other with narrow eyes. Our coaches paced up the sideline nervously. The game just changed, and we were back in it.

The next 10 minutes were a blur. We continued to fight and fight and fight. We threw numbers forward, chased down long balls, and still defended hard. UNC started going to the corner to waste time pretty early, so we had to keep the ball out of our half as much as possible. With about three minutes left, I was chasing down UNC's forward and going shoulder-to-shoulder with her. The ref whistled for a foul, and I threw my hands in the air. The ref had made cheap calls all game and it was getting out of hand. We won the ball back pretty quickly off the free kick and went up the field again. With 90 seconds left in the game, my heart started to feel heavy. We had just taken a bad shot, and the ball went out for a goal kick. We now had 60 seconds left to find a way.

All 10,000 Tar Heel fans were screaming and cheering already. There was so much energy going for UNC while we quite literally just had each other. With a minute left, Sunshine and Reilyn fought for the ball in the air, and Shine flicked the ball over the UNC back line. As the ball was bouncing towards their goalkeeper, Lexi came flying from the other side of the field to apply pressure. Between the defenders and goalkeeper, there was a miscommunication, and Lexi's pressure spooked them. They kicked the ball out of bounds, and it flew into the stands. Standing at the corner of the 18-yard box on the right side of the field, the ball girl tossed Maricarmen the ball, and she jumped up to catch it. She threw it into me, the UNC defender beat me to it, and we got another throw further up the field.

The clock was ticking down, and next thing I knew, there were 45 seconds in the game. 45 more seconds left in my career. I just kept thinking, "It can't end like this." "There's no way we are leaving Cary as losers." I ran towards the ball to throw it in, and I motioned to everyone to back out. I stood on the right side of the field, close to the endline, facing the 18-yard box. I chucked the ball into the mass of people. The ball got cleared out softly, Ally Lemos stuck her foot out, and it got played back out to me. It took one bounce, and the UNC defender ran toward me. Whether I consciously knew it or not, I knew I had to make some type of play. I timed it perfectly on the bounce, and I turned my body so that I was facing her. I wound up to cross. I hit the ball hard, the defender jumped up to block the cross, and the ball ricocheted off her back and sailed out of bounds for a corner.

Bend Never Break

There were about 30 seconds left in the game, and everything was moving in slow motion. This was our last chance. Our last opportunity to tie the game up. And, of course, it would be on a set piece. All throughout the fall, we struggled to be clinical on set pieces. We could score off set pieces, but we weren't known for that. Going into this game, we knew UNC's goalkeeper was susceptible on corner kicks. She wasn't very tall, and she struggled to defend her box. Marg would always tell us, "Make the keeper make a play." or "Serve the keeper." We had two corner kick specialists – Ally Lemos and Sunshine Fontes, and all throughout the tournament, they had been whipping corners in left and right. This was our last chance to turn the game around.

As the ball sailed out of bounds, I sprinted to the endline. The clock was ticking, and we literally had seconds left in the game. A UNC ball girl held the ball in her hands, and I held my arms out. She quickly tossed me the ball, and I looked over my shoulder. I was not in the mental space to take the corner kick, and luckily for me, Ally Lemos, our corner kick specialist, was already running over. Her ponytail was bobbing up and down as I tossed the ball to her. I didn't look at her. I didn't say anything to her. I didn't even stay over there to draw a player out.

Here I was, a 22-year-old fifth year leader, leaving our fate to an 18-year-old freshman. I handed her the ball and handed her our season all in a split second. I turned around and ran to the 18-yard box. I kept thinking, "Please keep it in bounds. Please Lemos, don't kick it out of bounds." I knew if she kicked the ball out, we had no chance. This was it. This was for all the marbles. All 10,000 UNC fans banged on the bleachers and screamed and yelled at Lemos. UNC set up in their unusual corner-kick formation. Their small goalkeeper had no protection around her, but instead had three girls standing on the goal-line. They lined up on either side of her, and then the rest of UNC's lineup was in the six-yard box.

Our team lined up in our usual spots. Jayden went and stood next to the keeper to box her out. Reilyn, Lilly, and Ally Cook got ready at the back post. Mari, Sunshine, and I flanked around the goal. Lauren and Quincy stood side by side in case the ball got kicked back out. As Reilyn watched Ally Lemos walk up to take the corner, she turned and looked at Mari. "Get it together." That's what she told Mari as Mari started to tear up. She turned around and yelled at Lauren to get into the box. She lined herself up near

Lauren, giving herself plenty of space to watch the ball and make a play. She looked at Lilly and told her, "Keep your eyes open when you head this ball". Whether it was her head, shoulder, or back, whatever it was going to be, Reilyn was going to have to make a play. I looked to my right, and Ally Lemos put her hand in the air. I held my breath as she ran up and kicked the ball with her right foot. It sailed over our heads and looked like it was going to fly out of bounds. All of Westwood, the bench, and our fan section stood in silence, watching the ball loop in the air. Reilyn had told Ally Lemos multiple times throughout the game to play the ball to the back post. She watched the ball hang in the air and dip to the back post. She whispered to herself, "Don't fuck this up Rei."

There were 16 seconds left, and we were moments away from complete euphoria or complete heartbreak. Securing herself next to the keeper, Jayden turned around and yelled, "Rei!" as the ball flew over her head. The ball almost looked like it was going to go in by itself, but then all of a sudden, out of nowhere, Reilyn freaking Turner jumped in the air and took the ball, herself, and three UNC girls into the back of the net. She watched the ball hit the top part of the goal as she held onto a UNC defender's shoulders to brace her fall into the net. Pandemonium ensued as Reilyn backflipped into the net, and the ball flew in. The smoke machines next to the goal shot up smoke, and the stadium went quiet. All you could hear was our bench, our 100 fans, and the 11 of us on the field. My arms flew into the air, and I looked straight over the stands. We had tied it up! Reilyn Turner scored at the death. We were still in the game. My teammates were going absolutely crazy – the entire bench was running on the field. We bend, but we don't break.

Our fans were jumping up and down, and back at home in Westwood, our local bar was going nuts. The water polo team bear hugged each other as the men's soccer team threw napkins in the air. The football team yelled at the TV while the volleyball girls jumped up and down, screaming. All of our family and friends watching on TV were screaming and running around their houses in shock. Girls on the field were running toward the girls on the bench and colliding mid-air. Reilyn pulled herself out of the goal and jumped into Ally Cook's arms. The UNC goalkeeper and defender were throwing tantrums, telling the ref to look at VAR, claiming that Jayden fouled the keeper. I put my head down in disbelief and started running towards midfield.

The UCLA fight song blasted over the stadium, and you could feel our Bruin Bubble take over. I high fived Lauren and Ally Lemos and took my spot in the right corner of the field. Tears brimmed my eyes, and I looked up to the stands where my parents were sitting. I knew that we were capable of winning and coming back from being down 2-0, but to watch it unfold in front of you is a surreal feeling. The crowd started to shout "boo!" as the replay showed on the jumbotron. So many thoughts were racing through my head as the ref blew the whistle for the last three seconds of the game. UNC kicked the ball off and fouled one of our players immediately. We sent a long ball in with hopes of finishing the game right there, but we couldn't capitalize, and the game went into overtime.

As I walked to the bench, I was in a trance. My teammates were jumping up and down and hugging each other. Our fans were leading chants, and our coaches were huddling together, figuring out a game plan. I was fighting so many emotions. I walked past my teammates and went and sat on the bench. I chugged water, and Jen walked over to me. She was asking if I needed to be stretched or anything. I was still blaming myself for the goals against, and I looked up to the stands, and I saw Marg's husband, Bates, standing right above me. He was pointing at me and kept saying, "Lead this team! This is your team." I snapped out of it.

I slowly started nodding and came back to life. I had worked way too hard to let this moment go to waste. In the midst of everything, Maricarmen walked straight up to Marg, Gof, and Molly and looked them dead in the face. She told them very confidently, but with emotional presence – "Marg, am I staying on?" Marg froze and just looked at her. With the most passion and heart one can have, Mari looked at her and said, "Believe in me. I can do this." Tears welled up as she stared directly into Marg's eyes. Marg replied, "100% we believe in you," and they kept her on the field.

I stood up and went back to my teammates, who were forming a huddle. Jayden was hyping everyone up, and we all looked at her in awe and inspiration. We had 20 minutes left in the game, and we were going to do everything we could to find a way. I pushed away my negative thoughts and locked in as I walked out back on the field. Music blasted over the stadium and Jayden and I were dancing away. We looked at the UNC girls, and any remaining hope was gone. You could tell they couldn't believe they just dropped a 2-0 lead.

Bend Never Break

This was our third overtime game of the tournament. The last two times, against UCF and UVA, we dominated. Our undeniable fitness was hard to slow down, and this was when we thrived. We had the most random lineup out on the field. Reilyn was right forward, Mari was left forward, and Ally Cook was center forward. Ally Lemos, Sunshine, and Jackie held it down in the midfield, and our back line remained the same. We immediately started on the front foot, whipping in crosses, winning any loose balls, and chasing down everything.

Any time UNC generated offense, we had three or four players swarming the ball. Lauren was chucking 30-yard balls out wide for fast restarts, Ally Cook was posting up against center-backs, and Sunshine was slipping balls through the midfield. Around four minutes into the first overtime, the cramping started. Ally Lemos had to be taken off, and Lex subbed in for her. Mari moved to the midfield, and Lex played out wide on the left. Reilyn was in downward dog, stretching out her calves. With about two minutes left, Sunshine played a perfect diagonal ball to Lexi, who was running hard up the left side of the field. She dribbled at the defender and whipped in a shot hard and low across her body. The UNC keeper stretched out and forced the ball out for a corner. *Could we do it again?* Since Lemos was out getting stretched, Sunshine ran over to take the corner on the right side of the field.

She set it up and whipped the ball as hard as she could with her left foot. The UNC keeper, surrounded by a sea of UNC and UCLA jerseys, made contact with the ball, and it fell hard. We scrambled for the ball, and it got played back out. One minute later, we earned another corner in the same spot, and Sunshine ran over again. The UNC players looked at each other and you could feel their nervous energy. Sunshine played another perfect corner kick, but we were unable to get anything on it. The ref blew her whistle, and the first overtime was over. We all high-fived each other, and the vibes were high as we headed back to the bench. I definitely felt the momentum shift, and for the first time this entire game, I felt we were in control.

As cliche as this sounds, our fitness and our ability to finish games off so strongly were a testament to the work we had put in months and months ago. In every overtime game we played, we flourished. As we huddled up again for what seemed like the 100th time this game, we got ready for 10 more minutes. 10 more minutes to finish out this game and walk out of here as National Championships. No one was even thinking of penalties; that's how much in control we were. Our arms intertwined with each other as our coaches told us the game plan. I squeezed my friends hard before letting go and heading back out to the field. Music continued to play over the stadium, and we ran out to the field. Gof pulled Sunshine and Lexi aside and told Shine to keep playing Lexi the ball. Lilly had her arms on Jackie's shoulders. Sofia Cook cracked her neck side to side as the freshman walked out on the field. In the stands, Bates and Rei's mom held a huge "UCLA" painted sheet that they were waving. I went up to the ref and expressed my frustration to her. Jayden came up to me with her hands open, and I high fived her hard as we took our positions on the right side of the field.

  Our lineup was the same backline: Sunshine, Mari, and Jackie in the midfield, and Lex, Ally Cook, and Sof in the front line. On the bench waiting to sub on were Ally Lemos and Reilyn. We started off with the ball and immediately started pushing forward. Minutes after we started the second overtime, Lexi collapsed on the field, holding her calves. She lay there as our athletic trainer, Nikki, and student athletic trainer, Abby, came running on the field. As she went down, Ally Cook was in the downward dog position, stretching out her calves. Nikki and Abby helped Lex up onto her feet, but Lex couldn't even walk. She wrapped her arms around them and was in tears as they carried her off the field. Reilyn ran on the field to replace Lex, and the crowd clapped for Lex.

  The minutes ticked down as we continued to push to create something. Sof Cook provided calmness for us as she dribbled circles around the UNC defenders. Maricarmen continued to run and run and run, and she soon earned us a throw in further up the field. I threw the ball into Ally Cook, and she quickly earned us a corner kick. Since Lemos was still out, Sunshine ran over to the same spot where Reilyn found the tying goal.

  She played another perfect left-footed ball into the mix, and the UNC defender point-blank headed it straight over the goal for another corner kick. Reilyn called over to Shine and slyly pointed away from the goal, signaling to Shine to play it a bit further away. They locked eyes, and Shine nodded. For the fourth time in the last 15 minutes, Shine lofted the ball to the back post. Reilyn, standing unmarked, headed the ball hard back across the goal. Jayden ducked out of the way, and it bounced on the endline before the UNC defenders cleared it out. It looked like it could've crossed the endline. Jayden and Mari threw their hands in the air, and our bench went crazy. Ally Cook looks over at the bench with her hands on her head, and our coaches stand up to go to the fourth referee on the sideline. In the meantime, UNC cleared the ball out, and Quincy and I were on a dead sprint back to win the ball back. As I passed the ball to Quincy, the ref blew her whistle and pointed to VAR: she was going to review the play.

    Our fan section went crazy, and I walked up to Mari and asked her, "Bro did it go in?" She said, "Yeah bro, I am pretty sure it did." The ref stood over the monitor and watched for a few minutes. The ball bounced on the endline, hit off the UNC's defender's shin, and almost went into the goal, before getting awkwardly cleared out. The ref backed away from the VAR, and we all held our breath, waiting to hear her verdict. She motioned that it was no goal. The entire stadium erupted in celebrations, and we all walked back to our spots on the field. In a way, that felt like our chance. We knew our corner kicks were so dangerous and felt that maybe we could get another goal off of one. In the next couple of minutes, we continued to have momentum, and the game started to turn more direct. The clock was ticking down and as the UNC center back winded up for another long ball, I positioned myself in front of my forward. The ball flew to me, and I ran forward to collect it out of the air. I wanted to one-touch play it to Sunshine, but the ball flew high into the air, right back where it came from. I let out a "Sorry Shine!" and she said, "It's okay Mads." The ball fell perfectly to Sofia Cook, who brought it down swiftly in one touch. She danced around the ball and started dribbling inside towards the left side of the field. Quincy, who had run a dozen miles over the last few days, took off on a sprint up the flank. Sof passed the ball in front of Quincy, and Q dribbled up to the field.

    She dribbled hard to the endline, and right then, cut the ball back to Ally Cook. The ball got pushed out in front of the six-yard box, and facing backward, Ally pushed her long, blonde ponytail behind her back and turned to face the goal. No one stepped up to defend Ally, and as she turned to shoot, she was off-balance and fell to the ground. As this is all unfolding, Maricarmen was standing, marked, outside the six-yard box. Ally's shot forced the UNC keeper to dive to her left to make the save. The keeper softly pushed the ball to her left. Mari, reading Ally's shot and the rebound, started to run towards the goal. As the keeper gave up the rebound, Mari was already running to the ball. The ball was about three yards away from the goal as Mari winded up with her right foot and shot the ball into the net. She fell over and rolled onto her back as her arms shot up in the air. The time stamp reads 3:23 minutes left in overtime, the same time stamp when UCLA won in overtime in 2013.

Tears fell down my face as Mari hit the ground. I threw my hands in the air and took off on a dead sprint towards her. She was lying inside the six-yard box, almost out of bounds, right behind a sea of UNC fans. Sof Cook ran to her and lay on top of her, telling her, "You did it Mari! You did it!" Mari was sobbing as she looked up to Sof. The smoke machine released smoke into the air, and our Fight Song blasted over the speaker. Reilyn penguin dived over to Mari and Sof, as Ally Cook raised her arms out wide and looked up to the sky. Quincy, Jackie, Sunshine, and I dog piled on top of each other. Lilly walked over to us, and I looked up to her; we were both crying. We were all hugging each other, and our bench was going crazy. Girls were running on the field, falling on the ground, crying, and hugging our coaches. Our fans were going nuts as they started chanting "UC....LA!" I was in the dog pile, and we all kept saying to each other, "We did it guys." Shine and I helped Mari stand up, and we all hugged each other. Mari was sobbing as she broke off from the group and ran towards the bench. Faith, Bridgette, Ame, and Ellie ran onto the field and hugged her. Mari sat on the bench for 80 minutes. A fifth year, and captain, who wasn't given any reason as to why she was benched, displayed the utmost, inspiring will to win. She didn't talk shit, she never complained, she didn't sulk during training or on the bench. She stayed loyal to the team, the program, the coaches, and most importantly, to herself. She cheered her teammates on, gave pointers at halftime, and fought like hell when her name was called upon. Her unselfish, resilient mentality was something we all can learn from.

We all ran back to our spots, looking at each other with admiration and pride. Also, with "holy shit" eyes. We were three minutes away from winning a National Championship after being down 2-0 with 10 minutes left in the game. It's hard to remember the exact feelings in that moment. All I can really remember is that we needed to do everything we could to not let them score. I literally held onto the forward I was marking, not letting her have an inch of free space.

At this point, UNC had lost any hope. Their 10,000 fans were silent. Their bench was silent. They had a foul throw-in with about two minutes left, and that felt as if it was the cherry on top. Unable to control herself, the coaches subbed off Mari and subbed in Brianne, another defender. We were now playing with five defenders in the back. UNC started flying numbers forward, but we just defended so smartly. Any ounce of offense they had we snuffed away. We moved our feet and made sure every tackle was clean. The clock was ticking down and all of a sudden, there were 60 seconds left. What is crazy to think is that when there were 60 seconds left in regulation, we were losing 2-1. We all knew that anything could happen.

Ally Cook, our lone forward, was chasing down everything. She continued to sprint at the backline and apply pressure on them. We cleared the ball up the field and stalled every bit we could. On the bench, Mari sat in the coach's chair as Lexi and Rei huddled around her, hugging her, and calming her down. Girls on the bench started putting their jerseys on and taking off their parkas. With 15 seconds left in the game, UNC sent a long ball toward our goal. Bri jumped up, and the ball flew over her head and rolled towards Lauren. Lauren let the ball roll all the way to the endline and baited the forward to run to her. The announcer started the countdown –

Ten. Lauren picked up the ball.

Nine. Sunshine threw her arms up in the air.

Eight. Mari stood up on the sideline.

Seven. Bates and Rei's mom turned the "UCLA" sheet around and now it read "National Champions."

Six. Girls on the bench got the Powerade ready to throw on Marg.

Five. Jayden turned to the crowd, her arms wide open, taunting them.

Four. Bri turned to me and said, "Mads." I looked over at Bri. We started crying as we embraced in a hug.

Three. The bench started to run out onto the field.

Two. Lauren punted the ball into the air.

One. We reached Competitive Greatness

I ran towards my fellow defenders, and we all hugged each other as our entire team came running onto the field. I was uncontrollably crying as my teammates were all lifting me up and hugging me. Everyone was emotional as the UNC girls dropped to the ground, crying. We all started running towards our bench and on my way there, Molly grabbed me, and I started sobbing in her arms. Next thing I knew, Erin Adkins came over and I was sobbing to her. The next 30 minutes were a complete blur. I remember us leading the crowd to an Eight-Clap and all our parents looking down at us recording our celebrations. We rallied around the trophy, lifting it in the air and starting our chant, "OLE, OLE, OLE, OLE, UC......LA!" The TV camera was in our faces as we embraced each other. "All I Do Is Win" blasted over the loudspeaker, and we were singing along with it. I was hugging everyone around me.

Ally Cook came up and gave me the biggest hug, and then I hugged Jayden and Lexi. As I made my way to everyone, I walked right to Martin Jarmond, our Athletic Director, and we locked eyes. I put my arms out, and he gave me a big hug and said how proud he was of me and our team. He thanked me for leading this team, and I thanked him for allowing this all to happen by hiring Marg. The next thing you knew, we were all being handed out T-shirts and hats. We all quickly adjusted our ponytails and pulled our T-shirts over our heads. I ran to grab my phone and started taking pictures and videos that would last a lifetime. There was a quick ceremony, and we all lined up together. The announcer went through all our names and presented us each with a mini trophy. I skipped up and received mine and continued to cheer on my teammates. We all gathered in front of the "National Championship" sign and took a team picture. As we all smiled at the cameras, confetti blasted behind us and startled all of us. We all looked up in awe at the confetti.

I lay down next to Lauren and Ally Cook and looked up at the sky as tears continued to fall down my face. As I lay on the confetti-filled ground, I held my trophy close to my chest and closed my eyes. I kept thinking about everything our team had gone through. We were literally 16 seconds away from losing. 16 seconds away from ending my career on a heart-wrenching loss.

We joked that 16 seconds could change your life. It honestly felt unreal. I danced next to Maricarmen and Bridgette, hugged Kylie and yelled, "we freaking did it!" I took selfies with Bri and America and captioned it "We fucking did it." I took pictures with all my teammates and coaches and posed for the NCAA photographer. I pulled down my bun into a low pony and secured my National Championship hat down. Lexi and I did our famous TikTok dance to Beyonce's "Freakum" and we took an iconic picture with Jayden and Reilyn and our trophies. Back in California, family, friends, UCLA students, our local bar, and everyone in between were going nuts. My phone was blowing up with "HOLY SHIT" messages, and believe me, I couldn't believe what just happened either.

Amidst all the celebrations, I ran to the stands where my family was waiting patiently. There is this incredible video of me climbing up to hug them. My mom was holding back tears, and my dad was helping me stay balanced. They kept saying how proud they were, and I started crying all over again. I hugged my Lala and Nana, and we took a picture of all of us together. My mom had my cousin on Facetime, so I said "Hi," to him. His girlfriend and him were going crazy. I will never forget the feeling of being so overwhelmingly happy.

John Wooden describes Competitive Greatness as "Having a real love for the hard battle, knowing it offers the opportunity to be at your best when your best is required." During the National Championship game, when the stakes were at the highest, we displayed that. We displayed that during the last 10 minutes of the game when we were down 0-2. We displayed that during the last 16 seconds left in regulation. We displayed that during overtime. We displayed that when Mari scored the game-winner. We displayed that when we beat Virginia in overtime. We displayed that when we beat UCF in PKs. We displayed that after our losses to USC and Stanford. We displayed that when we beat Duke and UNC back-to-back. We displayed that starting August 1st.

Chapter 27
The Celebration

Despite the what-ifs that raced through our minds, we loved the hard battle that the game presented. That's why we all were at UCLA to begin with. I'll never forget when we played UNC for the first time back in early September; I told the team in the huddle that we deserved to play on the biggest stage. We all came to UCLA to play in big games and in big moments. We didn't come here just to play college soccer; we came here to win. I know John Wooden was looking down at us, clapping his hands. I know he would be proud of us.

We displayed Competitive Greatness throughout our entire season. We displayed every single block of the Pyramid of Success and did it by playing elite, high-level soccer. Game by game, goal by goal, shutout by shutout, we climbed up the mountain, leaning on each other through the euphoric wins and stinging losses. Every Starbucks run, beach day, and team party contributed to our quest of winning a National Championship. We were being coached by a 31-year-old rookie head coach who was still figuring out her style and coaching philosophy. Her gutty-ness and bravery inspired me every day to encourage my teammates to buy in.

Quincy captioned her celebratory Instagram photo, "Thank you to the 35 badass women that show me every day how important it is to go after what you deserve." I think what is so poetic about our story and our group of girls is that so many of us deserved this win. From January to December, we all, personally and collectively, endured adversity and heartbreak that easily could have brought us down. We fought for our voices to be heard in the hiring process, adapted to our new coaching staff and their expectations, bonded through a mental health crisis, and rode the wave of a crazy college soccer season. For a lot of us, this was *years* of adversity coming to fruition.

We all knew that we deserved to play in the National Championship game, and it was going to take a relentless pursuit for us to achieve it. Every training, every lift, every extra run, every reserve training, every rehab session, every moment in between was us going after what we deserved. I think about us winning a lot. So much so that I wanted to write about it. All throughout the year, I told my teammates that "It was already written." Every win and every positive experience was supposed to happen; we were supposed to beat UNC and Duke, we were supposed to set the record for the best start in program history, and we were supposed to make it to the College Cup.

At the same time, every loss and every lesson learned was supposed to happen; we were supposed to lose to Stanford and USC, and we were supposed to lose the PAC-12 title, we were supposed to have tough conversations with each other. This belief that everything was already planned for us gave us the comfort of being okay when things didn't go our way. In our very first game of the year against Iowa, Maricarmen scored the game-winner off of Quincy's cross. She jumped into Ally Cook's arms, and we celebrated Marg's first win as head coach. 24 games later, number 24 Maricarmen Reyes scored the game-winner against UNC, off of a Quincy cross and an Ally Cook rebounded shot. Some people call it faith, but I call it being written. She scored at the exact same time that the 2013 team did. Unreal.

As we continued to wrap up celebrating on the field, we made our way to the locker room, where we continued the party. Lil Cheerio, Emma, was on aux, and she queued up banger after banger. I went on Instagram Live and documented everything. I was live for 10 minutes and sang, danced, and yelled into the camera. I went around to my teammates, and everyone had a little cameo. I went up to Sof Cook and called her "The young goat," to which she replied, "Grizzly season!" I stood on top of the chair and recorded Emma breakdancing to the popular song, "UCLA." The dance circle continued when "No Role Modelz" were next, and we all sang along – "ONE TIME FOR MY LA SISTERS!" The next thing we knew, Martin walked into the locker room, and started dancing with us. I looked around and everyone was in the moment. That was the best party I had ever been to, and it was with my best friends. In the background of my Instagram live, you could hear everyone saying, "Let's go back to the hotel!" We wanted to keep the good vibes going. We grabbed everything in the locker room, cleaned it up, and made our way to the bus. We waited for our coaches to finish up their interviews and then continued partying on the bus. I remember sitting next to Jackie and posting the NCAA graphic to my story – I captioned it, "We did that shit. Westwood see you soon." As we continued to sing and dance on the bus ride back to the hotel, our parents were getting ready for our arrival.

As the bus pulled up to the hotel, our parents lined up near the entrance with their signs, flags, and decorations all out. They cheered as we got off the bus one by one. One of the parents had gone out and gotten probably $300 worth of alcohol, which was passed out to every player over 21. We all went into the team room to drop off all our stuff, and I quickly went up to my room with Kylie. We both kept saying, "We did it." We showered, changed our clothes, and put our National Championship shirt back on. My waterproof mascara smeared underneath my eyes, and I took a makeup wipe to scrub off before heading downstairs to be reunited with my family and friends. The next two hours were some of the most fun I have ever had. We had the speaker going, and everyone was dancing and singing along. Our families were all with us, taking videos and pictures while the trophy was being passed around. I am so thankful that we got to celebrate with our families. They had been with us every step of the way, and getting to experience their joy is something I will never forget.

We all stood together at the bar, watching the highlights of our game being played. We booed the TV when the UNC coach was shown during his interview and cheered when the camera panned to them crying on the field. Finally, the biased UNC channel showed our goals, and we all broke out into an Eight-Clap. I went outside with the seniors, and we popped champagne and jumped up and down as another round of tears fell down my face. Throughout the night, I captured as much as I could on my phone, posting the most hilarious things to my Instagram story. I got a great picture of Marg and Martin together and captioned it, "Good hire my guy." Then, my next story showed Emma dancing with her shin guards on with a cut-out of Maricarmen's face. I rounded up Quincy, Lilly, Jayden, and Lauren, and we all took a defense picture, which I captioned "Defense wins championships".

The rest of the night was filled with cigars, champagne, and taking pictures. I responded to messages flooding in with selfies with my teammates and trophies. As midnight crept up, the bar stopped serving alcohol, so we continued the party in the lobby. The hotel manager was fielding complaints, but our parents were not going to let anyone rain on our parade. Halfway through the night, I realized that I hadn't eaten anything in hours, and somehow found a whole gluten-free pizza that was especially for me. I shoved three slices in my mouth and then continued the night. I remember going on Twitter and seeing "UCLA" trending, as well as seeing all the Instagram posts from Justwomenssports, ESPNW, UCLA Athletics, HighlightHer, and so many other accounts. Faith had her mini camera locked and loaded, and we took over the lobby for a photo shoot session. We all looked unbelievably tired and overwhelmed, but one day, we'll look back on those pictures and be glad we got them.

    Eventually, we all headed upstairs to get a little bit of sleep. It was almost 1 a.m., and we needed to be back in the lobby by 3:30 a.m. for our flight home. I hugged and kissed my parents and my grandmas and wished them a safe flight back to California. As we went up the elevator, I looked out the glass window and saw my friends passed out on the lobby couch, with their shin guards still on. At 3:00 a.m., my alarm went off and I woke up Kylie, who was fast asleep. I took a Snapchat video and said, "Kylie, wake up, we're National Champions!" My hoop earrings and smeared mascara were still visible as the white National Championship T-shirt clung to my body. Half asleep and half intoxicated, we quickly threw all our clothes into our suitcases and picked up our hotel room. I washed my face and put my Natty hat back on. We made it out of our room with 10 minutes to spare and headed onto the bus. I sat next to Jen as we sat in comfortable silence. Everyone on the bus was dead, but we all agreed now was the time to rest and recover because the next few days were going to be wild. It was Tuesday morning, and our team's banquet was Wednesday night.

    Prior to us leaving for North Carolina, the coaches had asked me to speak at the banquet, but I hadn't put anything together yet. I didn't want to jinx anything, so I planned to write the speech on the flight back to California, whether we won or lost. As we all sat waiting for our staff to check in our bags, Marg stood next to me and said, "Maddi what are you going to do now? You had a huge weekend." I looked down and said, "I don't know Marg." I hadn't really thought of it, but I knew that I needed to. During the weekend, a member of Mari's agency was at our games. I met her, established a relationship, and got her contact information. I had to start thinking about what was next, even though I really wanted to be in the moment. As we walked through TSA, we got stopped and either were congratulated or told that the last goal was a foul. Our team split up into two flights, so we said goodbye to our teammates, and my flight headed to Chicago. Once we landed in Chicago, we had a quick lay-over, but unfortunately, our flight was delayed quite a bit. We sat on the tarmac, and I remember telling Reilyn, "Rei, do you know what's crazy?" and she replied, "What, how we almost lost?" I started dying laughing. I forget what I was actually going to tell her. Our flight finally took off, and I started writing my speech. I had an idea of what I wanted, and thankfully, since we won, the words wrote themselves.

Once we landed in LA, it was immediate chaos for the following 48 hours. The flight before us was already at school and was greeted by news stations, UCLA staff members, members of the community, student-athletes, and fans. We raced back to Westwood, and as we pulled into the Mo Ostin drop-off, we were greeted by everyone. As we walked off the bus one by one, and reunited with our teammates, we were interviewed, hugged, and celebrated by our Bruin Bubble. I hugged my professors and Athletic Directors, and we all took a huge group picture. We went up to the locker room, and dropped off all our equipment, and went back to our apartments. That night, the water polo team was throwing us a party. I washed my National Championship T-shirt and met my friends. This would be the first party of the week. Everyone congratulated us as we sang "We are the Champions," on repeat.

The next day was our team banquet. *Thank God we won!* I kept thinking, *imagine how shitty this would've been if we lost.* Right before our banquet, we had a photoshoot with the trophy. We all put on our jerseys and took pictures with our classes. The pictures turned out great, and we all headed to the Alumni Center where the banquet was being held. My parents drove up from San Clemente and everyone's families were here to celebrate with us. The banquet was perfect. Each senior was highlighted, and I gave my speech:

When looking back on this year, the one thing that keeps coming back to me is how proud we are. Of every single person in this room. A year ago, there was so much uncertainty about our program and our team. The only thing that we knew for sure was that we had each other. We always had a strong culture built on friendships, hard work, and being inclusive. We were always super talented, fast, creative, dynamic, badass defenders, strong leaders, and we were always champions, but we never got the opportunity to show it. And that changed when our coaching staff came in.

We could go on and on about how much they helped our team, but at the end of day you guys were just the missing puzzle piece we needed. We needed a prepared, motivating, confident, and loving staff that had our best interests, cared about player 1 to 35, and wanted to win. And you guys did.

So, from the bottom of my heart, and we speak for the team when I say this, thank you. Thank you for making us run all winter quarter, thank you (and Paige) for making us lift heavy weights, thank you for spending months on teaching us how to play team defense, thank you for letting us be vulnerable, honest, and just giving us the space to be ourselves. We would not be champions without you.

The last thing we'll say is thank you to this team. Every single person in here has so much to be proud of. We faced so much personal and team adversity this year and handled it with such grace and love. The best thing about this team is how much we love each other. We wouldn't trade the beach days, the Starbucks runs, the themed gatherings, the team bonding activities and everything in between for anything. We've had so much fun this year. And we did it all winning game after game after game. Playing elite high-level soccer.

From dying during 300 shuttles a year ago to being National Champions we have so much to be proud of. And we want to say that this championship took everyone. From the injured girls who had the best energy on the bench, always cheering and motivating and making sure that catapults were put in and warm up was set up, from the reserves who pressed like Alabama better than Alabama themselves pressed, you guys are the reason why the starters felt so prepared and confident going into this these games, and to those who left everything out on the field for 110 minutes, we won this championship together. It took all of us from January to now and we couldn't be more proud. Our resiliency, competitiveness, and just undying belief we were going to win inspired so many people. There is no one who deserves this more than us. So, congratulations and thank you to our coaching staff, Nikki, Dr. Miller, Liza, managers, Paige, Melinda, interns, ADs, and everyone else who played a role in winning Number 120. And congrats to our best friends, we love you guys! We did it! We're natty freaking champions and no one can take that away from us.

I held back tears as I finished reading and looked up to all my friends, parents, and coaches as they tearfully looked back at me. It truly was a fairytale ending. My coaches awarded me the "True Bruin" award, which made perfect sense. They awarded Quincy the "Core Four" award, which also made perfect sense. We wrapped up everything, took more pictures, and got ready for the biggest celebration of the week.

The only bar in Westwood, Rocco's, was throwing a big party for us. We were all given wristbands for drinks, signed a jersey for the owner, and painted a huge "FUCK A TAR HEEL" sign that we carried with us down the streets. We moved with numbers in our white National Championship T-shirt down to the bar, where we celebrated all night. The DJ played "We are the Champions" on repeat, and we all raised our glasses in unison. On all the TVs, they showed our game's highlights, and everyone looked up and held their breath as Reilyn flew into the goal with 16 seconds left. The bar erupted, and it was fun being in everyone else's shoes, watching our fate on TV. Even though it was a Wednesday, during finals week, everyone showed up. The bar was filled with student-athletes from every sport, everyone coming up to us to relive the magic. This was our school's first National Championship in years, so everyone wanted to celebrate. It was the best party in my five years at UCLA and one I will never forget.

Right after we won, Reilyn, Lauren, Marg, and I were all on KTLA Live to kick off our world tour. Soon after the celebrations ended, my parents picked me up Saturday to head home to San Clemente. Before we headed south on the 405, I quickly ran up to our locker room to grab some last-minute things. I walked through the Acosta doors for the very last time. I stepped on campus as a 17-year-old, and was now leaving as a 22-year-old. I went up to the locker room and grabbed my cleats. Confetti and dirt were still stuck on them. I closed my locker for the very last time and looked at the empty room. The last five years were filled with change, different characters, and so many laughs, tears, and adversity. Despite the ups and downs, I was so grateful to have ended my time at UCLA with our 2022 family. Each one of my teammates embarked on their own journey after that win. Wherever they go, whatever they do next, I know that they'll do it with Competitive Greatness.

Epilogue
What's Next?

To celebrate the National Championship and to have a little graduation party, my parents hosted a party in December. Club teammates and coaches were invited, family friends were invited, and some of my UCLA teammates showed up. My parents catered from a taco truck and my mom made a shrine of all my pictures, mementos, and awards. I remember thanking everyone for coming, and more importantly for supporting me and my family over my career. I couldn't have done it without the army of people in my corner. I went back and forth for the next couple of weeks, deciding what I was going to do. Put my name in the NWSL draft? Sign with an agent? Go abroad? I had an offer on the table from a top team in Denmark's first division, but I was also getting traction from NWSL coaches. I had calls with a few NWSL teams and ultimately decided to enter the draft. With 48 hours left to spare before the deadline, on a family vacation in Hawaii, I submitted my information and put my name in. I had no idea what was about to unfold.

The draft was a week away in Philadelphia on Thursday, January 12th. On the 8th, Sunday night, our team had gotten tickets to a Pitbull concert at SoFi Stadium. We rented a party bus and continued our celebrations. Tuesday night, my mom and I sat huddled around our computer, looking at flights to Philadelphia. They were really expensive, but we decided to do it.

On the morning of the 11th, I woke up early and met Lauren at the fields near our house. We worked out for a little bit, and I took a Snapchat of us together and captioned it, "Next time I'll see you we'll be pros."

The next 10 hours were wild. Our connecting flight to Chicago was delayed, so we missed our flight to Philadelphia. We landed at the Chicago O'Hare around midnight and spent the night at the airport. We didn't sleep at all and boarded our 6 a.m. flight to Philly. Once we landed in Philly, we had about eight hours until the draft. My mom and I got to our hotel, showered, changed, and walked to the hotel to meet my agents. We hung out at their hotel, and I was introduced to some of the NWSL GMs and coaches. We got lunch and then got ready for the draft. I had a feeling I was going to get picked up but had no idea by who or when.

The draft was insane. I sat there for three hours next to my mom, hearing every other name announced but my own. Lauren was drafted in the third round to the San Diego Wave, and I remember cheering so loud for her. I sat through 4 rounds of the draft, watching my youth national team friends, college rivals, and people I had never heard of before getting drafted before me. I didn't understand. I had just come off this huge college season, and won a National Championship, but no one wanted me.

As the draft neared the end, it seemed as if there was no hope left. My agents were standing next to me, sweating, trying to work something out. All of a sudden, Houston Dash said they were going to trade the very last pick for me. Portland had the 48th pick, and it all came down to the very end. Houston traded money for the pick, and at the 12th hour, I was drafted. I cried as I went up on stage and thanked Houston for drafting me. My friends and family were going nuts at home, and I dedicated everything to my team and coaches. I couldn't believe what had just happened, but like everything in my career, it was another full-circle moment. I had spent my entire college career proving myself. I had spent my entire college career time coming back. Now, I was about to start my pro career in the same position: proving myself.

The United States Coaching Association's convention was also being held in Philly during the same time. My coaches were all there, and they came by after the draft to congratulate me and take pictures. Marg hugged me and said how proud she was of Lauren and me; we were her first pro players. With Lauren and I getting drafted, UCLA now led the country with the most draft picks. It truly was a beautiful moment for everyone. Marg, Gof, and Molly were named the 2022 United Soccer Coaches National Staff of the Year. They spent their time at the convention on podcasts, running sessions, and being interviewed. They couldn't walk 10 yards without stopping and being congratulated. They were the celebs of the moment.

Right before Christmas, our coaches messaged in our group chat that our team was going to be honored at the Rose Bowl Parade on the 2nd. I was supposed to be in Hawaii for a family vacation, but I decided that I couldn't miss it. My parents, being from the Pasadena area, agreed, and we moved my flight to that night. All of the California girls said we could go, so at the crack of dawn, we met in Westwood to bus out to Pasadena. We got to the meeting point and walked past all the beautiful floats to our designated float. We all wore our brand-new College Cup white hoodies and were given roses to hold. As the sun began to rise, we took pictures together, and the parade started. For the next three hours, we walked the parade and waved at the crowd. This would just be the start of our team being honored, and the start of the World Tour that ran through the first six months of 2023.

I headed out to Houston for pre-season, Lauren headed down to San Diego Wave, and Maricarmen signed her first pro contract with Tigres in La Liga Mexico. Kylie, Bri, and Kali all transferred for their fifth year. Jackie retired after her dream senior year, and Sunshine announced she was coming back for one more year in Westwood.

Over the next six months, the team was celebrated everywhere. They were announced during halftime at the UCLA men's basketball game, where they were given a standing ovation by thousands of people in Pauley Pavilion. They were honored at a Dodgers game, and Emma threw the first pitch, and was also brought out during an Angel City game. Marg was invited onto every sports podcast you could think of. Her schedule was booked with interviews, camps, and Zooms. Everyone wanted to talk to her and learn from her. She was named the U23 USWNT head coach and coached the team against NWSL teams during their pre-season. Around May, we found out that we were invited to the White House with all the other NCAA Champions in June. I asked my head coach at Houston if it was okay if I missed a training and a game to go, and he was so excited for me and said that I couldn't miss it for the world.

I landed in DC on an early summer evening and Ubered straight to the Abe Lincoln Memorial, where my team was. I cried as I ran up to them and hugged them. I hadn't seen any of them since January, and we were now reunited in DC. Mari and Lauren also got permission to go and everyone who had transferred also met us there. The next two days were the best. We went out in DC, went to Starbucks, went to the African American museum, walked around DC, and had a joint dinner with men's volleyball, who were also being recognized for winning in 2023. The day of the ceremony, we all dressed up, and wore our gigantic National Championship rings and headed to the White House. As we took pictures out on the lawn and admired the White House up close, Kamala Harris took the stage and honored all of the teams. It was perfect and felt like the best way to end our months of celebrations.

It took me two and a half years to write this book. It's crazy enough to think that is about half the time that I spent at UCLA, but when I was younger, time just went by a lot slower. I rode the high of winning the Natty for the first six months of 2023 and used that confidence on the field. Those feelings never fully go away, but they fade slowly. My rookie year at Houston had a lot of learning. I scored my first professional goal, and played with and against the best players in the world, but then my coach, who drafted me, was fired. I went into 2024 with big hopes but was eventually waived eight weeks into the season. I didn't write for a long time, probably close to a year. Time went by, things changed, and it took me a long time to find the mental and emotional strength to write about such a beautiful and successful part of my life. No one really talks about how hard it is to reflect in a happy way when you aren't your happiest. I knew I needed to be in a good place to write our story with the joy it deserves.

I signed with OB Q, played in the top division in Denmark, and by the end of 2024, I was able to write again.

When I was 13 years old, I sat on the couch and watched UCLA Women's Soccer win their first National Championship. I watched the confetti fall down as the players held each other, crying tears of joy. Two years later, I was 15 years old and committed to UCLA with one dream in mind: winning.

After I got injured, a lot of my dreams changed. I never really thought about playing professionally or playing in a National Championship. I remember watching my old teammates get drafted and thinking that there was no way that would ever happen to me. It's funny how dreams work. You put them aside or in the back of your head, and maybe one day, they become actually attainable.

I do believe wholeheartedly that we had luck on our side. A lot of things had to happen in order for us to win. However, we also created a lot of our luck. If us seniors didn't have the careers that we had, we wouldn't have won. Our adversity, our stories, our comebacks, and our full-circle moments are the reasons why we are who we are. They made us into the leaders and teammates that we are today. We wouldn't have won without Marg, Molly, and Gof. The will to win takes an unselfish, resilient mentality. If it's not inherent, it can be gained. And by the end of 2022, every single person on the team experienced what it truly feels like to want to win. I don't think I'll ever play on a team again with that much trust, talent, and joy. I thank UCLA Women's Soccer for giving me the best memories and friends I could ever have. No one can ever take Number 120 away from us.

Bend Never Break

John Wooden once said, "Success is peace of mind, which is a direct result of self-satisfaction in knowing you did your best to become the best you are capable of becoming." Read it twice. To me, Coach Wooden was saying that success comes from having no regrets. It's doing everything in your power to leave everything on the table. To be able to walk away when the whistle blows knowing that every box was checked. I knew going into the final that I did everything I could to have peace of mind. All we had left was 90 more minutes to finish the damn job. If we would have lost, it would've stung for a really long time. It probably would stay with me forever. But our season wasn't going to be decided in one game. We had already done the hard work, and this was just the circle finally connecting. It truly was written.

How we played, how we handled adversity, and how we treated each other was all a testament to our undeniable strength. Our disciplined, organized defense made it impossible for teams to find any hope in scoring. Our responses to tough losses and goals against made us scary to play against. Our ability to hold a high standard, and push each other to be better every day allowed us to be adaptable. The work we put in back in January motivated us to run the extra sprint. Our culture was cemented by friendship, trust, and resilience. We climbed up the Pyramid of Success, and whoever said it was lonely at the top was wrong. We stood strong at the top, side by side, and soaked in Competitive Greatness together. As the confetti fell down, so did any insecurities I had about how I led this team. Despite the doubts, changes, losses, and seconds away from losing it all, we never broke. Even though bamboo is a type of grass, it is three times stronger than timber. It has a tensile strength of 28,000 pounds per square inch, allowing it to withstand more tension before breaking. Bamboo bends, just like us.

Acknowledgements

I want to thank my parents and brother for their unwavering love, support, and guidance for the past 25 years. You guys allowed me to be me; on the pitch, off the pitch, and everywhere in between. I wouldn't be the person I am today if it weren't for you guys letting me follow my dreams.

Thank you to my Lala and Nana for coming to every single 2022 soccer game, home and away, and for texting me after all my games. I love you guys.

Thank you to all my family and family friends for supporting me through my career; whether that be driving up to Westwood or watching my games on TV. I had an army of people behind me and I could feel the love through all the highs and lows.

Thank you to Anish!! For being a loyal friend and helping me with everything. Promo, editing, social media, and picking up the phone. I appreciate you!

To Marg, Gof, Molly, and Chelsea- Thank you for trusting our team and believing in us. We would not have won a Natty without you, and that is something I am internally grateful for!

To my girls–my UCLA Soccer Baddies–our magical year is only a product of our love, joy, and trust in one and another. You all hold a special place in my heart and I am forever grateful for the laughs, tears, runs, goals, and championships we share with each other. I hope I did our story justice.

I love you all!

Bend Never Break

www.ingramcontent.com/pod-product-compliance
Lightning Source LLC
Chambersburg PA
CBHW060352190426
43201CB00044B/2100